Fading Scars:

My Queer Disability History

Corbett Joan OToole

Owned by disabled workers, Autonomous Press
seeks to revolutionize academic access.

Autonomous Press is an independent publisher focusing on works
about disability, neurodivergence, and the various ways they can
intersect with other aspects of identity and lived experience.

ISBN-10: 0986183512

ISBN-13: 978-0-9861835-1-5

Cover photography & model: Chun-Shan *(Sandie)* Yi

DEDICATION

Do Not Lose Heart
We Were Made For These Times[1]
By Clarissa Pinkola Estes

"Ours is not the task of fixing the entire world at once,
but of stretching out to mend the part of
the world that is within our reach.
One of the most calming and powerful actions you can do
to intervene in a stormy world is to
stand up and show your soul.
Soul on deck shines like gold in dark times.
The light of the soul throws sparks,
can send up flares, builds signal fires,
causes proper matters to catch fire.
To display the lantern of soul in shadowy times like these,
to be fierce and to show mercy toward others,
both are acts of immense bravery and greatest necessity.
When a great ship is in harbor and moored,
it is safe, there can be no doubt.
But that is not what great ships are built for."

---

1. Source URL: http://www.awaken.com/2012/11/do-not-lose-heart/

Table of Contents

Foreword

The 1960s and 1970s were an incredibly important period in American disability history, and the events that transpired during those two decades changed the world. The author of this book, Corbett Joan OToole, lived that history intimately and provides us with a richly woven narrative from a different perspective than what is found in most textbooks. We see through her eyes and feel through her body as a participant in those pivotal moments. We follow her journey through the 1980s and 1990s and the new millennium as new avenues opened for people with disabilities, although amongst many setbacks.

This book starts us off at the very beginning of modern social disability history—from the first dormitory for students with disabilities at the University of California Berkeley in 1962 to the founding of the Center for Independent Living in the city of Berkeley in 1970. The author herself moved to Berkeley in 1973 and was involved in the early days of the Berkeley CIL and the community around it. There she took some of the first courses in Disability Studies ever offered in the world and she was one of the brave individuals who staged a sit-in protest at the San Francisco Federal Building during the 504 Movement of 1977.

The actions of the 504ers helped bring disability rights to millions of Americans by forcing the government to fulfill earlier promises made in the Rehabilitation Act. The 504 protests and protesters—and more importantly the social networks and organizations that were created to support them, along with a newfound optimism for progressive social change—helped lead to the passing of the Americans with Disabilities Act a little over a decade later.

The author's standpoint in these momentous events provides new insight—the pivotal role that other activists and community members played in the creation of the Berkeley CIL, the significance of the help provided by Black Panthers in the 504 Movement, the excitement and sensuality of the dances and events held during those early times. She supplements her rich narrative and personal history with archival research and interviews from other people involved in the movement that are part of the Disability Rights and Independent Living Movement oral history archives at the University of California, Berkeley.

It goes without saying that without the political, social and artistic movements that disability activists started in the 1960s, millions of people with various disabilities in the United States and around the world would still be living in institutions for their entire lives, without jobs and without the right to claim full participation in society. The Americans with Disabilities Act of 1990 helped inspire other countries to adopt similar legislation focusing on disability rights as a civil rights and human rights issue, not as a welfare and medical problem.

In 1995, the author organized a group of women with disabilities to be part of the Beijing Women's Conference, helping to bring disability, gender, and the family to the forefront of the world stage. By this time, the author was a mother with small child, and she weaves in her own stories of parenting and disability. She is also an avid athlete, and her chapter about her experience participating in team sports rivals the best sports writing in its ability to bring a rush of adrenaline to the reader. She also helps create the Axis Dance Company, a globally renowned dance company that brings together both disabled and non-disabled bodies, as well as organizing the first international Queer Disability Conference. Throughout the book, the vivid description of bodies, of gazes, of touches, and of scars emotional and physical, only partially healed, brings to the fore the deep humanity of the movement.

While this book reminds us of how far we have come, there is much of the past that we are at risk of losing. A good part of the richness of this book comes from the oral histories of people with disabilities that are at UC Berkeley. But there are only 100 oral histories in this archive, just a tiny portion of the total number of people who are part of our collective disability history. Many people who were active in the 1960s and 1970s have now passed on. The author provides us with a clarion call that we need to recapture this part of our history and provides resources with which people can record and protect their memories and legacies.

The book closes by also reminding us that there is still much to do. Full social participation is not possible for many within disability communities, especially for those with developmental and psychiatric disabilities. Unfortunately there are still rifts and boundaries that separate our communities along lines of race, poverty, sexuality, and sexual identity. And while the 2006 United Nations Convention on the Rights of Persons with Disabilities declares that we all have a fundamental right to have families, many people with disabilities have had those rights taken away from them—preemptively through sterilization or abortion, or post-facto through the taking of children by courts and child protective services. In this vein, parents with disabilities and parents of children with disabilities encounter myriad levels of discrimination in trying to work with school systems. There is still much work to do, and I hope this book inspires a new generation of young activists, artists, and community organizers to take up her call for action.

This book is a must read for everyone, disabled or not. Part autobiography and part history, it is also part of all our history and biography. We must read it to get a different perspective of disability history, to be reminded that behind the stories of "founding fathers" there are many other people whose stories are just as important and moving. It is a story about alliances and friendships and care and love. It tells us that we are all part of a history in the making and in the past. It is our story.

Karen Nakamura
February 7, 2015
Yale University
New Haven, CT

Editorial Preface:

One Elder is a Whole Library

When I was in grade school in Portland, Oregon, I was lucky enough to be included in outreach activities by a coalition of local Native American tribes who made a practice of inviting children on field trips to traditional Potlatch events, to share between cultures. Like many cities in the U.S., Portland was constructed on ground—some of it holy —taken from a variety of tribes. While many people went to reservations in the middle of the eighteen hundreds, a relatively large number remained in the growing urban center, and helped give it the character for which it is still now known.

A Chinook woman told me I was bound to like fry bread, despite my idea that very few things were actually edible, and unlike myself, I rightly believed her. Then, having discerned my love of reading, she told me a much more important thing.

"Respect your elders," she said, "And hear what they have to say. One elder is a whole library."

This has stayed with me always, and it is why I became interested in epistemology, which has to do with how people know things, and what it means for them to know them, and what kinds of knowing there can be.

People can know by thinking, and also by doing, for example. The knowledge held by an elder is doubly powerful: elders have done the things, and also thought about them. More is written about this elsewhere, but what must be said here is that Corbett OToole was there in key moments of disability culture even before people had written that there is such a thing as disability culture and named it. She is also friends with other people who write about disability culture and history, and so knows in a lot of detail what she thinks about the things she has done and seen in many different ways.

This book spans decades, major events and topics, and comes from a point of view called "autoethnographic," which is another word for writing about one's own life in order to show larger culture to the reader. It is a memoir with educational purpose. It is from the horse's mouth, as they say: a play-by-play written by someone inside the action, telling us what happened then and there.

Fading Scars is absolutely essential reading in courses about disability studies and provides an excellent voice to complement histories written by historians, who have access to other kinds of knowledge about our collective past. Karen Nakamura is right to say that this is not only to be read by students of disability culture and history, but also by everyone. As Kim Nielsen says in *A Disability History of the United States*, disability history is the story of our nation. And the future of disability history (and queer history) is the kind of intersectionality and coalition we learn about in these exciting pages.

Elizabeth J. Grace
February 10, 2015
National Louis University
Chicago, IL

I.

Celebrating Crip Bodyminds

"'Abled' is nothing but a sop to the pernicious toxic focus on ability that ruins the lives of disabled people."[1]   — Alice Sheppard (disabled)[2]

Summary

Disabled people are imaginative, interesting, capable people. Yet we are often viewed as incapable. I love being disabled and being with disabled people (in person and online). This long essay talks about ways that disabled people are discriminated against, how disabled people learn a lot from each other, and how disability organizations pay more attention to white people with physical disabilities than to other disabled people.

I write about why I wrote this book, and why I organized the book in this way. For example, I say whether the person in this book is disabled, nondisabled or unknown. I also tell a lot of stories about myself.

I love being disabled. That's not a statement you hear too often outside of disability circles.[3] Pretty much everyone assumes that given a choice

---

1.   Single quotations are added by the author.

2.   Alice Sheppard earned a Ph.D. in Medieval Studies from Cornell University and was an Associate Professor of English and Comparative Literature at the Pennsylvania State University. She is now a professional disabled dancer and philanthropist. This quote is from Alice Sheppard on Facebook, Dec 14, 2014.

3.   I am using the word "circles" throughout this book to name the informal, non-organizational groups of disabled people. I discuss this more fully later in this essay.

disabled people[4] would rather be cured than disabled. And it's certainly true that lots of us would gladly give up the symptoms of disability that are inconvenient such as pain and loss of function, as well as the daily hassles of dealing with ableism.[5] But for many of us the reality of being disabled, the ways our bodyminds[6] function, is cause for celebration. Once we stop seeing ourselves from the medical perspective of sickness, diagnosis, and aberration, and find circles of disabled people, we can often feel pride about who we are, the skills we've learned and the interdependent circles we've created. As Laura Hershey[7] (disabled)[8] reminds us: "You get proud by practicing."[9] Being disabled gives you lots of opportunities to practice.

Disability, as it is typically framed by nondisabled people, is all about loss and rarely about ableism, which is the systemic discrimination against disabled people. Nearly every article about disability in mainstream media is by nondisabled people for nondisabled people. These articles focus on the imagined distress at the losses that will occur if nondisabled people became disabled and almost never on the systems that create the perceived losses. Sometimes the concern is about the change in their bodymind, but typically the primary focus is their changed social status should they become visibly disabled or be unable to hide their disability from others. Society overlays the experience of physical or mental impairment[10] with enormous social stigma. Let me give you an example.

---

4. In this book, I am using "disabled people" to include all forms of disabilities and impairments— physical, sensory, mental—everyone. Although in other writings I have alternated between "disabled people" and "people with disabilities," for this book I chose to only use "disabled people."

5. Ableism is the systematic discrimination against disabled people. Similar to sexism, ableism privileges people who are closest to the nondisabled mythical norm, that is a white, middle class, nondisabled male.

6. Instead of saying "bodies and minds," I am using Margaret Price's phrase "bodymind." Price states, "mental and physical processes not only affect each other but also give rise to each other—that is, because they tend to act as one, even though they are conventionally understood as two—it makes more sense to refer to them together, in a single term." from "The Bodymind Problem and the Possibilities of Pain" by Margaret Price, in the journal *Hypatia*, Volume 30, Issue 1, pp. 268–284, Winter 2015. URL: http://onlinelibrary.wiley.com/doi/10.1111/hypa.12127/full

7. Laura Hershey, MFA, (1962-2010) was a writer, poet, disability activist, and consultant. She was a 2010 Lambda Fellow in Poetry. Her poems and essays explore diverse topics including body, nature, community, activism, social justice, and much more.

8. Throughout the book every person has one of three identifiers: disabled, nondisabled, or unknown. I used publicly available information to determine the appropriate identifier.

9. Laura Hershey's poem "You Get Proud By Practicing" is widely referenced, particularly among disabled activists. The Australian comic Stella Young (disabled) had the phrase tattooed on her arm.

10. I am using "impairment" to mean a specific medically defined condition—that is, the way that the medical system would classify someone.

In the mid-1980s I attended the women's conference of a progressive national organization. That is to say, these women had thought deeply about issues of societal inequalities, including race and gender. At one point in the conference, women proposed topics for small groups. Marj Schneider (disabled), from the Womyn's Braille Press,[11] and I proposed the topic of disability. Marj and I put up sign that said "Disabled" and another woman put up a sign that said "Not Disabled." There was a long pause then a third woman in the group put up a sign that said "Not Sure." When Marj and I were the only ones to show up for the "Disabled" group, we wandered over to the "Not Sure" group.

As we listened to their stories, we found that the 40 women who joined the "Not Sure" group were all women that Marj and I would easily consider to be disabled. They had significant impairments that impacted their daily lives. Some of them would have days when they couldn't leave the house. Their disabilities varied—some had mobility impairments, some had hearing impairments, some had mental impairments. Yet not one of those women wanted to be associated with the word "disabled," nor did they associate with disabled people. This affected them in two ways. First, they didn't have any language for being disabled, so they were isolated in their own worlds. Second, they were working intensely to hide the fact of their disabilities from the people around them.

Many women told stories of being unable to work for a day or week and calling in sick with a "bad flu." These women were in great distress. They were clinging desperately to their former nondisabled lives, asking the people intimately involved with them to maintain the secret of their disability. Now, if this were a news article, the reporter will be telling you about how their distress was caused by their disabilities, but I believe that their distress was caused by their isolation both socially and politically, their lack of disability community, and by their internal belief about no longer being considered "normal."

Inside disability circles are years of experiences and resources for solving common impairment-related problems. So for example, women with breast cancer often find important resources by connecting with other women with breast cancer.[12] Disability justice writer and activist

11. Womyn's Braille Press (WBP) was founded in 1980 in Minneapolis, Minnesota to produce feminist literature on tape or in Braille for the visually impaired and non-print readers. Because of financial difficulties, in 1994 the WBP donated their collection to the Florida Library for the Blind, where it is available to eligible readers by interlibrary loan from National Library Service for the Blind and Physically Handicapped (NLS). WBP ceased operations in 1996. URL: http://socialarchive.iath.virginia.edu

12. Asbury, F.D.(unknown) et al. (1998). *One-on-one peer support and quality of life for breast cancer*

Naomi Ortiz (disabled)[13] says:

> Even disabled people connecting with another person who has a
> different disability can provide support and creative problem-
> solving. For example, someone with a psychiatric disability
> could connect with someone who has multiple sclerosis over
> the complications of integrating daily medications that make
> some symptoms worse and others better. Being disabled is a
> cultural experience which shares many commonalities, even
> with others with very different disabilities.

During the past two decades researchers have documented that
support from peers and personal resourcefulness are keys to having
successful lives for disabled people.[14] Through the Looking Glass's
research found that one of the main characteristics of disabled parents
(meaning people who are both disabled and parents) is creative
problem-solving.[15] Living with a disability and being a parent both
require flexibility in often-changing situations. As my cousin told me
when I became a parent, "From now on, all plans are changeable
because you never know what your child will need."

The vast majority of people with permanent disabilities[16] face
enormous social and economic barriers.[17] We have learned to be very

---

patients. Department of Public Health Sciences, University of Toronto, Canada. Email:
cappe@netcom.ca

13. Naomi Ortiz (disabled). *Inquisitive Writer about Self-Care for Social Justice Activists, Deep
breathing Poet, Cares About The Process, Loves to Laugh, Disability Justice Activist.* Twitter:
@thinkfreestyle

14. "The psychosocial functions of effective mentors include counseling, friendship, role modeling,
acceptance, and confirmation (Kram, 1983). Peer support can foster personal growth and provide
relevant information that cannot be obtained in any other manner. Peer mentors often provide
information about local support systems and the 'ins and outs' of dealing with them (Mason,
2008). Peer support can provide an avenue for dealing with personal and complex issues." from
Kruck, A.D., et al. (2011). *Building an effective peer support program.* Independent Living Research
Utilization (ILRU). Houston, TX.

15. Kirshbaum, M. (disabled). (June, 1988). "Parents with physical disabilities and their babies." *Zero
to Three.*

16. In data these folks are often called "severely disabled" but that only means that their disability
continued for 12 continuous months.

17. "Persons with a disability are likely to have limited opportunities to earn income and often have
increased medical expenses. Disabilities among children and adults may affect the socioeconomic
standing of entire families. It is estimated that over 40 million people in America have some level
of disability, and many of these individuals live in poverty (U.S. Census Bureau, 2006). Although
the Americans with Disabilities Act assures equal opportunities in education and employment
for people with and without disabilities and prohibits discrimination on the basis of disability,
people with disabilities remain overrepresented among America's poor and undereducated. Some
data suggest causal relationships between low SES [Socio Economic Status] and the development
of disability in late adulthood (Coppin et al., 2006). These barriers contribute to discrepancies in
wealth and socioeconomic opportunities for persons with a disability and their families." From

creative in solving the problems that occur. Unfortunately, that information is locked away inside disability-specific circles of people with similar impairments, such as support groups, both online and face-to-face. That information is rarely known by nondisabled medical professionals, who are almost always disconnected from the broader disability communities.[18.]

Research in the United States shows that disabled people who are connected through disability circles have a much higher quality of life.[19.] Notice that I did not say that they have fewer impairments. Their quality of life goes up because, often for the first time, they are surrounded by people who see their wholeness, in contrast to the medical system that primarily sees their brokenness. Being around other disabled people can provide: a mirror of positive self-reflection; a source of peer support; a place to get answers and resources and an opportunity to change minds from a perspective of tragic loss to a new vision full of pride—not in spite of the disability, but including it.

Even a decade into the new millenium, we don't have a societal vocabulary for telling each other about the beauty and ingenuity of disabled bodies. We lack what Judi Rogers (disabled)[20.] calls "visual history."[21.] For example, we as a society have a mental image of how someone with arms would drive a car, but we have no image of how someone without arms would drive a car. Yet we can know from observing drivers without arms that they use one foot on the pedals and one on the steering wheel. In addition, media distortions make disabled people's accomplishments seem individual and extraordinary, rather than expanding our ability to imagine new possibilities. This failure of vision is what makes people tell a new arm amputee that they can never drive.

The current U.S. media representations of disabled bodyminds

Disability and Socio Economic Status. American Psychological Association. URL: http://www.apa.org/pi/ses/resources/publications/factsheet-disability.aspx

18. National Council on Disabilities. (2009). *The current state of health care for people with disabilities.* URL: http://www.ncd.gov/publications/2009/Sept302009#Professional

19. Nario-Redmond, M.; Noel, J. & Fern, E. (2013). "Redefining disability, re-imagining the self: Disability identification predicts self-esteem and strategic responses to stigma." *Self and Identity,* 12:5, 468-488. DOI URL: http://dx.doi.org/10.1080/15298868.2012.681118

20. Judith Rogers (disabled), O.T.R. (Occupational Therapist). Judi works as an occupational therapist at the National Resource Center for Parents with Disabilities at Through the Looking Glass in Berkeley, California. She has designed, developed and researched the impact of adaptive baby care equipment for parents with disabilities. Having children inspired her to write a book on pregnancy and disability entitled *Mother To Be: A Guide to Pregnancy and Birth for Women with Disabilities.* She has provided hundreds of consultations and interventions to parents and professionals.

21. John Berger (unknown), 1972, *Ways of Seeing,* examines how the images in our art and culture determine how we see the world. The text is widely used by feminist scholars.

demonstrate a profound failure of imagination. We're constantly fed media messages of "the happy and always smiling person with Down Syndrome," or the "tragedy that confined him to a wheelchair." The messages are endless, and so woven into our culture that they are rarely challenged outside disability circles. We are so flooded with these simplistic and inaccurate messages that we fail to imagine a world that already exists—one where disabled people are interesting, competent, resourceful human beings.

Without a doubt, American society is geared not only to promote the nondisabled body and mind but to actively discourage any other image. We as a society hold tightly to the idea that there is a bodymind called "normal" as a valid and useful standard. When deviations from "normal" occur, our society reacts as if all efforts should be made to bring the deviant back to as close to normal as possible, and if that is not possible, to eliminate the deviant.

During pregnancy, parents in the U.S. are encouraged to test for "abnormalities" early, so they can abort a pregnancy that is not "normal." When such tests are available to parents, the birth of children with identifiable conditions such as Down Syndrome dramatically decreases. Many people would say, "Yay. That's a good thing." I would say, "A good thing for whom?" I know many people with Down Syndrome. I don't go around wishing they were never born. I enjoy their double-jointedness, the way that their face and body tell us right away "I am disabled." In my lifetime, I have seen the beliefs about people with Down Syndrome change dramatically. When I was a child, people with Down Syndrome were routinely institutionalized. When I was in college studying special education, people with Down Syndrome were categorized as incapable of learning. And now, largely through changes in belief systems rather than from any medical or educational advances, people with Down Syndrome are literate, voting, and leading full and rewarding lives. Some folks even drive.

These changes did not occur because suddenly medical science figured out a better way to minimize the impairments of Down Syndrome. These changes occurred because people with Down Syndrome and their families pushed against the stereotypes and asked not, "What is wrong with me?" but instead, "What is right about me?" They developed new educational approaches and support systems that allowed many people with Down Syndrome to live outside institutions.

I like to use the example of people with Down Syndrome for a number of reasons. One is that people like me with physical disabilities rarely talk and act in a way that includes people with intellectual disabilities, who sometimes prefer the term "self advocates,"[22] in our work and our world. Many disabled people, and particularly national disability rights organizations, distance themselves from anything where they are perceived as not being smart, and promote instead a notion of "we're just like you but we're sitting down." This approach is extremely problematic.

Trying to pretend that disabled people are not different from nondisabled people, and that disabilities can be managed in such a way as to be non-impairing (not needing accommodations), presumes that the only disabled people welcome in society have, as I saw on one job application, "unimpairing handicaps."[23] If successful, this approach would allow only a small sliver of the disabled population to gain access to the privileges of the nondisabled world, where the hypothetical "normal" white middle class man resides. In many cases, this is exactly what has happened. Unfortunately, many national disability organizations have promoted this idea as well, which in the end leaves many disabled people behind. This also results in the continued exclusion of all the non-white, non-male, poor people with impairing handicaps. My friend Naomi Ortiz (disabled) calls these mythical white disabled people, promoted as "just like you but sitting down," *disability pretty*. If they used their entrance to open the doors for the rest of us, I wouldn't mind so much, but embedded in the "we're just like you but we sit down" approach is the idea that only people who can approximate "normal" will be allowed access to nondisabled opportunities.

All bodyminds are on a continuum.[24] At different points in our lives, we have more and less function and move closer or further from the "normal" end of the spectrum. "Normal" is an artificial construct built upon the white, middle-class, male, nondisabled bodymind. Any deviation from that bodymind is considered "not normal."[25] Western

22. I am informed by my younger friends that people in their 40s and 50s use the term "self advocates," while younger people prefer the term "intellectually disabled."

23. During the 1980s the City of Oakland, California's nondiscrimination clause on job applications read: "we do not discriminate on the basis of race, gender … and unimpairing handicap." I love the honesty of that statement because this is the true rule that employers use.

24. "Personal characteristics, as well as environmental ones, may be enabling or disabling, and the relative degree fluctuates, depending on condition, time, and setting. Disability is a contextual variable, dynamic over time and circumstance." from The Center for an Accessible Society. *The new paradigm of disability.* URL: http://www.accessiblesociety.org/topics/demographics-identity/newparadigm.htm

25. "The matter of what is normal can't be and must not be a mere statistical nicety. It can't be and must not be 'normal' to be a Christian just because 95% of your community is Christian. It can't be and must not be 'normal' to be attracted to someone of the opposite sex just because 90% of the general population is heterosexual. It can't be and must not be 'normal' to own slaves just because all the landowners in your state own slaves. 'Normal' can't mean and must not mean

cultural beliefs hold that the closer one is to "normal," the more deserving they are of the highest rights and privileges.

I argue that "normal" is for suckers. Nobody is normal. A group of young disability rights activists created a website called "I am Norm,"[26.] which takes a humorous approach to this exact problem. As long as we culturally subscribe to the notion of "normal," disabled people will never be seen as anything but "abnormal." While I love the ways that we reclaim ourselves as outsiders, and I love flying my "freak" flag, in reality I am only a "freak" if one believes that there is one human standard, and that is called "normal."

Embracing the concept of "normal" means embracing the concept of "not normal." Looking at U.S. statistics, it is easy to see that a society that leans towards "normal" creates significant disenfranchisement for everyone who is "not normal." If one is not middle-class, not male, not able bodied, not white, one will experience significant barriers to accessing the services and privileges provided for people who are "normal." Most disabled people fall into multiple disenfranchised categories, and have little to no access to "normal" privileges.

In the richest country on earth, the United States currently has: the most incarcerated people in the world,[27.] the lowest living birth rate among industrialized nations,[28.] the highest rate of gun violence,[29.] and significant gaps in educational achievement[30.] and economic access.[31.] In short, for anyone who is not a white, middle-class, nondisabled man, there are significant economic, educational, employment, and societal barriers. What is the justification for all this disparate treatment? The

---

'what we see all the time' or 'what we see the most of.' It must have a different meaning from that for it to mean anything of value to right-thinking people." from Maisel, E. (unknown). (November 15, 2011). "What do we mean by 'normal'?" *Psychology Today.*

26. URL: http://iamnorm.com/

27. At 716 per 100,000 people, according to the International Centre for Prison Studies, the U.S. tops every other nation in the world. URL: http://www.prisonstudies.org

28. Ingraham, C. (unknown). (2014). "U.S. lags behind other wealthy nations in infant mortality." *The Washington Post.* URL: http://www.washingtonpost.com/blogs

29. The U.S. has 88 guns per 100 people and 10 gun-related deaths per 100,000 people—more than any of the other 27 developed countries studied. URL: http://abcnews.go.com

30. "The term 'achievement gap' is often defined as the differences between the test scores of minority and/or low-income students and the test scores of their White and Asian peers. But achievement gaps in test scores affect many different groups. Some groups may trail at particular points, for example, boys in the early school years, and girls in high school math and science. Differences between the scores of students with different backgrounds (ethnic, racial, gender, disability, and income) are evident on large-scale standardized tests. Test score gaps often lead to longer-term gaps, including high school and college completion and the kinds of jobs students secure as adults." from the National Education Association. URL: http://www.nea.org/

31. A Pew Research Center report finds wealth gap between America's top 20 percent of earners and rest of country has stretched to its widest point in at least three decades, according to *The New York Times* (December 13, 2014). URL: http://topics.nytimes.com

embodied reality of assumptions and beliefs about people who are not white, middle-class, nondisabled, men. It's ironic how pervasively people buy into the idea that "normal" is a good thing and we should all aspire to it. As Naomi Ortiz reminds us,

> Acknowledging that there is no 'normal' doesn't mean that everyone experiences disability as a political and social identity. Acknowledging that there is no 'normal' creates a society where difference can be recognized without being diffused or ignored. It does not take away the culture of disability, only adds an opportunity and awareness for us to be more integrated into society as a whole.

Presuming Competence

Close to the concept of "normal" is the concept of "competent." Disabled people are usually viewed as "not competent." This assumption permeates and constrains the life of disabled people, and is embedded in our societal psyche. Often hidden beneath layers of stereotypes, many of which appear benign, disabled people's competence is challenged in myriad ways. An easy view into the destructive outcomes of presuming the incompetence of disabled children is through educational tracking, a century-old practice that privileges the students who are closest to "normal" and disenfranchises the students who are the farthest away from that standard.

Disabled youth frequently report how assumptions of incompetence are placed on them by nondisabled educators.[32] In a recent U.S. example, Emma (disabled), blogs at Emma's Hope Book[33] and writes about sitting in middle school special education classrooms and being read books written for toddlers. There was never any presumption by those "special" educators that she was capable of learning, since her verbal communication is significantly impaired. Once her parents became aware of this, they took her out of public school and allowed Emma to create her own curriculum. This semester Emma, now age 12, decided to tackle German, chemistry, math, Shakespeare, American history and creative writing. Emma did not magically change

---

32. I want to reiterate that I believe that all disabled people are competent just as they are, however they express themselves or appear. Competence as I am using the term is not about performing in ways that are acceptable to nondisabled people. Competence is core to the person, whether others perceive the disabled person to be competent or not. This section talks about the impact of not being able to 'perform;' competence means that incompetence is presumed and systemic discrimination based on that assumption occurs.

33. URL: http://emmashopebook.com/

and become less competent in school settings and more competent outside of them, but the presumptions about her changed dramatically. A significant problem in American culture, as in many Western cultures, is the presumption that performing "normally" is required for competence to be presumed. So not only are disabled students presumed incompetent, but also students who speak English as a second language, who speak in African American Vernacular English, who are kinesthetic learners, etc. And disabled students are in all these groups.

Presuming the competence of some people, those closer to the "normal" standard, and presuming the incompetence of the "other," is built into the fabric of our society. High unemployment rates for disabled people do not reflect the inability of disabled people to work, but instead reflect the pervasive presumed incompetence of disabled people to work in nondisabled environments as they currently exist, as well as a systemic ableist unwillingness to build work around people's capabilities.[34] This is seen very dramatically in the fact that 40 years after the first disability civil rights law, Section 504, and 25 years after the passage of the Americans With Disabilities Act, both of which legally mandated equivalent opportunities, or at least a lack of discrimination, the number of disabled people who are employed still hovers around 27%.[35]

It is important to note that presumption of incompetence encompasses not only disabled people but also people who deviate from "normal" based on race, language, age and class. Many, if not most, disabled people are members of multiple groups that are rarely seen in their wholeness, their rich complexity. The disabled people of color leading Sins Invalid, a performance project based in Berkeley, California, address the insidious categorization of "others" in their vision statement: "Sins Invalid recognizes that we will be liberated as whole beings—as disabled/as queer/as brown/as black/as genderqueer/as female- or male-bodied—as we are far greater whole than partitioned."[36]

---

34. "Industrialisation in Britain exacerbated this segregation by creating social divisions between those who were deemed to be of use in the workplace and those who were not. Those not up to the physical and mental standards required for the work-place [sic] were thus considered useless. This is consistent with the dominant capitalist ideology which values individuals according to their productivity: from this perspective inability to produce results in low or no value. As Oliver suggests, disability is 'culturally produced through the relationship between the mode of production and the central values of the society concerned' (1990: 23). As a result, disabled people are six times more likely to be out of work than non-disabled people (DfEE, 2000)." from Thomas, N. "Sport and disability." in *Sport and Society*. B. Houlihan, ed. (2008). Sage Publications. Thousand Oaks, CA.

35. "By severity, 27.5 percent of adults with severe disabilities were employed compared with 71.2 percent of adults with non-severe disabilities" from http://www.census.gov/prod/2012pubs/p70-131.pdf

36. Sins Invalid. (2009). *Our Vision*. URL: http://sinsinvalid.org/vision.html

My Story

This book is my story. Well, part of it anyway. No one (at least not me) can write it all. Some I am holding back because I made a pact with myself to do no harm with this book (and in some places that was harder than I expected). Some moments of history I can no longer recall (a side effect of a lifetime of dissociation). Sometimes I just could not bear to tell the truth publicly. I've shown this book, or parts of it, to many people. They've all been intrigued, shocked, and/or laughed at parts of it—rarely the same parts. Whether these stories will resonate with you, I cannot know. I only know that I am telling you the best truth I can at this point in my life.

These stories are not complete. I can only tell you what I saw from my seat on the late 20th century U.S. disability history bus. I remember details, and, as I've become aware, they are mostly about white people, about women and girls, and about disabled people. Those are the lenses I've worn. If you are a person of color who was there, and/or you were not female when I knew you, and/or you were not disabled, I hope you tell your story, for we need more stories. The ones we have of 1970s U.S. disability history focus on white, middle class people with physical disabilities and their organizations.[37] I am glad those stories are preserved, and I am deeply sad that those are the only ones that have been preserved permanently.

I am a unique package shaped by abuse and Irish history and immigration and the Boston superiority that spreads all the way down to the working classes. I am a woman who was taught she was not a woman by virtue of her long steel leg braces, and lace up, high top, boys' brown leather shoes (the better to accommodate the leg braces). I was never supposed to be married, to have children—according to my family and community. At best, I was supposed to get a job, support myself, and be the spinster aunt to my siblings' children. Being freed from the societal expectations of females created a wonderful recipe for letting me know that being a lesbian was a great option.

My writing buddy, Naomi Ortiz (disabled), laments the rigidity of books. What we write is preserved, critiqued and analyzed, yet it is only a snapshot of our thinking at that time. Hopefully, it is our best thinking, yet we know that it is and will be full of contradictions and half-formed ideas. A week after publication we will realize the importance of changing a now unchangeable sentence. That book will

---

37. See note 36.

go into the world locking the writer into that version of the truth.

These essays tell my story of only one moment. And like a photograph, the point of view decides the story that is shared. The photo viewer never knows what lies outside the picture's frame.

I share disability history with all the others who lived it. We all had many different observation points, so our stories are necessarily contradictory. My filters allowed me to see and remember the white people much more clearly than the people of color; the women more than the men; the children more than their parents; the kind people more than the mean ones; the queers more than the straights. I am a white girl from a white neighborhood who went to white schools and whose biggest historical achievement, the 504 sit-in, depended on the Black Panther Party from Oakland, California, for our success. I love the irony. I was taught to hate and fear powerful Black men, yet my survival and my first major activist political success depended on them.

My history is messy. There are lots of contradictions, gaps, confusing realities. I connect best with people who are poor, yet educated; fierce, yet kind; strong, yet vulnerable. At my best I am these things, at my worst I am not.

I cannot tell you my stories of joy and surprise and sometimes even inspiration if you do not know that I also carry within me the shame of being a burden, a problem, an unexpected and unwelcome intrusion. I can craft stories of pride and community and impress you with my resilience and cleverness. But unless I draw back the curtain, you might believe that people like me, with impairing disabilities, live in the same world you do. But we don't. At least I don't.

My world is multicultural. In the mainstream world, I am a fat cripple. In the disability activist world, I am a queer. In the queer world, I am a dissatisfied disability activist. I am all of these and often none of these. I have learned the academic skills demanded of white people, so I can participate in the educated upper class white world. This saved me many times from being forced to live in institutions. I have learned the disability cultural norms that allow me safe passage through gnarly[38.] bodies and creative minds to the beauty and resources deep within. I learned the mannerisms of soft butch, to pass enough to get laid in queer communities.

I am all of these and none of these. I am told to believe that I belong everywhere, but mostly I know that I belong nowhere. Each of my worlds does not want the other parts present. So my stories are messy. No neat margins here. My life spills in too many directions to be

---

38. I intentionally use the word "gnarly" here in homage to Cheryl Marie Wade (disabled), a poet who greatly influenced me.

contained. Sometimes I cannot be seen because my life overflows community boundaries. Other times parts of me lie invisible.

There are scars all over my body. The visible ones tell stories of surgeries to force my polio-atrophied muscles to obey, in the attempt to make me more like "normal." After decades, my body rebels, tightens up and returns to its original polio state. The body always wins.

In 1950s Boston I grew up in a family where I was the wrong gender in the wrong body. My mom promised my dad that their first child would be a boy. Dad decided I would be named Michael. But when I arrived with female genitalia, my mom named me Joan as the closest female name to his, Joe. I am forever grateful that she did not choose "Josephine." The mis-gendered assumptions foreshadowed the myriad ways that I would forever be mis-assigned, mis-understood, and mis-labeled. I learned early that mystifying people often angers and disappoints them.

Is it a boy or girl? Is everything all right? These are the questions people ask of new babies. Providing expected answers to gender assignments and health status maintains societal expectations. My gender disappointed my father, who impregnated my mother annually to get his promised son (whom he, inexplicably, called Stephen).

For my first birthday, in 1952, I received the gift of polio, an infinitesimally tiny gift, but one with enough power to shape my whole world. Having a child with polio meant that my family got the gift of major medical expenses. Polio in 1952 meant steel leg braces, numerous surgeries, an orthopedic corset, and wooden underarm crutches. My mother's already frail back now had to lift my toddler body, encased in a toe-to-neck plaster cast. My newborn sister had to wait for care, because now there were two bodies unable to do anything for themselves. We all also received gratuitous and often hurtful comments from strangers every day.

"What's wrong with her?" was by far the most common comment during my childhood. "Isn't she cute? What's her name? How old is she?" These were the questions asked about my nondisabled sister. Everyone reminded me that how I was, which I often interpreted as who I was, made them uncomfortable. My very presence in their universe was unexpected and unwelcome.

Fighting my way through the neighborhood questioning prepared me to fight my way through unwelcoming schools. After a successful kindergarten year at my local public school, the principal told my mom that I would not be allowed to return for first grade because the classrooms were all upstairs. Even after my mom pointed out that we lived in a second floor apartment, the principal remained adamant and so did the school district. My mom marched me down and registered me for the local Catholic school, forcing my siblings to attend as well. High school graduation led to college, with a degree in Special Education, because even then I wanted to be connected to other disabled people and that was the only way open to me.

Life took an unexpected turn when, in 1973, I moved to Berkeley, California with a friend from college who was going to attend graduate school at UC Berkeley (which in this book I refer to by its common nickname "Cal"). I didn't know anybody else, so I spent a good deal of time wandering around Cal. Being in the city of Berkeley in 1973 was heady stuff. By then I no longer needed my leg braces and corset, and I walked with one cane. So, depending on the situation, I could pass or not pass as nondisabled. Yet, even though those heavy steel leg braces were not on my body anymore, their invisible scars were present and they were always an ongoing part of my image of myself.

In March 1974, at the International Women's Day celebration at Cal, I met Susan Sygall (disabled) staffing an informational booth for the Disabled Women's Coalition. Through the Coalition, I connected with adult disabled women and decided to start a disabled women's support group, which in those days was called a "rap group." Curtis "Kitty" Cone (disabled), who would later be a national leader in disability activism, but at that time was a lowly employee at the new Center for Independent Living, joined the group right from the beginning. With Kitty's guidance, the group became both a support system for members and a hotbed of activism. I ended up working at the Berkeley Center for Independent Living, and while there became involved in 1977 with the 504 sit-in in San Francisco.

After the sit-in, I became a trainer with the new 504 Training Project. The 504 Training Project brought me to the attention of the newly forming Disability Rights Education and Defense Fund, and with their support and fund raising I ran the three-year First National Educational Equity Project on Disabled Women and Girls. In 1983, when my project ended, I began volunteering with various disability circles. In 1992, I organized workshops on sexuality, a favorite topic of mine, at the National Council on Independent Living conference in Oakland, California. In 1995, I organized North American disabled women who wanted to participate in the Fourth World Conference on Women in Beijing, China.[39] At both the Beijing conference and the subsequent International Leadership Forum for Women with

---

39. URL: http://www.un.org/womenwatch/daw/beijing/

Disabilities in 1997,[40.] I interviewed and videotaped dozens of disabled women from around the world. In 2002, I co-organized the first international Queer Disability Conference.[41.]

Along the way, I worked on a lot of other conferences, gave numerous presentations, and became a parent to a disabled daughter. In the mid-1980s, I stopped focusing on educating nondisabled people, and turned my focus to supporting work led by members of different disability circles. Since that time, I've followed the philosophy of doing the work that was right in front of me. This has led to a rewarding, if somewhat meandering, path through feminist communities, disability studies, and more recently the arts.

I'm now 63 years old, quite old for a person with polio. I often joke that, for those of us with lifelong disabilities, no matter our chronological age, disability adds 20 years. It's very important to me during my elder years to ensure that the disability history knowledge that is locked in my head is passed on.[42.]

The Book

Obviously there's a lot that needs to be written about the U.S. histories of disability circles from the 1970s to 2002. In this book, I write about two general topics: disability history that I participated in and disability topics that I am passionate about. I've lived through an important period in disability history. For many of us, we are the first generation who had the possibility of living our entire lives outside of institutions. That does not mean that the threat of institutionalization is gone, only that now there are enough options that, with a lot of resources and support, the possibility of staying outside institutional clutches exists.

---

40. "The International Leadership Forum for Women with Disabilities was one of the most heralded, far reaching and successful events of 1997. Held June 15-20 in Washington, D.C., the Forum attracted legislators, artists, advocates, organizational executives, trainers, international assistance experts and grassroots development specialists from around the globe. As a follow-up to the United Nations 4th World Conference on Women held in Beijing in 1995, the Forum served as an international progress report on concrete implementations of the Beijing Platform for Action benefiting the world's estimated 300 million disabled women and girls." from The Center on Human Policy at Syracuse University. URL: http://thechp.syr.edu/women-and-disability-conference-proceedings/

41. Queer Disability Conference URL: http://www.disabilityhistory.org/dwa/queer/

42. I am extremely grateful to Elizabeth "Ibby" Grace (disabled) and Autonomous Press for asking me to be part of their inaugural book series. Every word of this book was read (often multiple times) by Naomi Ortiz (disabled), who offered loving guidance as my writing buddy and Ginger Barnhart (nondisabled), who made sure that every word was spelled correctly, that my citations were complete, and turned my sloppy references into useable information. Michael Monje (disabled) managed all the formatting, copy editing, and printing. Paula C. Durbin-Westby (disabled) indexed the book. Without them this book would never have happened.

Disability history is extremely hard to tell. It's a story of community but also of individuals. Disability history is embedded in politics, identity, violence, assumptions, and enough written misinformation to fill the Smithsonian. It's also a history that is largely unexplored and undocumented, even though disabled people have always been here.

We live in a time where disabled people are tolerated, but not welcomed; where violence against disabled people is an everyday occurrence; where much of society, from schools to hospitals to employers, get to choose whether or not they allow us in. This is despite significant state and federal legislation that purportedly guarantees our rights, but in reality merely guides people's decisions about whether or not they want to include us.

In many ways this book is a push back against the pervasive disregard for disabled peoples' lives. My journey reflects a common trajectory. I was a disabled child that only met one disabled adult until I was 18 years old, and that adult was the director of my disabled kids' summer camp. Yet quite by accident I found my way to Berkeley, California, in 1973 just as the disability rights movement[43] was blossoming. In Judy Heumann (disabled)'s oral history, she talks about the difference between large city disability activism, such as in New York City, and smaller community activism, such as in Berkeley, California. Her interview was conducted far after the extremely successful 1977 504 sit-in, so she has the long view of history. She noted that while the east coast disability circles have numerical supremacy, the Berkeley disability activists have a passion and tenacity rival to none. Many social justice movements have strong ties to the Berkeley area and the history of the Student Movement, the Black Panther Party, National Council of La Raza, the American Indian Movement, gay rights, and many other social justice movements provided expertise and support for the developing disability rights movement.

I'm telling my stories of disability history not because they're the most important stories to be told, or even the least known, although some of them certainly are. I'm telling them to leave a trail that future scholars can follow. Forty years is a very long time to live in a vibrant and ever-changing activist community. I was privileged to watch some of the most important moments of disability rights happen, to sit next to the national leaders, and to watch a movement grow. Living in the Berkeley area immersed me in dialogues about disabled people and society that deepened my thinking and continually challenged me. This book shares the insights I've gained by being near power but never in

---

43. "Disability rights movement"'refers to the disability civil rights work that is conducted by organizations run by and for disabled people.

power, by being part of the disability community and yet always a queer outsider, and by watching far too many disabled people die without leaving their stories archived.

Terms

To reduce confusion and to differentiate, when I am referring to the City of Berkeley I use the city name "Berkeley," and when I'm referring to the University of California at Berkeley I use the university's popular designation of "Cal."

Throughout the book, I always default to the terms preferred by different disability circles. So sometimes you will see the word "deaf" written as "Deaf" and sometimes as "deaf." Sometimes you'll read me writing about "people with" certain kinds of disabilities, such as people with cancer, and at other times I will just name the disability as in "hemophiliacs believe..."[44]

I was very intentional in the methodology for this book and want to make transparent my decisions in hopes of opening further discussions. In no way do I see my conventions as complete. I prefer that the reader think of them as question marks for further discussion.

Perhaps most jarring to readers who are unfamiliar with my work is my intentional decision to record the disability status of everyone named in the book. So for example I might say Judy Heumann (disabled). The other two categories I employ consistently are (nondisabled) and (unknown). I want to note that all qualifiers are based on public statements, either in the writings of the person or in their public presentations, and not based on my personal interpretations or knowledge. So for example, if I know from personal experience that someone has a disability but they have chosen not to disclose it in any public way, I will list them either as nondisabled (if the public record shows that that's how they have represented themselves), or as unknown (if there is no public record indicating disabled or nondisabled).

---

44. "I believe that taking the words that we use for ourselves too seriously is a sign that we're uncomfortable with who we are and the whole like "People First" movement, like no blind people refer to themselves as people with blindness. And if they do it's because they're not comfortable with their blindness. And the whole calling yourself a blind person, you know would you ever say if you're rich are you a rich person or are you a person with wealth right?.... And I think that interestingly enough the people first language is actually in direct conflict with identity language by saying I am a blind person that's putting blind first because I'm proud of it. If I put it second, that means I'm trying to hide it. And I'm a grown up now and I'm proud of the difference that I have. I am no longer ashamed of the differences. I think they add to who I am." Josh Miele (disabled) (2014), at The Story Corps Project, for the Disability Visibility Project. URL: http://disabilityvisibilityproject.com

A few other conventions that should be noted are the ways in which I'm categorizing different parts of the disability worlds, such as the "disability rights organizations," "disability circles," and "disability justice groups."

When I write "disability rights organizations" I mean those organizations set up by and for disabled people, that maintain that their mission is to fight for the rights of disabled people, and that most frequently ally themselves with the 1970s concepts of disability rights and independent living. Examples of these organizations are the independent living centers, state and national independent living organizations, and national disability-run groups. A typical mission statement focuses on the need for equal opportunity and enforcement of disability rights laws, like this one from National Council on Independent Living (NCIL): "NCIL advances independent living and the rights of people with disabilities. NCIL envisions a world in which people with disabilities are valued equally and participate fully."

Often when I write the phrase "the disability community" I mean those groups aligned with the principles of disability rights and independent living, whether they are organizations or not.

"Disability circles" means the formal and informal networks among disabled people. These groups provide welcome to new members, support and invaluable community knowledge. They are run by and for disabled people and rarely involve professionals. These circles are often loosely organized, so for example, if I need to find polio-related information, I contact the local post-polio support group, which is an informal monthly gathering of people with polio. With them I have the option of getting my information from their website, from their phone contact person or by attending a meeting. These circles are the social networks that teach advocacy and problem solving not through formal classes, but through one-on-one sharing of information. The vast majority of disabled people who are connected to other disabled people do so through these loose but very important circles. An example of how one of these circles defines itself:

> San Diego Polio Survivors is an unofficial, all volunteer, non-commercial, organization that meets to share information about polio and post polio syndrome (PPS) for those who live in the San Diego County area and for anyone else regardless of where they live.[45]

---

45. San Diego Polio Survivors. URL: http://polio.home.mindspring.com/

When I refer to "disability justice groups," I mean that the organization, at its foundation, examines and commits itself to prioritize the principles of justice above access; that the organization's leadership is disabled people of color; and that whatever services are provided, the organization equally commits to social justice activism. Sins Invalid, a disability justice performance group quoted above, created this clear statement of welcome:

> Sins Invalid is a disability justice-based performance project centering disabled artists of color and queer / gender non-conforming disabled artists. Our work celebrates the embodied humanity of disabled people, and we understand all bodies live in a multitude of very real social, political, economic and cultural contexts.[46.]

In addition to performances, primarily comprised of disabled people of color and disabled queers, they also train social justice organizations on disability justice. Their intersectional work is articulated in their vision statement:

> Sins Invalid is committed to social and economic justice for all people with disabilities—in lockdowns, in shelters, on the streets, visibly disabled, invisibly disabled, sensory minority, environmentally injured, psychiatric survivors—moving beyond individual legal rights to collective human rights.[47.]

Just to recap for clarity. In this book I am using "disability rights organizations" to mean disability-led organizations based on the principles of independent living and individual disability rights. The team "disability community" means both individuals and organizations who follow the principles of independent living and disability rights. The term "disability circles" refers to groups of disabled people who have no ongoing paid staff, but who provide important peer support and invaluable resources because they are connected through affinity (such as queer, black, Deaf, etc.). The term "disability justice groups" means those groups led by disabled people of color whose work publicly advocates for the needs of all disabled people, especially those from multiply marginalized communities.

---

46. Sins Invalid blog. URL: http://sinsinvalid.org/blog/

47. Sins Invalid. (2009). *Our Vision*. URL: http://sinsinvalid.org/vision.html

Kitchen Table Activist

I am a kitchen table activist. For me, if it can't happen around the kitchen table then it's not worth my limited energy. What I mean by that is that I believe in the power of simple conversation, a basic human connection, as the most important way to move equality and justice for disabled people forward. In my parents' house everything happened at the kitchen table. Being a kitchen table activist means that I want to create spaces for conversation, for interactions, that provide respect and access for everybody at the table. I like to mix it up, and having lots of different kinds of people at the table at the same time definitely makes for more interesting conversations.[48.]

My kitchen table is working class. People stop by and sit around the table to have a cup of coffee (or water or juice). It's where you talk to your friend and neighbor while you are folding your laundry. It's a place of welcome and nurturance. And even though I say "sit at the table," in no way do I mean that people need to sit down. Only that we're close enough to communicate.

Plain Language

When I was growing up my dad would sit at the kitchen table and read the newspaper every day. We were lucky that we were in Boston, a city that likes a good newspaper, so he was reading the Boston Globe. All my grandparents were Irish immigrants. They could read and write well enough to get by, but that was about all. My dad struggled with reading as a kid. He didn't like to read books, but he loved to read the newspaper. And he loved to talk about what he was reading.

When I sat down to write this book I thought about my father a lot. He's been dead a long time, but the lessons he taught me have stayed with me. I wanted to write a book that someone like him could read. My dad was a smart guy, but he never learned any kind of fancy academic jargon. Oh, he could talk his way around the parts of a car, but he certainly could not have a conversation about political theory.[49.]

When I first moved to California, I hung out with a lot of women who called themselves feminists. I loved what they were fighting for, I

---

48. Zach Richter (disabled) critiques the dining room table as a site of distress and sometimes violence against bodyminds that do not sit still. At my kitchen table all are welcome to bring their authentic bodyminds. I saw Zach present his initial thinking on this at the 2014 Queer Spaces, Queer Places Conference at The Ohio State University.

49. Although he needed to translate the car mechanics information into plain language for me.

loved the ways they made the world bigger for women and I loved the freedom I felt being around feminists. But sometimes I would end up at political meetings where people were going on and on about "the working class," and it always struck me as ironic that the people they were talking about, people like my parents, would not have understood a word that was being said in the room.

I have no interest in any political movement unless we are all welcomed, even, and perhaps most especially, the movements for the rights of disabled people. So while I certainly know some of those fancy words, a benefit of my mom teaching me to read and sending me to college, and of being mentored by many friends with Ph.Ds, I've intentionally chosen not to use them in this book. At the beginning of this book project, my friend Ginger agreed to read every word and do the editing for me. To keep her entertained, I would occasionally slip in a big word knowing that she would delete it during the editing. It became a running joke for us, as I tried to find the silliest and least known word to slip into the text. I want my friends to be able to read what I've written. I want us to be able to have deep and thoughtful discussions based on the content of what I'm saying, without the words that I use being a barrier between us.[50]

Some people call this "plain language," others say "clear language" or "accessible language." For this book, I'm using the term preferred by organizations such as Self Advocates Becoming Empowered,[51] who call it "plain language." Whether you call it plain language or not, the point is the same, to make sure that the words are written in such a way that all the people who want to be part of the conversation can be.[52]

One of the issues I want to challenge by intentionally using plain language is the presumption that using plain language means making the information simpler, the ideas less complex. "Dumbing the material down" is the way that I've often heard it said. That phrase is incredibly ableist, meaning that it insults people by presuming that plain language is a less intellectual way of communicating. Choosing to not write in plain language is just like putting steps in front of a building instead of a ramp. It tells some people they are welcome and makes sure that other people never get in.

For some people, reading is a chore, a horrible, exhausting chore.

50. I also benefit from plain language when I am with my academic friends. They can present information with the specialized vocabulary of their academic training, but they often choose to use plain language so that I can participate in the conversation.

51. Self Advocates Becoming Empowered. URL: http://www.sabeusa.org/

52. See Elizabeth "Ibby" Grace's excellent article on this: "Cognitively Accessible Language (Why We Should Care)." (November 22, 2013) *The Feminist Wire*. URL: http://thefeministwire.com/2013/11/cognitively-accessible-language-why-we-should-care/

Each chapter in this book begins with a Summary which has the following requirements: short (1-2 paragraphs); plain language (no jargon) and easy to find. Having a short Summary helps folks decide whether or not it's worth it to read the whole chapter right now.

In writing each essay, I tried to use plain language as much as possible. I've been thinking about the topics in this book for decades. As I've talked to a lot of different people about these ideas, my thinking on these subjects has become more complicated and nuanced. I felt completely comfortable writing these topics mainly using plain language. Any places where I deviated from using plain language in the essay itself is probably due to my ego and a failure of my imagination.

In addition to writing in plain language for the Summary and essay, it's important that the more technical parts of the book are as accessible as possible. At times, this meant deviating from traditional methods of documenting information.[53] When I had to choose between academic standards and accessibility (which I think of in this context as making the information as easy to use as possible), I always deferred to access.

I struggled to find a way to reference materials and still make the book readable for people who are distracted by typical academic styles, such as putting author information into the text. There were many times in writing this book when I longed for the ease of a website link. In the end, it seemed that including small numbers in superscript was the least intrusive.

I could not subject my readers to citations like this: "Disabled people are poor (U.S. Census Bureau, 2012) and unemployed (Department of Labor, 2010)." When I could just reference it with superscript: "Disabled people are poor[1] and unemployed.[2]"

If I am giving a reference, a small number appears next to the word and a reader can look at the the bottom of the page for the footnote. The footnotes do not follow a traditional formatting protocol. Instead, they point to references but explain points that might be confusing (such as why sometimes a person is "deaf" and other times a different person is "Deaf"). As you have seen, I have a lot to say about each topic, and many times the footnotes are extremely long. (I guess that's why book people make the type size on them so small.) I worked hard to make the language that I use in the footnotes as close to plain language as I could.

Many times when I am reading a document that has a lot of information, I have a hard time finding the information again when I need it. To help others like me, I created two sections of useful

---

53. Footnotes, references, bibliography and the like.

information and put them at the end of the essay, making them easier to find. At the end of each essay, the reader can get the historical information in a summary at "Just the Facts, Ma'am." This helps people know the time and place the events occurred. I also wanted to provide a few easy-to-find resources, so I created "Resources."

Throughout out the months spent researching this book, I intentionally depended heavily on online sources. This is also not common in academic publications. My decision to use online sources is intended to increase access for both readers and scholars, especially community-based scholars like myself.

Extremely few people, disabled or not, have access to academic sources either in print or online. The printed sources, such as books, are usually in places that require special identification and passes, such as university libraries. (I don't mean that you need special identification to check out the book. I mean that you need special university identification to be allowed into the library.)

The online sources, such as journals and academic websites, also require special passes. Typically, a university library buys a pass to an academic website and provides their own university people with that password. The richer the university, the more book and online websites they provide access to. If you do not have the special university password for online websites, then sometimes you can pay for them yourself if you really need to see that one article.

I, like nearly all disabled scholars, don't have university privileges, so I cannot get to the expensive books or professional journals. I rely on the open internet for my information.[54] I am typical of the vast majority of disabled people—permanently unemployed, poor, with limited resources[55] —and I depend on the internet to connect me with people and also to be my library. I saved a massive bibliography of everything I found while researching this book. Many of these are folded into the footnotes, but there is also a master bibliography at www.CorbettOToole.com.

One of the reasons I decided to have this book published with Autonomous Press was because of their deep commitment to maximum accessibility. Not only is this book coming out in print, but at the same time it will be available through Bookshare, a service for people with print impairments,[56] which provides books that people can

---

54. I have lots of friends with university privileges, and I am extraordinarily grateful to them for sharing their access with me. But since this is not available to many disabled scholars, I am not including it here.

55. U.S. Census Bureau. URL: http://www.census.gov/people/disability/

56. "Print impaired" means people that either can't see the printed page, can't hold the book easily,

listen to or read. They have made a lot of advances in the voices available for reading aloud, but I don't think that they've mastered the working-class queer Boston voice yet. So you'll just have to imagine my voice as you listen to the book.

So I ask you: What words do you use? Do you use plain language? At your job? In your community? In your writing? And if you do not, Why not?

Disability-Specific Language

From writing the first sentence, I needed to ask myself how I was going to talk about disabled people. Was I going to use the academic language? Was I going to use the language of service professionals? Was I going to use the disabled peoples' self- and community-identifiers? How should the time (late 20th century) and place (United States, more specifically Berkeley, California) shape the language choices?

While a blind person might use "blind" in formal contexts, they might also refer to themselves as a "blink" in a blind-only gathering. They might use "visual disability" to include all people who deviate from "normal" vision. There is a whole world of professional language to isolate and separate different visual levels. I do not use the professional language, as it rarely comes from the disability community.

Throughout the book, I defer to disabled people's "formal" word choices. So while I use "disabled" to cover all disability groups, I also use: hearing disability (D/deaf), physical disability (wheelchair user, etc.), mental disability (consumer/survivor), visual disability (blind), intellectual disability (self advocate), health disability (cancer, diabetes, etc.), and so on. Although it seems pretty clear that I am someone who would follow the lead of disabled people, I became aware of many places in the text where using that language, which is unfamiliar to many people outside disability circles, might create confusion.

Just looking at one community gives a bit of perspective. People who are prescribed medications by psychiatrists use many different terms for themselves.[57] People might refer to themselves as "mad"[58] (and having Mad Pride), "a consumer/survivor,"[59] and the variation

---

and/or can't read easily. Bookshare URL: https://www.bookshare.org/cms

57. All these examples are from national organizations run by and for people with mental disabilities.

58. "Mad Pride participants use and refuse a variety of labels. We choose "mad" as an umbrella term." URL: http://www.theicarusproject.net/article/mad-pride-creative-maladjustment-and-mad-cartographies

59. "While most of us are psychiatric survivors," Mind Freedom. URL:

"psychiatric survivor," "having a mental disability," "diagnosed as mentally ill/with mental illness,"[60] and "people experiencing (or labeled with) madness, mental health problems or trauma."[61]

After extensive consultation with people with mental disabilities, I decided to use "consumer/survivor."[62] I know this term is not much used in the nondisabled world, but it is widely used by people with mental disabilities.

There is no standard grammatical structure in how people use their chosen disability-specific terms. People with hemophilia call themselves "hemophiliacs." The deaf community has a convention of using "Deaf" to mean people that are affiliated with the cultural and linguistic community of people who use American Sign Language, and "deaf" to indicate that someone has a hearing disability but is not necessarily tied to the cultural and linguistic capital "D" Deaf community. People with intellectual disabilities refer to themselves as "self advocates," while people who are neurodivergent[63] reject that term.

Confused yet? This is a little bit of a rabbit hole, and it's very easy to get lost in a language. Ironically, there is a ton of material written primarily by and for nondisabled people that addresses the issue of "What do you call a disabled person?" I don't know the 'right' answer, but may I suggest calling him by his name, Bob? But I digress.

I made a decision in this book to use the terms the people from different disability-specific communities use. I started by looking at organizations and online materials created by and for people from those specific disability communities. When there was a conflict of language terms, I looked to organizations with the highest percentage of disabled people and the lowest percentage of nondisabled people, and followed their convention of the words that they used. It's not a perfect system, but it's what I could do.

---

http://www.mindfreedom.org/truth/mfi-truth-200907.pdf

60. Icarus Project: "The Icarus Project is a support network and media project by and for people who experience the world in ways that are often diagnosed as mental illness." URL: http://www.theicarusproject.net/ Also, "people diagnosed with mental illness" and Psych Rights URL: http://psychrights.org/index.htm

61. "The Center for the Human Rights of Users and Survivors of Psychiatry (CHRUSP) provides strategic leadership in human rights advocacy, implementation and monitoring relevant to people experiencing (or labeled with) madness, mental health problems or trauma." URL: http://www.chrusp.org/

62. Also known as people with mental disabilities.

63. "Neurodivergent." Typically this term means people who are Autistic, and often it is used in a larger sense to encompass people with neurology-related disabilities such as mental disabilities, cerebral palsy, brain injuries, etc.

Communities, Circles and More

I've been part of the world of disabled folks for over 40 years, so I have a veritable encyclopedia of disability knowledge. When I began to write this book, one of the most confusing things to communicate was all the different ways that disabled people come together in various communities.

I spend a fair amount of writing trying to succinctly communicate a lifetime of learned nuances, such as why there are many disability communities but only one disability community. See what I mean? This section teases out the subtle differences.

I live in multiple communities, which I call "circles" in this book: some disability-focused and some not. I am part of these circles: people with polio, disability rights activists, queer people, disabled queer people, parents, parents of disabled children, disabled parents, disabled parents of disabled children, adoptive parents, athletes, disabled athletes, wheelchair athletes, abuse survivors, poor people, unemployed people, people living on government benefits, etc. Each of these circles intersect in my life but rarely do these circles interact with each other. Each of these circles contain people who are parts of many other circles such as Black people, working people, etc.

In this book I attempted to narrow the categories of disability groups down to just a few: disability rights organizations, disability circles, and disability justice groups. I talk about disability groups because nearly all the important knowledge for surviving as a disabled person is hidden in those groups. By hidden, I mean that the information is located in rooms (both online and offline) that have some kind of disability label attached to them such as 'sickle cell anemia' or 'independent living.'

Getting to that information is hard unless you know, and are willing to use, the language of the group holding the information. This information can range from the mundane such as which car rental companies offer vehicles with hand controls, to the critical, such as the hospital is refusing to get a sign language interpreter for me in the emergency room; what do I do?

Nearly always the best source of disability information is other disabled people, so knowing how to navigate into those circles is an important skill. People will read an essay in this book and try to navigate the disability world, so I want to make it as clear as possible what types of groups I am speaking about.

At an individual level I am part of many disability circles. I am also part of a larger disability community that is tied together by a belief in the principles of disability rights and independent living.

Identifiers

We go through life with our individual self-chosen identifiers as well as those assigned to us whether we agree with them or not. As a society, we refer to people by their social roles, such as parents; by their occupational roles, such as store clerk; by their perceived gender, such as male; and by many other societally assigned labels. Some of our self-chosen identifiers are more public than others—and that changes over time and with different circumstances. So while I am widely known as being queer in disability circles, I was much quieter about being queer when negotiating school services for my disabled daughter. I was no less queer, but the school environment was significantly less friendly to queer parents than to non-queer parents. So I prioritized my daughter's need for services over my own need to educate them about queer and disabled parents.

In my writing I pay a lot of attention to identifiers. I notice how they can be wonderful ways of reclaiming negative words for some people, especially when we choose them. And how they can be used as instruments of hate against people as well, often when they are chosen by others to negate and hurt us. However they are used, identifying labels can give us common reference points.

Disabled people get written out of history all the time, in nearly all societies, in all time periods. We are ignored, overlooked, mislabeled, discounted, omitted, and sometimes intentionally not discussed. While disabled people have written about themselves in all time periods and parts of the world, their work is often marginalized and ignored. If it's not ignored, their disability experience is often glossed over or omitted making it difficult to find disability history.

Every contemporary author who writes about disabled people faces the dilemma of how to include or ignore disability identity information when writing about disabled people. The more closely aligned the author is to the prevalent medical model where disabled people are seen as "sick" and "impaired," the more likely that author will only use disability information in ableist ways. Ableism in writing often takes one of two forms either omitting the disability information or presenting the disabled person's life as unique and inspiring. Unfortunately most contemporary U.S. writers chose to use existing "professional" practices that continue to erase us (as I show below). I did not want to do that with my work. My solutions are preliminary and crude, but it's a start.

What do I mean when I say disabled people are written out of contemporary history? There are many ways this occurs. Sometimes the writer is saying, "a person's disability is not important." So, for example, people write articles about the author Alice Walker, and yet no one discusses how her artistic vision is influenced by growing up with vision in only one eye. That seems like a relevant point of inquiry to me.

Another common belief from writers is that naming someone's disability is lowering their status. This happens a lot with people who are well-respected. So actress Whoopi Goldberg's learning disability is rarely mentioned, nor is Albert Einstein's. For generations President Franklin D. Roosevelt's daily use of a wheelchair was never reported or documented. Of the nearly 35,000 photos in his presidential library only three show him seated in a wheelchair, even though he used one daily.[64]

When the popular stories about Helen Keller's childhood are told, the visual disabilities of her teacher Anne Sullivan never appear. It seems as though the role of "miracle worker" conflicts with the role of "disabled person."

Of course, the other trap happens as well, with "I can only see you through your disability," which happens in writings about Frida Kahlo, Stephen Hawking, Temple Grandin, and many others. Media stories about U.S. economist and former Labor Secretary Robert Reich always comment on his height.

I love disabled bodyminds. I feel nourished when people share their experiences, their resources, the ways that they navigate the world. It intrigues me that we have so many different ways of accomplishing the same task.

I want to celebrate disability creativity, the presence of disabled people in the world, so it is extremely important to me that I leave a trail for future scholars to follow about who was and was not disabled at the time I was writing this book.

I've raised this topic in a number of different settings, at the community level and at the academic level. At the community level, talking about people's disability status and people's relationship to disability is expected. Everyone is pretty free with that information. It

---

64. "There was a gentlemen's understanding with the press that photographs displaying FDR's disability were not published. Consequently, only candid photos of FDR in his wheelchairs have survived. The Roosevelt Library owns three of them." FDR Library. *Roosevelt facts and figures.* URL: http://www.fdrlibrary.marist.edu/facts/

carries no shame, no judgment; it's just a fact among friends who are accepting of difference. I do not want to imply that there's not a hierarchy of disability, because there definitely is. It's most clearly seen in who is and is not allowed to represent the disability community in public. But I do want to say that within a community that accepts disability difference, disability specific information is considered a positive thing to know about someone, not a negative.[65.]

I love being disabled, and I love hanging out with other disabled people. It's important to me that we don't erase ourselves when we write down our histories. There are not many ways that people have tackled this in print. The most common way is for people to refer to someone's disability, or the fact that they are disabled, in a fairly oblique way. For example in a paragraph about a woman there might be the words "she has a disability" buried somewhere in there. That style of information is extremely challenging for a lot of disabled people, because the disability information is so hard to find. And to me it kind of implies a level of shame by the writer about communicating disability information. I did not want to do that.

I want to be out and loud and proud about people's relationship to disability. I've been pushing for the last 10 years to have some nuanced and new thinking happen on this topic. There's been a lot of push back, meaning a lot of people have been fighting with me about even wanting to do something as simple as I've done in this book, which is to say "Maria (disabled)." I truly wish that we were at a time in history where we'd spent the past 25 years of doing Disability Studies really thinking about our relationships to disability, developing new theories, developing new language, but we haven't. So instead I'm left with this very crude method of communicating the information.

Some of the pushback has been a concern that people's disability information should not be made public without their consent. I completely agree that disability information, when made public, should come from the person themself. So in this book I have three possible designations: disabled, nondisabled, unknown.

Before I chose any one of these three identifiers for a person, I looked at how they have identified themselves in public contexts. Have they said that they're nondisabled? Have they said that they have a disability? If I didn't know this information, I started digging through their writings and presentations to see if they stated it somewhere. If I could not find something that they themselves had said or written about having a disability or not having a disability, then I put that

65. Siebers, T. (disabled). (2010). *Disability Aesthetics (Corporealities: Discourses of Disability)*. University of Michigan Press. Ann Arbor, MI.

information into the unknown category. Even when I had personal knowledge that was in conflict with public statements, I always deferred to a person's public preferences for how I listed their identity. And in a few cases where I couldn't find anything public, I contacted the person directly and asked them which of these three identifiers they preferred that I use.

I argue that hiding a person's relationship to disability diminishes both disabled and nondisabled people. Relationships such as "parent of a young disabled child," "lover of a disabled person," "best friend of a disabled person," provide important information about how closely that person has observed, and sometimes shared, the oppression of ableism. By lumping these people into one category of "nondisabled," important differences are masked in their relationship to disability and from that of most other people. Each of these people is sharing the experiences of disability discrimination when they are out with the disabled person, and grouping them under the category "nondisabled," with people who have no connections to disabled people, ignores their valuable experiences with ableism.

Refusing to explore language options for people's relationship to disability harms the nondisabled people by ignoring the ways that ableism also impacts them as they go through life with disabled people. When I speak about individuals where their relationship to a disabled person is known, and relevant to my text, I include it. I yearn for deeper public discussions about relationships to disability that are not marred by knee jerk reactions of "you're saying that only disabled people are important" which shuts down any possibility of advancing our thinking.

I intentionally chose not to use any impairment-specific information, even when it's widely known. So for example, while Erin Esposito, a national leader on domestic violence particularly as it impacts Deaf women, is well-known to be culturally affiliated with the Deaf community, in this book I merely say Erin (disabled). I am aware that within the Deaf culture what I am doing is an heretical act,[66] but I did not feel comfortable saying Erin (Deaf) and then saying Jessie (blind). Even though both of their impairment statuses are well-known, it introduces the problem that if I then say "Maria (disabled)," I am essentially hiding a more stigmatizing impairment by not giving her an impairment-specific label. In every case I relied on only those three identity choices unless, as is the case with Erin, I was specifically speaking about her work in the Deaf community and I wanted to position her in relation to that community. So I did say "Erin (disabled),

---

66. Many Deaf communities reject the idea of being lumped under the term "disabled," because it obliterates the linguistic and cultural aspects of the Deaf person.

a Deaf professional."

All of this is complicated by the fact that people move in and out of a relationship to disability. Does the phrase "parent of a disabled child" still relate when that "child" is now an independent adult? Or does that parent become a "family member" to honor that their relationship is now adult-to-adult and not parent-to-child? Also, many of the people who I write about from the 1970s have a different relationship to disability now than they did then. I adopted the convention of keeping people's disability status related to the time period when I wrote about them. So when I write about Hal Kirshbaum in the 1970s, he is presented as a white man who moves around with one cane, even though now he uses a wheelchair.

I feel very strongly that a great deal of harm occurs when disabled people are invisible in our writings. It makes it impossible for subsequent scholars to build on our work, since to find this information they need to re-do our research. And I find incredible ableism in this push for intentional omission. I am proud of being disabled, I find great joy in discovering other disabled people in print, and I am committed to sharing whatever disability information I can.

Who is a Scholar?

Throughout the book I use the word "scholar." Frequently I use the word to refer to a contemporary person who holds great knowledge, such as myself or Leroy Moore (disabled), but who does not have any institutional titles or affiliations. We are working as scholars while living on welfare and not having access to academic resources.

I attempt to accomplish two goals with this approach. One, I want to honor the many community scholars who do important work but who are rarely recognized for their scholarship. Two, I want to tie together university-trained scholars and grassroots scholars under one title, "Scholar," recognizing that while each group has different perspectives and access to academic resources, both provide important data.

Many disabled scholars became interested in research and writing as a direct outgrowth of their work as activists. Fighting entrenched systems is hard work, and often having statistics on your side can help with that fight. Yet there is a poverty of data, mostly because the questions that communities are asking are rarely the questions that academics are researching.

Some committed individuals help activists become scholars through mentoring, support and publishing opportunities. For many years I was a disability rights activist. I knew many academic scholars, but did not have the money or available resources to attend graduate school. In the late 1980s people kept urging me to write for publication, but doing that required skills I did not possess. My friend Tanis Doe (disabled), an extremely accomplished and well-published scholar, decided to mentor me. As she co-wrote numerous articles with me, she taught me the rules of academic writing. She showed me how to shape my thoughts into coherent paragraphs and topic areas. She brought my work to the attention of the people who decide what gets published. She built my confidence and crafted me into a competent scholar.

As I learned my skills, I began to recognize the many other disabled scholars around me. Although their work is rarely, if ever, recognized as "academic scholarship," it is rigorous and thought-provoking. Sometimes the work is dismissed because the topic is not considered academic enough. Leroy Moore (disabled)'s work on disabled Hip-Hop artists, which he calls Krip-Hop,[67] is an example of overlooked scholarship. Disabled scholars may also be discounted because their bodymind deviates from what is acceptable in a presenter. Scholars with speech disabilities are often asked to submit written work, but not to do public presentations, because of deep-seated prejudices against people without fluent speech.[68]

But most often, scholarship by community-based disabled scholars is dismissed simply because of economic factors. Disabled scholars are poor. This means that they cannot attend professional conferences where they could meet other scholars and discuss their work, because they cannot afford the hundreds of dollars in registration fees, plus hotel room and travel expenses. Access to learning the skills needed to write for peer-reviewed journals is hidden behind expensive gates—primarily university graduate programs. Without rigorous graduate program training it is extremely difficult to acquire the academic skills to write for a peer-reviewed journal.

Few non-university-based disabled scholars are published in peer-reviewed journals. Their work is further disregarded by academics because they are publishing in blogs and online magazines. In a brilliant reclaiming of community-based knowledge, POOR Magazine's Race, Poverty and Media Justice Institute's Staff Directory lists Tiny

---

67. Leroy Moore - Black scholar/activist. URL:
     http://www.amoeba.com/blog/2008/07/jamoeblog/krip-hop-project-s-leroy-f-moore-on-being-black-disabled.html

68. My understanding of the impact and privileges of speech fluency have come from these scholars: Devva Kasnitz, Harilyn Rousso, Robin Stephens, Zach Richter, and Joshua St. Pierre.

(nondisabled) and Leroy (disabled) in this way: Tiny (aka Lisa Gray–Garcia), Poverty Scholar; and Leroy Moore, Race, Poverty and Disability Scholar.[69] Recognizing the important contributions of all scholars, with and without institutional affiliations, is an important step in creating a deeper and more inclusive research base.

The Myth of the Benign Myth

One of the most destructive problems facing disabled people is nondisabled people's assumption that their beliefs about disabled people are benign, which is yet another aspect of ableism. Nondisabled people believe that the stereotypes they hold and repeat are accurate, are not harmful, and are respectful towards disabled people. These stereotypes are everywhere. They are dangerous because when nondisabled people act on these stereotypes, they cause great harm to disabled people. Unfortunately they rarely realize it.

Most Americans realize that stating a stereotype that demeans another person is considered harmful. Saying that one group of people is "better" than another group of people, based only on stereotypes, is generally considered to be a devaluing of the "lesser" group.

Many people believe that people with permanent, visible disabilities are "worse off" than nondisabled people. We know this because if they thought it was cool to be disabled, people would be signing up to join us.[70] Yet the widespread belief in the inferiority of disabled people is often masked by the myths that are repeated. The myths tend to match the hierarchy of disability. People with higher status disabilities tend to have "nice" myths assigned to them such as: "People with Down Syndrome are loving." "That wheelchair man is so brave." "Blind people hear so much better than we do."

These myths quickly transform into negative ones as soon as the disabled person expects to have the same rights as a nondisabled person. Using those same examples, if each of these disabled people became a parent, the societal message about them changes rapidly. "People with Down Syndrome are not capable of knowing how to raise a child." "That wheelchair man's nondisabled wife takes such good care of the children, who must be adopted." "Blind people cannot safely care for

---

69. POOR Magazine's Race, Poverty and Media Justice Institute URL: http://www.racepovertymediajustice.org/staffDirectory.html

70. Native Americans often point out that white people feel very comfortable asserting their belief that they have a Native American relative in their family tree without any historical evidence. They just think it's cool to have a dead Indian relative. But that never translates to taking any actions to support Indian communities or causes.

children by themselves."

Throughout this book, I push for remembering that the nondisabled world neither expects nor wants disabled people as full and equal members. They willingly dismiss our gifts in order to maintain the superiority of the imaginary nondisabled body and mind in the full belief that they are part of the "normal."

I push for us to presume the competence of disabled people, to recognize the gifts disabled people bring by being disabled, not in spite of their disabilities. Being disabled in a nondisabled world teaches great problem solving skills and requires constant creativity to navigate endless barriers. Maintaining the myths about disabled people, even when they seem benign, is supporting a discriminatory world.

Fading Scars

Scars on my body mark my differences, show others how and where my "deficits" are the most severe and label me as permanently different. I had all my surgeries as a child. I remember the smooth skin that after surgeries is open, bleeding, painful. I remember the stages of healing: cuts changing from raised red welts that slowly pale, swelling lessening, leaving shiny lines surrounded by small stitch dots. My scars are precious to me, reminders of both my powerlessness to stop being cut open and my resilience at surviving. I rarely allow anyone but a lover to see my scarred legs. I keep them hidden, holding the intimacy of the now faded markings.

My scars of medical and societal abuse are invisible to nondisabled people but often seen very clearly by other disabled people. The public strippings in front of rooms of young male medical students, repeated touchings of my body without my permission and constant discussions about what is wrong with me leave scars all over my bodymind. The medically-caused scars overlap with societally-caused scars, daily reminders that I did not belong, that I was not welcome in public spaces such as schools, that I was a 'bother' and 'inconvenience.'

I have a bodymind full of scars, some from my infancy, some from last week. Like all scars they initially cause great pain, but slowly get integrated into my bodymind, creating tight places where tension is permanent, flexibility restricted.

My scars define me. I have often wanted to host a Scar Camp where I can celebrate and mourn my scars with other disabled people, where being scarred is the norm. Where we share knowledge only learned from surviving the physical and virtual scalpels. Where we sing and paint and write and perform our scar stories.

Growing up scarred created the container of my life, determined my options, shaped my future. Scars never disappear, although they fade over time. My bodymind, while incredibly resilient, does not allow the incisions to go unnoticed. Scars remind me that the traumas of my past will always accompany me, faded though they may be.

I named this book *Fading Scars* to name both the abuse and my survival. The two are permanently entwined. I do not wish to pretend that I am not scarred, for that dishonors my life and work. My scars, as much as my race and gender and family, defined the parameters of my early life, provided me with the options and tools that I used to build my adult life. I have created an interesting and challenging life not in spite of my scars, but in full acknowledgement of them.

The cover photograph of Sandie Yi (disabled) wearing her handmade art was my first choice for this book's cover. I love the way that she embraces her body, how the shorts are cut away to showcase her hip's scars, her two-digit hands. The blatant sexuality of her image reminds me to celebrate my bodymind's twisted places, embrace my scars, and revel in the glory that is the disabled body.

Fading scars never disappear. We carry them in our bodyminds forever. This book shows you some of my scars. I entrust to you, dear reader, these scarred stories from my life.

Structure

I wrote the book as a series of stand-alone essays. There are many disability stories to tell, and far too few of them get preserved. In order to make this information as useful as possible to many different communities, I wrote separate essays on each topic. Naturally, there is overlap between essays, but by and large, they stand alone.

Five essays look at specific incidents in disability history: the Berkeley Center for Independent Living, the 1977 San Francisco 504 sit-in, the founding of the first Disability Studies program, the 1995 United Nations Forum on Women in Beijing, and the 2002 international Queer Disability Conference. Some historical events are woven into larger thematic essays. The founding of the Axis Dance Troupe lies within the essay on disability culture, the genocide of an entire generation of hemophiliacs lies within the essay on queers and disability. Some essays provide historical perspective without being tied to a single event or organization. I write about issues that are widely misperceived or ignored outside disability circles including parenting, race, culture, sports and violence.

"Center for Independent Living, Berkeley" tells of the early 1970s at the Berkeley Center for Independent Living (CIL) and the ways in which it is and is not connected to Cal. In this essay I dispel a number of myths about CIL, particularly the most persistent myth which states that Ed Roberts founded CIL, because it is well documented he did not. I trace the actual history of the Berkeley CIL, relying on the 109 oral histories contained at the University of California Berkeley's Bancroft Library's Disability Rights Independent Living Movement Collection. This collection heavily favors white people, as 102 of the 109 individual interviews are white people.[71] This collection also heavily favors people with physical disabilities (64), the vast majority of whom are people who use wheelchairs. Nondisabled people (29) are the next largest group. And there are token numbers of people from other disability communities (21), queer people (7), and parents of disabled children (4). Even with these limitations, the oral histories are enormously valuable, particularly as they capture a number of people who have since died, but who provide critical historical information.

"Flexing Power: San Francisco" recounts the 1977 504 sit-in in San Francisco, in which I participated, as well as the subsequent 504 Trainings. I was merely a participant at the 504 sit-in, but sometimes that's the best seat in the house. A few years ago, I asked some disability historians, Kim Nielsen (nondisabled) and Susan Burch (disabled), what parts of my disability history they most wished I would write about. They told me they wanted to know two things about the 504 sit in: why it was successful and what one day at the sit-in looked like. I hope that I have answered their questions.

This essay also covers the 504 Trainings that were conducted by disabled people from 1979 to 1982. Disability rights organizations convinced the federal government that merely having a civil rights law meant that people needed to be trained how to use the new law. The federal government, specifically the Department of Justice, funded three years of state-by-state trainings for disabled people and parents of disabled people. I was fortunate enough to be a trainer with that program and worked throughout the American West.

"Hal Kirshbaum's Grand Experiment" looks at the field of Disability

---

71. In the University of California Berkeley Bancroft Library Disability Rights Independent Living Movement collection there are 109 personal oral histories and two institutional histories. A further breakdown shows: 102 white people; 9 people of color; 60 males; 54 females; 64 people with physical disabilities; 10 people with visual disabilities; 1 deaf person; 1 person with mental disability; 6 people with chronic health disabilities; 3 people with intellectual disabilities; 4 nondisabled parents of disabled children; 29 nondisabled, non-parents.

Studies.[72.] Although the United States history of Disability Studies often starts with the formation of the Society for Disability Studies (SDS), an earlier program, created and directed by Hal Kirshbaum, existed in Berkeley from 1975 to 1977. Hal proposed the Disability Studies Master's program and seated it at Antioch University West. Antioch University, a private liberal arts college based in Yellow Springs, Ohio, had set up a satellite program in San Francisco called Antioch University West. Since there was no wheelchair accessible public transportation in the city, Hal convinced Antioch to rent classroom trailers, which he placed in the very large parking lot of the Berkeley Center for Independent Living. Until I'm proven wrong, I am asserting that this was the first Disability Studies graduate program in the United States.

In Berkeley in the early 1970s, people with disabilities grew political and cultural circles. Along with Cheryl Marie Wade (disabled), I had the fortunate task of being the midwife for the Axis Dance Company, a physically integrated (disabled and nondisabled) dance troupe. In "Dancing Through Life," I relive those heady days of multiple companies of disabled performers. Disability arts have always flourished within disability circles, although they are rarely honored or funded. Yet all disability circles have depended on our artists to reflect back to us our joys, our struggles, and our triumphs.

In 1995, the United Nations hosted the Fourth World Conference on Women in Beijing, China. In "From Berkeley to Beijing" I recall what happened when disabled women from around the world decided to storm Beijing after having been effectively excluded from the three previous United Nations conferences on women. Unprecedented international activism brought over 200 disabled women to the conference. My personal involvement was to get 50 North American disabled women there. While there, I also conducted a series of interviews with disabled women from around the world. These are in the process of being digitally uploaded.

The "Disability Queered" essay explores the intersection of the queer and disability communities. In 1992, I attended the National Council on Independent Living's conference in Oakland, California. At that conference, I led workshops on sexuality. I was shocked by the level of intentional ignorance about safe sex, and by the outright homophobia when Independent Living Center directors stated publicly that their agencies refused to serve people who had AIDS or men they perceived as gay. This disheartened me deeply. I began to yearn for and

---

72. In academic texts the term "disability studies" is never capitalized. I have chosen to flaunt convention here to make the discipline of Disability Studies more clear.

network to create a gathering that supported, validated, and shared extensive knowledge of disabled queers. With a brilliant team of organizers, in 2002, the first international Queer Disability Conference happened in San Francisco, California. This essay also includes an examination of the ways the disability rights movement ignored the deaths of thousands of hemophiliacs and the decisions that excluded people with HIV/AIDS from disability service organizations.

The remaining essays, sprinkled throughout the book, are thematically based essays. They address topics that are threaded throughout the historical events, and that dramatically affect the lives of disabled people.

"Race and Disability" has floated in and out of my table of contents more times than I can count. Race is the topic that white-based disability rights organizations rarely address, and when they do, they rarely implement the recommendations that emerge. Disenfranchising disabled people of color, by far the numerical majority of disabled people, is a long-standing practice in the disability community. This essay examines some of the challenges, and hopefully shines a little light on a few examples of the amazing work that has been done by disabled people of color.

In 1993, my friend Atsuko Kuwana (disabled) asked me during a break at a meeting "Corbett, would you like a baby?" My immediate and resounding "YES!" shocked the onlookers. For over a decade Atsuko and her husband Michael Winter (disabled) had seen me play with everybody's kids and offer to babysit. My longing for a child was well known. Through Atsuko's contacts, my daughter came home to me. To provide her with at least a veneer of confidentiality, in this book she is referred to by the name "Joy," which I selected for how I feel every time I think about her.

In typical queer fashion, I had to "crip" parenting. One essay is "Welcome to India: Parenting Disabled Children." A separate essay covers "Disabled Parents," which is a much larger number than you might imagine. Each of these essays explores the intersections of parenting and disability from different sides.

I love being an athlete, so I wrote "Court Crips." I have always loved sports. One of my favorite parts of the disabled kids' summer camp I attended every year as a child, Camp Caravan, was the ability to play competitive sports unfettered. In my home life and my school life, where I was the only disabled person, the kid with the leg braces and the crutches, I was never included in sports. But at camp I could shoot a bow and arrow and get archery certificates. I could fish, hike, play competitive volleyball. In other words, I could just be a kid. It was disappointing to me as I aged out of camp that there were no more opportunities for me to play sports. At age 30, when I began to use a manual wheelchair, I was thrilled to find that a women's wheelchair basketball team was forming near me. When my basketball days ended, I floundered for about a decade before I discovered power soccer, a sport for people using power wheelchairs. In this essay, I look at both the history of wheelchair sports and also the role that sports plays in disability community.

Perhaps the hardest essay to write, and therefore the most researched one, was "Violence Against Disabled People." It's really hard to look at all the ways that nondisabled society enacts violence on disabled people. From bullying, to seclusion and restraint, to surgical procedures, and incarceration, disabled people have a constant threat of violence hanging over our heads. I soon realized that I had an entire book just on violence, and so this essay became what would be considered an introductory essay to a book on violence and disability.

The bulk of the book looks backwards in time, so I wanted an essay that looks forward, where I can share the exciting and vigorous work of new disability scholars and activists. I have been surprised and delighted by the new forms of disability activism that seemed to go hand-in-hand with the onset and growth of the digital world. Not only has it opened up information sources so that more information is available for disabled people without leaving their homes, but it's also opened up cross-disability communication in a way that has never been possible before. The robust ways that young disabled people are using the Internet surprises, enlightens, and at times baffles me. I have to admit that I love the ease of being able to go into an online group and say I can't find a reference on a topic and within five minutes somebody will post a reply. The "Dancing Forward" essay gives you my perspective on some of my hopes for our communities.

In closing, I want to acknowledge that writing, for all of its solitary moments, is for me very much a collaborative act. Dozens of people invested time and energy over the years to give me the knowledge I possess today. They mentored me, challenged me, and taught me critical skills. They did so without any payment, without any hope or expectation of a return on their investment. They did it because they believe in passing on knowledge, of strengthening disabled people, and of creating networks.

I chose not to include an acknowledgment section in this book, not because there are not people to thank but because listing the people who helped me over 40 years would fill many more books than just one. I am truly grateful for all of the people that have created disability circles whether in their homes, on the phone, in print, as performance, through art, and on the Internet.

I've often told young disabled scholars that it's important that we write for each other and for the disabled people coming behind us, because so much that's written even by disabled people is written to explain ourselves to the nondisabled world. We need more writings that celebrate and validate disability pride, disability resilience, and disability brilliance. Make no mistake about it, disabled people are severely oppressed, and we have barely begun to have a toehold in society. There are those seeking to destroy us through the selective abortion of disabled fetuses, the restrictions on medical services, the incarceration of disabled men (particularly disabled men of color) and the mass institutionalization of disabled elders. These forces are strong and persistent. We must create support for and resistance among disabled people. I hope this book provides some history, insights, and resources to help with that effort.

If you are reading this book because it was assigned to you in school, I will try to make the information enjoyable and outrageous enough that you might actually read what you are assigned all the way through. If you are reading this hoping for some juicy gossip, please buy me a drink, for that is a much better way to get that information. If you are disabled (whether you use that word or not) and want to get a glimpse into those who went before you, please know that I am typically atypical, in that crip freak way (much more on this later in the book). If you are related to someone with a disability, please know that I embrace my weird and loving disabled circles, and I invite you to find that pleasure with your own folks too. For everyone, please buckle up your seat belts and enjoy the ride.

JUST THE FACTS MA'AM

In the University of California Berkeley Bancroft Library Disability Rights Independent Living Movement collection there are 109 personal oral histories:

white people = 109 / people of color = 7;
males = 60 / females = 54
Physical Disability = 64 / Visual Disability = 10 / Intellectual Disability = 3 / Deaf = 1 /
Nondisabled, non-parents = 29 / nondisabled parents of disabled children = 4

RESOURCES

Clare, E. (2007). *The marrow's telling: Words in motion.* Homofactus Press, Ypsilanti, MI

Wood, C., Ed. (2014). *Criptiques.* May Day. Blog URL: http://criptiques.com/

Emma's Hope Book URL: http://emmashopebook.com/

I Am Norm URL: http://iamnorm.com/

Naomi Ortiz. (disabled) Twitter: @thinkfreestyle. "Inquisitive Writer about Self-Care for Social Justice Activists, Deep breathing Poet, Cares About The Process, Loves to Laugh, Disability Justice Activist."

Maisel, E. (November 15, 2011). "What do we mean by 'normal'?" *Psychology Today.* URL: http://www.psychologytoday.com/blog/rethinking-psychology/201111/what-do-we-mean-normal

U.S. Census Bureau Disability Statistics. URL: http://www.census.gov/people/disability/

A full bibliography is available at my website: www.corbettotoole.com

2.

Flexing Power: San Francisco 504 Sit-In

"We shall not be moved" — Civil Rights Anthem

Summary

In 1973 one sentence was added to a rehabilitation bill, in Section 504. That one sentence gave disabled people in the United States their first civil rights law, but the law could not be enforced until the federal government wrote down what that one sentence did and did not cover. The President appointed the U.S. Department of Health, Education and Welfare to write the first regulations. Some people wanted the one sentence to mean that all forms of discrimination against disabled people were covered. Other people wanted the regulations to be as weak as possible.

By 1976 the national disability community was fed up with waiting. They met and decided to ask each presidential candidate to support the disabled community and to promise to sign the 504 regulations without any new discussion or changes. Jimmy Carter promised to do that. But when he became President in January 1977, the man he put in charge of HEW refused to sign the regulations. Disabled people marched into all the regional HEW offices in April 1977 and occupied them, saying they were staying until the regulations were signed. In all the cities except San Francisco the protesters were thrown out quickly. But the San Francisco protesters occupied the HEW offices for 28 days, until the regulations were signed.

After that, disabled people went around the U.S. training people in every state about the Section 504 regulations so that people could use this new law to fight for their rights. I was part of the San Francisco protest and I also was a trainer in the 504 Training Project.

In April 1977, over 100 disability rights activists occupied the San Francisco federal building for 28 days, the longest occupation of a federal building to date. Part of a nationwide protest, the San Francisco demonstration was by far the most successful of all the protest sites. It resulted in the establishment of a law that mandates civil rights for all disabled people. Although an important historical event, very little has been written from the perspective of participants in the occupation. My account here is merely one perspective. There are numerous stories yet untold that will present both complementary and conflicting accounts, exactly what is needed for this complex history to be told.

The 504 Sit-in

Section 504 is one sentence written into the Rehabilitation Act of 1973. The sentence reads: "No otherwise qualified individual with a disability in the United States, as defined in section 705 (20) of this title, shall, solely by reason of his or her disability, be excluded from the participation in, be denied the benefits of, or be subjected to discrimination under any program or activity receiving Federal financial assistance or under any program or activity conducted by any Executive agency or by the United States Postal Service."[1]

The United States Department of Health, Education and Welfare (HEW)[2] was tasked with providing the implementing regulations.[3] Many congressional aides and disability rights organizations consulted with and monitored HEW's attempts to create these regulations.[4] By 1976, when there was still no action toward implementing the law, disability advocates got tired of waiting. 1976 was an election year, and national organizations got together and decided to approach the

---

1. Department of Labor. URL: http://www.dol.gov/oasam/regs/statutes/sec504.htm

2. In 1979, the Department of Health, Education and Welfare was separated into two departments: the Department of Education and the Department of Health, and Human Services.

3. After a law is passed, one federal agency is designated the "lead agency" to write the regulations that will guide how the law will be implemented. The U.S. Department of Health, Education and Welfare (HEW) was designated as the lead agency for Section 504.

4. James Cherry and the Action League for Physically Handicapped Adults sued the government in 1975 for issuance of 504 regulations. From Brown, S. (2000). *Freedom of movement*. URL: http://www.ilru.org/freedom-movement-il-history-and-philosophy

presidential candidates on this issue.[5] When he opened his presidential campaign at Warm Springs, Georgia, Jimmy Carter, the democratic candidate, publicly stated that he supported the disability community and would sign the 504 HEW regulations without any new changes or reviews to the law.[6]

On November 4, 1976, Jimmy Carter was elected president of the United States, and on January 20, 1977, he was sworn in. He appointed his Cabinet, and selected Joseph Califano as the head of HEW. The disability rights community rejoiced and expected Califano to sign the 504 regulations immediately as Carter had promised. Instead, Califano announced that he and his staff would review the 504 regulations and possibly make changes. The disability community was made furious by Carter's broken promise. The national organizations met, strategized, and issued an ultimatum to Carter: "Keep your promise or we will protest." At that point in American history very few groups of disabled people had organized publicly and when they had, they rarely succeeded. Califano and Carter seemed confident in ignoring the ultimatum.

On April 5, 1977, disability activists across the United States met with HEW regional secretaries in their offices, and then refused to leave. This occurred in all 10 regional HEW offices. In San Francisco 150 people showed up for the meeting with the Region IX (Region 9) HEW secretary, Joseph Maldonado. Many people were surprised that 150 people showed up with the intention of staying as long as necessary, even if it meant sleeping on cold office floors without any support structure in place. To be honest, most people who showed up had very little idea of why we were protesting, since we'd never had a civil rights law before and almost none of us understood the legislative process involved. What we did understand was that Judy Heumann (disabled), Kitty Cone (disabled), and other national disability leaders had been working on this issue for four years and had decided it was time to put our collective feet down.

So off we trudged, all 150 of us, with huge backpacks. We were trying to hide our food and medical supplies, as well as sneak in some sleeping bags. I'm really not sure why they let so many of us in for the meeting, but the security staff did not seem to communicate with their

---

5. The Action League for Physically Handicapped Adults, Disabled in Action, The American Coalition of Citizens with Disabilities, to name a few. From Brown S., see note 4.

6. At Warm Springs, Georgia, Franklin D. Roosevelt, 32nd president of the United States created an accessible retreat for himself and other disabled people. Roosevelt returned to use the therapeutic waters at Warm Springs every year, except 1942, from his first visit in 1924 until his death there in 1945. From the National Park Service. URL: http://www.nps.gov/nr/travel/presidents/roosevelts_little_white_house.html

chief administrative staff, so by the time anyone figured out there was a problem we were all inside and up on the fourth floor. A few people went into Maldonado's office for the meeting while everybody else stayed outside in the hallways. The purpose of that meeting was not to get the regulations signed, since the Regional Director, Maldonado, could not accomplish that. The purpose was to send a message to HEW Secretary Califano.

Before too long, Maldonado and his secretary left because of the protestors, his three-room office was empty, and we were making it our headquarters. People brought materials they'd found on the street and we duct-taped them around the air conditioning unit to create a refrigerated space for medications. We set up a small medical center next to the air conditioner.

The HEW offices were only three rooms on an entire floor of offices. We found a large meeting room, which became the center for all of our meetings. Not everyone fit inside, so we created informal circles for easier communication. All the groups were connected through their previously established social networks. Some people were tied together by similar disabilities (such as intellectual disabilities), others through their geography (such as San Francisco), and others through identities (such as queers). Representatives from each social circle would attend the meetings. Then we would take a break for everyone to discuss the issues in their informal circles, and we would come back together to make final decisions. No decisions were made unilaterally or by a small committee. All decisions came before everyone who was a part of the protest. For efficiency we created committees for communication, food, safety, and other issues. At our daily meetings the representatives from those committees would bring all decisions that needed to be made to the whole group.

I'm spending time describing our process because it is at the heart of the success of the sit-in. Every single person believed that their voice would be heard and their opinion attended to, even if it went against the trend of the discussion. Making decisions this way takes time and a commitment to the process. Luckily we had lots of time. By the time the FBI ratcheted up their efforts to eject us, our pattern of trusting our communal decision-making process prevented them from succeeding in their divide-and-conquer strategy.

The occupation of the building lasted 28 days. For the first week the media ignored us. We believed that this was at the behest of the FBI. Overall that was our least comfortable week, since we only had what we had brought into the building with us. By the second week the tide had turned, and the media started covering us as a civil rights protest. By the third week we sent representatives to Washington, D.C. By the fourth week, we were planning our triumphant exit from the federal building.

Setting up an encampment for 150 disabled people in a federal office building was a major challenge. For the first day or so, a few people had unrestricted access and could come and go from the building. They would go out and solicit donations for food and bring it back to the rest. I've seen some historical accounts that talk about us getting food from Safeway and McDonald's. But my memory of that time was that those businesses believed they were donating in the vein of "help the handicapped" and not supporting civil disobedience. As soon the protest hit the news, those sources of food dried up, a crisis that could have potentially ended the protest before it really began.

The solution for our food needs came from an unexpected source: the Black Panther Party. Headquartered in Oakland, the Panthers ran an extensive network of community supports including a health clinic, a school, and a free kitchen. Two members of the Black Panther Party, Brad Lomax (disabled) and Chuck Jackson (nondisabled), Brad's attendant, were participating in the sit-in. Brad used a wheelchair and had been working to build connections between the Berkeley Center for Independent Living and the Black Panther Party in Oakland. Even with the full support of the Panthers in making this connection, he had limited success, mostly due to a lack of commitment by CIL.[7] While there were always disabled people of color hanging around CIL, they were rarely hired as staff.[8] Brad's work to bring disability services to the poorer communities of Oakland was largely done by him, with the support of the Panthers.[9]

I was surprised when two nondisabled men from the Panthers arrived a few days into the protest and asked permission at our daily

---

7. Elaine Brown, chair of the Black Panther Party, met numerous times with Ed Roberts, a key disability rights figure in California. Ed expressed support for directing services into impoverished neighborhoods, but no formal commitment was ever made. From Elaine Brown, interviewed by the Paul K. Longmore Institute on Disability, (July 26, 2014). *Patient No More* Exhibit.

8. For a more complete discussion of this see the essay "Race and Disability" in this book

9. From Brown, note 7: "So we were not thinking just of rights under the law, we talked about the freedom of everyone and eventually we met with and learned about the Center for Independent living and met with Ed Roberts, but I think probably our consciousness was raised around this issue of the independence and the rights and freedom of people who were oppressed because of disability because we had a brother in the party who had become afflicted with MS who showed us that he was black and he was poor, but we didn't think about how he was going to get around and be in the Black Panther Party if he didn't have a physical ability to be in the party, so we had to transform our own thinking, which we did, which wasn't difficult because we were already recognizing our own aspects of oppression throughout the world and within the United States. So we decided to put our energy and attention into participating in any efforts on the parts mostly led by the Center for Independent Living."

meeting to feed our entire group dinner for the duration of the sit-in. In fact, I was completely and totally shocked. My knowledge of the Panthers at that time was completely limited to the white media stories of them as dangerous. After the meeting, I turned to one of the men and asked him why the Panthers were contributing this considerable resource to support a group of people that had consistently ignored Oakland's disabled people of color. He told me there were two reasons, both rooted deeply in understanding the struggle for civil rights in America, neither of which I, a naïve young white woman, understood. He told me that Brad and Chuck's commitment to the sit-in automatically guaranteed that the Panthers would support them. "Okay," I said, "I understand why you would feed Brad and Chuck, but I have no idea why you would feed the rest of us." He turned to me and said, "We support you because you're asking America to change, to treat you like human beings, like you belong. We always support people fighting for their rights."[10]

And support us they did. Every single night the Panthers showed up with a hot meal.[11] They never asked us for money, which was a good thing, since we didn't have any. They showed us what being an ally could be. We would never have succeeded without them. They are a critical part of disability history and yet their story is almost never told.[12]

Feeding over 100 people in an office building that did not have a kitchen was challenging. It was complicated by the fact that the FBI soon shut down the building, limiting which people could come and go. Once a protestor left, they told us, they would not be allowed to reenter. This kind of obstacle, restricting our movement, was old hat to us, and we quickly strategized around them. We got them to agree that safety was a priority, and that attendants and sign language interpreters needed to be allowed to come and go, as well as any healthcare professionals. Since the security staff had no knowledge of American Sign Language, if someone needed to leave the building and come back we taught them enough signs to get past the security people.

---

10. From Brown, note 7: "Our issue was systemic change and that would sweep, we presumed, all of the people who had been oppressed and left out and marginalized. Same thing with being disabled. If you cannot have all the things that you need, which includes your human dignity obviously, but if you do not have all the things that you need then you are an oppressed person, because if someone is making you pay extra for something, denying you a place to live because you can't get in and out of it, denying you freedom of movement because you can't get on transportation so we saw it from that perspective. We were very very serious about it"

11. Elaine Brown states that they also sent over food for breakfast. They did two runs every day.

12. Schweik, S. (2011). "Lomax's matrix: Disability, solidarity, and the black power of 504." *Disability Studies Quarterly*, 31(1).

Although most people think of the sit-in as exclusively about the people inside the building, the people who gathered outside the building were critical to ensuring the success of the sit-in. Organizers erected a stage, got a sound system, and rallied every single day outside the building so that the public knew what was going on. They also brought food and medical supplies and delivered them to the people inside. But it was their presence outside, within the sight lines of San Francisco city hall, the main library, and major public transit lines that kept our struggle in the eyes of the public. A little known fact is that some people who came to support us outside the building later decided to join us inside the building.

During the first week the FBI worked hard to isolate us from sources of support. I happened to be in the lobby the first night that the Black Panthers brought us dinner. The FBI blocked them and told them to leave. The Panthers, being extremely sophisticated about how to manage police interactions, merely informed the FBI that they would be bringing dinner every night of the occupation. They would bring the food, they would set it up, and they would leave. If the FBI prevented them from doing that they would go back to Oakland and bring more Black Panthers until the food got delivered to the protesters. The FBI soon backed down.

1977 was well before the advent of personal computers, cell phones, and any digital technology; it was even before the age of the fax machine. So when the FBI shut off the pay phones, we were in communication isolation. Being resourceful, we soon figured out a way around it. Because our coalition included people with a wide variety of disabilities and allies such as attendants and sign language interpreters, we had strength in numbers and many communication options. The Deaf people suggested that we could easily use sign language to overcome the communication barrier.[13]

The people outside the building wanted daily updates of what was happening inside the building, and we inside the building needed to know what was happening in the media outside. The people outside would get on the stage with a microphone and the ever-present sign language interpreters and call out to us on the fourth floor asking for an update. Someone from the communications committee would formulate an answer and one of the Deaf folks, usually Olin Fortney (disabled) or Steve McClelland (disabled), would sit on the deep granite windowsill and sign our answers to the interpreter on the stage, who

---

13. Capital "D" Deaf means that people are tied to each other through the culture and language of American Sign Language. Small "d" deaf means that people have a hearing impairment. So all Deaf people are deaf, but not all deaf people are Deaf.

would speak them into the microphone.[14] It was an elegant solution that came directly from disability experience and completely confounded the FBI with its simplicity and its effectiveness. Once we established this simple and brilliant communication system we used it every day.

With the communication challenge addressed, we turned to other basic needs. During the first week everyone was sleeping on the floor in a sleeping bag, if they brought one. We were washing up in the office sinks. The very nature of the sit-in meant that we were completely interdependent. Whenever something was needed, whoever was nearest pitched in to help. That meant that everybody was both a giver of help and a receiver of help. One of the things that was striking about the sit-in, and that's rarely been reported, was the strong presence of nondisabled people. Some of them were parents of disabled children, a few of whom were also in the building. The majority of them, though, were in the building giving up their paid work in order to ensure the safety of the disabled people inside the building. There were numerous personal care attendants as well as a number of sign language interpreters.[15]

A typical day in the first week consisted of everyone slowly waking up and helping each other with our different morning routines. That might mean emptying someone's leg bag or finding a cup of water so they could take their medications.[16] After breakfast, which everybody ate wherever they were sleeping, we'd gather for our morning meeting. Like birds, we gathered when we had critical mass, so while we aimed for meeting at the same time every day, in fact the meeting time was always dependent on how fast or slow we were all moving that day.

After the morning meeting, people would disperse. The folks who attended the meeting would have conversations with their social circles and discuss the issues that we needed to come to consensus on. People would also go to their work assignments, which were all voluntary. Lunch was often the time when people gathered across social circles and shared information and learned about each other's lives. By the

14. In Deaf circles my decision to put (disabled) after the names of Deaf people is extremely controversial and may be considered disrespectful. Although I respect the wishes of each community to define their terms, for this book I am using "disabled" to encompass people who fall under federal legal definitions of disability. In this specific context, and following my (disabled)(nondisabled)(unknown) protocol for this book, I am choosing to name them both as disabled. For more on the identity naming, see the essay "Celebrating Crip Bodyminds."

15. Personal care attendants such as Avril Harris and ASL interpreters such as Jadine Murello, Lynette Taylor, and Joe Quinn.

16. A "leg bag" is used by people who have a catheter (tube) that carries their urine and stores it in a bag tied to their leg until the bag is emptied.

afternoon meeting we were generally ready to form a consensus on the issues discussed in the morning. After the dinner provided by the Panthers we would play cards, sing, and plan the strategies for the next day.

While the first week was challenging—because, really, who wants to live with one hundred other people and sleep on the floor—our belief in the rightness of what we were doing, even when some of us didn't know why we were doing it, kept us focused. But as each day passed and we hadn't been ejected, we grew confident in our belief that we would win. In 1977 none of us knew of any place in the U.S. where visibly disabled people had been successfully arrested.[17] There were no accessible jail cells, no sign language interpreters on police interpreter lists, no Braille copies of mandatory consent forms. We had the arrogance of youth, the righteousness of our cause, and the naïveté to think that we were invulnerable. The disabled people of that era who survived to go out and live in the community did so without any institutional support. Not giving up led us to occupy the San Francisco Federal Building. We knew how to survive under adverse conditions.

As the days wore on, the local media found it increasingly difficult to maintain the news blackout. Our highly visible protesting outside the building meant that more and more people were coming to us, instead of the media, for information. Other disenfranchised groups, such as people from queer communities, also came around to see how they could help.

When the media started covering us, the attention rippled support locally, regionally, and nationally. We already had some local media connections, particularly with ABC local reporter Evan White (nondisabled). He covered the burgeoning disability rights movement and was one of the few mainstream media reporters who thoroughly knew our issues. He quickly became our go-to person for any breaking news announcements. His television coverage attracted the attention of the national press, and by the end of the second week the media descended upon us.

With positive media coverage, the political climate warmed up. San Francisco Mayor George Moscone (nondisabled) visited, and publicly supported our occupation. The Director of the California Department of Health evaluated our situation and declared us to have emergency housing needs. He obtained mattresses, blankets, and even rudimentary bathing supplies. To us, those thin emergency shelter mattresses and

---

17. People with mental and intellectual disabilities were routinely arrested in 1977, but without any accommodations for their disabilities. The folks with physical and sensory disabilities required access in order to be arrested.

blankets felt like precious presents. With the new bathing supplies, we hooked up a hose to the sink faucet in the two-stall women's bathroom, and sat or stood in a baby's bathtub that we put on the floor in front of the sinks. For the rest of the sit-in that was our primary way to bathe.

Once the media communicated our message, particularly in the San Francisco Bay Area, many supporters came forward. People brought us casseroles, clean clothes and board games. One of my most favorite donations was when Ollie (nondisabled), who owned a lesbian bar in Oakland, and her girlfriend, who was a nurse, asked us what we needed. We all said we really wanted to have clean hair. So the next afternoon they showed up with arms full of towels and gallons of shampoo and cream rinse. They opened the janitor's closet, cleaned the industrial sink, and proceeded to wash the hair of anyone who wanted. That simple act of generosity was the best gift I have ever received. They asked us what we needed, listened to our answer, and provided it for us.

With the media attention came a change in our focus. During the first week our objective was to survive and not be ejected. Now our goal shifted to getting the message out and putting pressure on HEW Secretary Califano and President Carter. In addition to communicating with the national press, we began to strategize with legislative staffers. On Friday, April 15, ten days into the sit-in, Congressmen Philip Burton and George Miller began to hold official congressional hearings in our occupied meeting room. While everyone was welcome to attend, the presence of the congressmen, the tables for them and for us to testify and the media coverage meant that our room capacity was significantly less than it had been, so people wandered in and out, catching parts of the hearing. Our usual system of having a few people in the room communicating to their social circles outside the room helped to spread the word. Anyone who wanted to testify was welcome to do so. Judy Heumann (disabled) and Kitty Cone (disabled) framed the issues explaining our frustration with the four-year delay in getting the HEW 504 regulations in place.

Getting a congressional hearing during the occupation of a federal building, over the objections of the FBI as well as HEW Secretary Califano, was a huge coup. Congressman Burton declared that our occupation of the HEW offices was now a temporary congressional office, and he ordered pay phones installed in the hallways. This was the first time we'd had personal communication options since the sit-in began. Restrictions were also eased on who could come and go from the building, since we were now a temporary congressional office.

When it was clear that we had won the media war on a local and state level, we turned our attention to strategizing how to impact

Secretary Califano and President Carter, who so far seemed unmoved by our protests. We decided it was necessary to take the fight to them and began to figure out how we were going to do that. We knew that in order to be successful we needed to take a representative group from our protest of over 100 people inside the building, as well as the hundreds outside the building, to Washington, D.C. That meant flying the representatives across country, feeding and housing them, and, perhaps the biggest challenge, transporting them.

After a lot of networking with various allies, we raised enough money to send 22 people to Washington, D.C. Naturally everyone wanted to be one of the 22, not only because it seemed like the more glamorous work, but also because it seemed to be the new frontline. Soon everyone realized that was impossible, and we began days of discussions of how and who to select to go. Early on, decisions were made to include representatives from all of the disability groups, from the various racial and ethnic communities and to include attendants and sign language interpreters. How many people from each group could go was going to be extremely limited. It did not matter whether a person had been the head of the committee or a quiet participant. It only mattered that the people in the protest, whether it was the broader disability community or their individual social circle, respected that person enough to want them to represent our issues in Washington. As soon as we made the decision to send a diverse group, I knew that my demographic (white, physically disabled female) excluded me, because I shared it with many of the "must go" leaders. While I was disappointed, I put my energies into helping different social circles find consensus to decide the people for the final Washington, D.C. slots.

In the end, the 22 people were chosen within a few days. Sometimes there were heated discussions. We discussed everyone's concerns until we all were satisfied that the group, as a whole, represented all of us. The Washington group was tasked with putting pressure on Secretary Califano and President Carter to force the signing of the 504 regulations without any changes. The larger group, the one remaining in the building, was tasked with holding the building until the regulations were signed. It was a critical, if far less glamorous, job. Our primary leverage was occupying a federal building. Although all 10 regional HEW offices were visited at the beginning of the sit-in, only a few protests succeeded in occupying the buildings overnight, and by the end of the third day only San Francisco's protesters still remained inside an HEW office.

I chose to remain with the San Francisco protesters, but I will briefly discuss what happened with the D.C. contingent.[18.] After a long cross-country flight, the D.C. protesters were transported in the back of an industrial truck to the basement of a church.[19.] The April weather was still fairly cold in D.C. and sleeping on the hard floor was far less comfortable than the mattresses and blankets available in San Francisco.

After a few hours of rest, the protesters drove to HEW Secretary Joseph Califano's house. They greeted him good morning with protest signs and singing. Neither he nor his upper class neighbors were happy with our morning serenade, and one protester reported that Califano cut through his backyard to avoid encountering our protest. Over the subsequent days we attempted to meet with Califano at his office, but he locked us out. On Sunday morning, we stood across the street from President Carter's church holding protest signs. The national media was covering all of these actions, so even though Califano ignored us, the White House staff soon got involved in attempting to defuse the situation.

Nearly one month earlier, Califano and the FBI had successfully ejected the local D.C. protesters from the HEW building. It seems that they believed they would be able to control our San Francisco contingent as well, but they underestimated our resolve, our resourcefulness, our Berkeley activism. By the time the White House staff intervened, it was clear that we were not going away until the 504 regulations were signed unchanged.

Prior to being admitted to the White House West Wing, protesters were required to agree not to sit-in at the White House. In fact every attempt was made to keep the protesters as far away from the Oval Office as possible. Unfortunately staff preparation was lacking a bit in one very significant area: bathrooms. Kitty Cone used a power wheelchair and required a wheelchair accessible bathroom. During a break in the meeting she requested to use the accessible bathroom. After considerable investigation, the White House staff realized that the only wheelchair accessible bathroom in the entire complex was the one installed by President Roosevelt to accommodate his wheelchair, and it was located in the Oval Office. So our chief negotiator and strategist, a card-carrying socialist and member of the Student Nonviolent Coordinating Committee (SNCC), was escorted to the Oval Office to

18. This reporting is based on oral histories by protesters from the D.C. contingent. I was not present in D.C., but the two groups, through geographically separated, were on the same mission, so we freely used "we" when discussing the actions in both locations.

19. In 1968 the Architectural Barriers Act, originally called the Architectural and Transportation Barriers Act, had been passed, but clear standards and regulations were not established until the Section 504 regulations were signed and then, later, the Americans with Disabilities Act (ADA) in 1990. Source URL: http://www.access-board.gov/the-board/board-history

use the bathroom.

Even though the tide was turning decidedly in our favor, Secretary Califano was determined not to be forced into signing the 504 regulations. However, it soon became apparent to White House staff that the occupation in San Francisco continued to be successful and the San Francisco protesters in Washington, D.C. were gathering media momentum. The only way to stop us was for Califano to sign the regulations, and after a few days he did.

Back in San Francisco the days got a lot more boring at the sit-in. The strategic agenda was just to hold the building. The FBI believed, mistakenly, that we were a hierarchical organization and that once our "leaders" had left we would be easy to evict. They were so very wrong. Without the distraction of national media and daily planning meetings, we had one very simple job. We would not let the D.C. protesters down by losing the building.

The FBI tried many tactics to evict us. The fire alarm would go off at 3:00 a.m. They would come through the building with dogs and tell us there was a bomb in the building. During this time they engaged with us more directly than at any other time during the occupation. It really didn't matter what they tried, because we knew that we had won. It was really just a matter of time until the regulations were signed, and two things that disabled people are really good at are waiting and problem solving. Sometimes it feels like our lives consist of long waits for access, scattered with intermittent periods of chaos. It might be that the elevator for the subway is broken, or that the required meeting with a services staff person has just been cancelled. When we are not waiting, we are often handling situations that require us to be good problem solvers, such as how to get the bottle of beer opened after you just dropped the bottle opener someplace you cannot reach.

We spoke by phone with the D.C. protesters every day and kept up with their activities on the national news. It really didn't take long for D.C. to fold. President Carter ordered Secretary Califano to sign the 504 regulations. On May 4, 1977 the 504 regulations were issued. We waited a few days for the protesters to come back from D.C. and scheduled our exit from the building to occur on Saturday April 30, 1977, when our community allies could come. The building where the HEW offices were housed also held offices for many other federal agencies, and to thank these many other federal employees who had put up with our occupation, on Friday we handed out flowers and offered them our thanks. At various points in the sit-in, we had answered their phones saying "504 sit-in. How may I help you?", borrowed their office supplies, taken showers in their bathrooms, had sex in their hallways, and generally disrupted their lives. Throughout it all they were gracious and kind to us.

A group of disabled people winning against the federal government provided a lifetime of momentum in the fight for civil rights. Each of us came away from the sit-in, whether we were inside or outside the building, knowing to our core that we had beaten the federal government and won our civil rights. This was our hero's journey. A group of disenfranchised disabled people who were widely excluded from society fought back to claim our rights.

We won doing everything the way we had succeeded as disabled people: we created an interdependent support system, we relied on the knowledge and expertise of other disabled people, we worked cooperatively, we came to our decisions by consensus, and we created the opportunity for everyone to participate. We succeeded because we did *not* do it the nondisabled way. Our success came directly from the skills we'd learned in order to survive as disabled people.

For those of us involved in the 504 sit-in, our lives were profoundly changed. Going up against the federal government and winning has that effect on people. A new generation of disability activists emerged. New leadership identified itself through working on the sit-in. New cross-disability connections were made. No matter where we went in our personal or professional lives, we carried with us that incredible experience.

A friend once asked me why our protest succeeded when so many other protests have not. I have attempted to answer that here. For me, it was because we brought the best of ourselves: our power, our humor, our trust in each other as disabled people. All those years of bonding in special education classrooms, at disabled kids' summer camps, in the medical clinics, it came to fruition at the 504 sit-in. We brought the best of ourselves and shared it with each other, and together we got the 504 regulations signed. In the process, we created momentum for decades of disability activism. So if you see me sitting and staring off into the distance with a smile on my face when you ask me about the 504 sit-in, know that I am remembering the heady joys of those days, tempered with the sadness of who has passed. The number of protesters who have died is slowly outnumbering the protesters still alive.[20] We did our job and we did it well.

---

20. The Longmore Institute at San Francisco State University recently attempted to compile a complete list of 504 sit-in participants. They found that 40 people have died.

The 504 Training

After the protests and sit-ins that got the 504 regulations signed, there came the problem of notifying disabled people and parents of disabled children of their new rights. The Department of Justice, under pressure from national disability rights organizations, put out training contracts for each of the four U.S. regions. The newly created Disability Rights Education and Defense Fund, Inc. (DREDF) was granted the contract for the 13 western U.S. states and territories.

Mary Lou Breslin (disabled), co-founder of DREDF with Robert Funk (disabled), ran the project. She hired Alan Kalmanoff (nondisabled), a professional trainer, to design a program for training the 504 trainers, who would in turn teach 100 people in each state to become the local and regional 504 community experts. As part of their selection process, local experts each agreed to provide instruction to disabled people and parents of disabled people in their new 504 rights. With a 3 year contract, we trained 100 people in each state for each of the first two years, for a total of over two hundred 504 trainers per state.[21] The final year we did advanced training to create a deeper cadre of 504 experts who often served as the 504 legal experts for their areas, since few trainings programs existed for the designated state and local enforcement officials.

Logistics presented a huge issue for the 504 Training administrators. Few airlines were equipped to transport one wheelchair and we often brought three. Nor were there many hotels with any wheelchair accessible sleeping rooms, and we needed at least ten. The local sign language interpreters were unlikely to have an experience with government jargon. In short, if we needed it, we had to plan to bring it ourselves.

By 1979 Mary Lou was using a power wheelchair. Although it gave people great mobility, the technology was primitive. Power wheelchairs broke down frequently and did not do well with jostling. Airlines in the late 70s had little experience with transporting power chairs and frequently broke parts of them during transport. Mary Lou knew that going to 13 different states while taking a minimum of 26 different flights was going to create havoc for the wheelchair users, so she designed the training staff to include a traveling wheelchair technician. She knew enough about the business to hire the most qualified repair people.

---

21. People who lived in U.S. Territories joined the 504 Training in the state closest to them.

Working with deaf people had also taught her that sign language interpreters had a wide variety of education and language skills. So not only did we need to train the deaf trainers, but we also need to train the local sign language interpreters.[22] The language of 504 was new, so the American Sign Language signs for the new legal and regulatory terms were not yet established. Our interpreters, in consultation with deaf community members, created a standardized vocabulary of the key 504 terms and concepts. In the evenings after the trainings, the deaf trainers and our sign language interpreters supplemented the day trainings with deaf-specific instruction for those who wanted it.

By having trainers who were blind, we were able to insure that the access for people with visual disabilities and the Braille handouts were done correctly. Access to both the trainings and materials required careful planning. As training participants identified additional access needs we strove to meet them. In some trainings we provided cots so people could lay down, fans to minimize environmental toxins, and we turned off the florescent lights.

For each of the 504 Trainings we sent a travel team that consisted of: one travel coordinator, three trainers from different disability communities, one wheelchair repair technician, two personal care attendants and two certified sign language interpreters. On site we hired additional attendants and interpreters as well as general support people for staffing the registration tables and handling local logistics.

This model of including access into the planning was extraordinarily rare at that time. Most disabled people, including the 504 trainers, could not participate in competitive employment because the organizations who might hire them did not provide reasonable accommodations that were needed, such as Braille, wheelchair accessible bathrooms, etc. The early work of Berkeley's disability activists, as well as the successful 504 sit-in, demonstrated that without support built in, disabled people are unable to work successfully. The 504 Trainings intentionally built in disability supports to enable both trainers and participants to have a successful training experience.

---

22. Training the local sign language interpreters was a huge part of the 504 trainings. American Sign Language is the first language for deaf people and English is a second language. But the 504 complaint process required everything to be in English. Having interpreters who knew the correct 504 signs as well as the 504 English equivalents was critically important to having deaf people be able to fight for their rights.

Training the Trainers

The 504 trainers were selected based on their ability to lecture without putting people to sleep, their ability to work on a cross-disability team, and their strong connections to various disability communities. We were a bunch of disabled folks from around the San Francisco Bay Area, none of whom had previously done more than talk in an occasional college class about our own experiences.

For the first round, all of the trainers had visible disabilities. People with no visible disabilities would be added as trainers as the years went on, but that first year it was important to establish that visibly disabled people, although often unemployed and widely considered unemployable, were in fact the leaders and trainers for enforcing Section 504.

The selection of trainers involved a rigorous vetting process. Trainers had to demonstrate the ability to communicate complex ideas in clear and simple ways, a pleasant manner, a dedication to disability rights issues and enough endurance to work 12 hour days for a minimum of three training days, plus two travel days.

Training teams were carefully balanced by both topic areas and disability needs. We would not send three Deaf trainers or three wheelchair users. Nor did the legislative analysts get paired up together. We intentionally modeled cross-disability cooperation and leadership designed for success. This was, in large part, to reflect back to the audience of disability leaders that they deserved professional training by people who, like them, were disabled.

A typical 504 training took three days. Each day we sat in a conference room from 9 to 5 going over the new requirements from the HEW regulations that were going to guide enforcement of Section 504. This was the disability community's first civil rights law. People were ecstatic. Everyone was experiencing discrimination but had nowhere to turn. A few states, notably California and New York, had state laws that provided some civil rights protections for people with disabilities, but in general there was very little legal protection. While public schools were covered by Public Law 94–142,[23] students who were not covered by that law could now get services by being covered by 504. This was

---

23. When it was passed in 1975, P.L. 94-142 guaranteed a free appropriate public education to each child with a disability. This law had a dramatic, positive impact on millions of children with disabilities in every state and each local community across the country. This law was the precursor to IDEA. Source URL:
     http://www2.ed.gov/about/offices/list/osers/idea35/history/index_pg10.html

particularly important in the state of New Mexico, which had categorically refused to accept the education monies from the federal government because it required them to adhere to Public Law 94–142.

Our trainings covered employment law, education, and public accommodations under Section 504. People had some protections with other parts of Section 5, but we did not cover that. A large part of our job was to take complicated legal concepts and translate them into usable information for advocates and parents. At the same time we needed them to know the law well enough to use it in situations where they had to prove that what they were asserting was in fact legally correct. We had a huge binder of the regulations with the examples and interpretations.

There was very little case law at this point, and what was there was contradictory. The same facts often yielded two different legal decisions in two different federal circuits. Take the example of a person who uses a wheelchair sitting at a bus stop and asking to board the bus when it arrives. Since no public transit at that time had any lifts or mechanisms for allowing a wheelchair onto a bus, there was effectively no public transportation for wheelchair users. One court said as long as the bus driver gave the wheelchair person permission to ride the bus, then the requirements of 504 were met. In a different Federal Circuit, when presented with the exact same facts, the courts ruled that just passively allowing the person on the bus did not in fact constitute access, that without a mechanism to get the person on the bus, such as a lift, the disabled person was effectively prohibited from riding the bus. Until the 504 regulations were issued by HEW, we had no guidance as to which was the correct legal interpretation, though it was perfectly clear to disabled people which interpretation in fact provided access and which did not.

My job in the trainings focused on teaching the public accommodations and the educational components, because I was a former special education teacher. I also led groups for parents of disabled children in the evenings, and I learned from the other trainers. By the end of a year, I was pretty knowledgeable about all the parts of Section 504.

Trainers rotated through the assignments so that each trainer went to approximately 1/3 of the trainings offered each year. The most popular assignment was Hawaii. The least popular assignment was Idaho, with Montana coming in a close second. Even in the late 1970s, Berkeley was a foodie community. We gotten used to the good stuff and it was hard to go and train in places where Denny's was considered haute cuisine.

As we traveled, we encountered unexpected and often silly problems. For example, when we had to fly from Phoenix to Tucson, we had to go through a separate security screening. The security man, who looked like a "good old boy" in his white shoes and white belt, freaked out when he saw a circular metal object in one of our suitcases. He refused to believe us that it was not harmful, and we were forced to pull it out and show him that it was the metal ring of a vaginal diaphragm for birth control that he was misinterpreting as handcuffs.

Many of the places we went had no unified disability community. Of course Deaf people will always find each other and network. So do Little People. For the rest of us, disability can sometimes be a very lonely experience. It was uncommon in most communities for disabled people to be out and about in public or in groups of more than one or two people at a time.

You could imagine the surprise of some restaurant patrons as our group of seven or eight disabled people would tromp into their local eating establishment. Our gaudy Berkeley clothes, our loud urban style, and our air of self-importance challenged the stereotypes of disabled people in many localities. People would not only stare at us but occasionally come over to tell us how inspiring it was for them that we were out in the community, meaning they were surprised that we were let out of the hypothetical group home where they always envisioned people like us would be. It was always tricky to navigate those moments, because we did not want to make it harder for the local disabled people. We knew that we were brash and a little bit obnoxious, but we are also full of enthusiasm about sharing our new rights.

We were so excited to be traveling around the country talking to other disabled people and parents, telling people their rights, giving people hope that the discrimination they were facing might end, or at least being mitigated by these new laws. We were offering people tools for fighting back against the discriminations they were facing every single day. Although we goofed around a lot, and many times felt like young hippies, there was also a solemnity about us and our work. We had the certainty of conviction, the fire of changing society, the deeply instilled hope that if people only knew their rights then the wrongs caused by discrimination could be worked out.

I look back now 40 years later and remember fondly what it felt like to be fighting for the cause, to know that you are right, that you are fighting on the right side, and that you are giving people the tools to fight for themselves. We were nourishing our souls while we were nourishing others, and it was like water in the desert. Much of the work itself was tedious, teaching the regulations, teaching the importance of the minutia of the regulations, but each place we went, 100 people looked at us as friends and mentors. Our job was to give them the skills and tools to make changes in their communities.

For those of us who participated in the 504 sit-in San Francisco, our passion for this work came directly from the high of having occupied a federal building for 28 days to win a major concession from the federal government. At that point we believed we could accomplish anything, that there was absolutely nothing that could stop us. We figured if the FBI and the entire weight of the federal government had not stopped us at the 504 sit-in, then there was nothing at a state level that we had to fear. We talked from our hearts, melding our passion with the regulations. It was important to us to show other disabled people that their struggles, their commitment, their dedication matched to our own.

For many of us early disability rights Berkeley activists, our 504 activities in both the sit-in and subsequent 504 Trainings shaped the rest of our careers. Fighting and beating the federal government gave us enormous confidence that we carried into the next decades of our work. I learned that when disabled people come together, work cooperatively, and stay focused on our goal, we can accomplish anything. That message got encoded in my 26 year old brain and gave me the confidence to reach for all my dreams.

JUST THE FACTS MA'AM

1973 — Rehabilitation Act of 1973 is passed, including Section 504 which prevents discrimination on the basis of disability in any program receiving federal funds.

April 5, 1977 — Disabled protesters enter all ten offices of the Department of Health Education and Welfare, intending to stage a sit-in until the Section 504 regulations are signed. 28 days later, the regulations are signed into law.

May 4, 1977 — 504 Regulations are issued.

RESOURCES

Cone, K. (n.d.) *Short history of the 504 sit-in.* URL: https://dredf.org/504site

Disability Rights Independent Living Movement interviews, especially: Curtis "Kitty" Cone, Mary Lou Breslin and Judith Heumann. URL: http://bancroft.berkeley.edu/collections/drilm/index.html

DREDF celebrates disability rights history – YouTube post of 'As We Are' Video from 1978. URL: http://www.calegaladvocates.org

Schweik, S. (2011). "Lomax's matrix: Disability, solidarity, and the black power of 504." *Disability Studies Quarterly*, 31(1).

Tanaka, T. L. (Summer, 1997). "A moving wave." Reprinted from *The Independent.* URL: https://dredf.org/504site

A full bibliography is available at my website: www.corbettotoole.com

3.

Center For Independent Living, Berkeley

"I dream a world where all/Will know sweet freedom's way"
— Langston Hughes, "I Dream a World"

Summary

In 1970 a group of disabled people in Berkeley, California created a new organization and a new philosophy. They believed that disabled people could and should run their own lives. They called this idea "Independent Living" and named their organization the "Center for Independent Living" which many people call CIL. They did not mean that the disabled person had to do everything for themselves. They meant that the disabled person was in charge of all the decisions in their lives. When disabled people from other places found out, they were excited and came to Berkeley to learn how the Berkeley people were making this idea a reality.

I moved to Berkeley in 1973 and became part of CIL and the broader disability rights movement. In this essay I talk about how CIL was structured, some of the projects we did, and some of the fun we had. I was lucky to be there at the beginning as these new ideas were developed.

❖ ❖ ❖

The Center for Independent Living (CIL) in Berkeley, California emerged from decades of disability activism both in the city of Berkeley and at the University of California Berkeley. For clarity I will refer to the city as "Berkeley" and the university as "Cal." Disabled people, both individually and through organizations, directly impacted the 20th century history of Berkeley.

In the 1850s, when Cal was founded, and through the 1960s protests, Berkeley had been a site of innovation and growth. From an historical perspective it was to be expected that the city would provide a nurturing environment for growing a disability rights movement. Although the sanitized and often erroneous story of Berkeley's independent living movement has been repeated many times, in this essay I provide a deeper and more nuanced telling of that history.

As early as the 1860s, disabled people came to Berkeley to attend the university. While they made many changes on campus, their long lasting impact has been to the city itself. The social justice activism of the 1960s created an environment that nurtured and provided political guidance for disabled people. By the mid-1970s Berkeley was a recognized international leader in disability rights and a training ground for spreading the new model of independent living. Over the past 40 years these ideas have spread worldwide. In this essay I'll examine the roots of the disability rights and independent living movements, present historical facts to correct to some widespread misassumptions, and document some histories that have remained untold.

A Bit of History

One common misconception is the belief that disabled people only began attending Cal in the 1960s when Ed Roberts (disabled) attended. Disabled people have attended Cal since it opened in the 1850s.[1] Just as there have always been disabled people in America, there have always been disabled people in higher education.[2] The numbers increased dramatically in 1869 when the School for the Deaf and the School for the Blind shared a campus on land adjacent to Cal.[3]

---

1. University of California Berkeley was originally called the College of California. URL: http://berkeley.edu/about/hist

2. Newell Perry was the first blind person to be accepted for enrollment and to graduate from Cal in 1896 (Source URL: http://www.aph.org/hall/bios/perry.html). I am unable to determine who was the first deaf person to graduate from Cal.

3. The School for the Blind and the School for the Deaf changed names many times in their combined histories. For clarity, I am only referring to them by their current names. Their origins begin in 1860 when they were founded in San Francisco as the Society for the Instruction and Maintenance of the Indigent Deaf and Dumb, and the Blind in California. In 1869 they moved to Berkeley. Later the name was changed to the Asylum for the Deaf, Dumb and Blind. In 1906 the name was changed to the California Institution for the Deaf and Blind. In 1914 the name was changed to the California School for the Deaf and Blind and in 1922 the schools were legally

When the students from the School for the Blind or the School for the Deaf had learned as much as they could from their teachers, they would walk down the hill to take classes at Cal, with school staff accompanying them to provide needed accommodations. So, for example, a deaf student who had learned everything they could at the School for the Deaf would attend classes at Cal with a staff sign language interpreter accompanying them.[4] Many students took classes but did not graduate from Cal, such as sculptor Douglas Tilden, who graduated from the School for the Deaf and enrolled at Cal in 1879, but later dropped out.[5]

The earliest disabled person I could find who graduated from Cal was Newell Perry in 1869.[6] Perry was a student at the School for the Blind, who later became the Superintendent at the School. He also mentored Jacobus tenBroek, one of the School's most famous graduates, who later joined Cal as faculty.

Finding disabled students in the historical records is challenging, because disability is always categorized as a negative, so it is often not noted in archived documents. There are many ways this happens: the disability information is not written down (meaning even though it is known the person has a disability, the index doesn't record that information); there is no overall "disability" or "handicapped" index, it's by the specific disability (meaning I cannot search on "disability," but I need to search on "blind," "lame," etc.); the person had a disability, but hid it so it never got recorded; or the person's disability is well-known but the historians don't mention it because of the negative (ableist) connotations. Until archives are indexed for disability, the research will be slow. In reviewing Cal's student-based historical media for just an hour, I found the presence of disabled people. For example, in 1924 a blind student posted a fund-raising appeal in the student newspaper asking for help to raise the funds to get a guide dog.[7] I suspect a more

---

separated. From Tat, L. (October 23, 2009). "California School for the Deaf celebrates 150 years." *Oakland Tribune*. URL: http://www.insidebayarea.com/argus/localnews/ci_13621228; **Also** California School for the Blind. URL: http://www.csb-cde.ca.gov/History.htm

4.   Some disabled students audited classes, some registered and completed classes, and some took degrees from Cal.

5.   Cal honored his connection by purchasing and prominently displaying one of his statues "Football Players." The university has Douglas Tilden's papers at this URL: http://www.oac.cdlib.org/findaid/ark:/13030/tf3t1nb05j/admin/#did-1.3.1.

6.   See note 2.

7.   OToole, C.J. (2010). "Deaf man wheelchair: How Dale Dahl brought the Deaf community to the Center for Independent Living in Berkeley." In Burch, S. & Kafer, A. (Eds.), *Deaf Meets Disability*. Washington, D.C.: Gallaudent University Press. URL: http://www.corbettotoole.com/publications/dale-dahl-judy-heumann-deaf-man-disabled-women-allies-in-1970s-berkeley/

thorough investigation would yield more disabled students.

Cal's population grew with each successive decade. By 1940 Cal had 23,000 undergraduates. Also, by the 1940s a very small number of disabled people had acquired professional training, including Jacobus tenBroek (disabled), a blind constitutional law scholar.[8] In 1942 he joined the faculty of the Speech department at Cal where he remained until his death in 1968.[9]

Jacobus tenBroek was hugely important in American law. As a leading civil rights scholar, he worked on many cases, the most famous being Brown v. Board of Education. His 1951 book, "Anti-Slavery Origins of the Fourteenth Amendment," is credited with having contributed significantly to the landmark 1954 Brown decision, which desegregated public schools in the U.S. During preparations for the famous racial justice case, tenBroek ran mock debates to help Thurgood Marshall and his team prepare their defense for the Supreme Court. TenBroek also founded the National Federation of the Blind,[10] and drafted many Federal laws and policies that created legal protections for blind people.

In 1962, Ed Roberts became the first disabled student to live in campus housing who used a wheelchair and an iron lung.[11] Polio had weakened his body.[12] He could talk, turn his head, and move two fingers. He slept in an iron lung, a large metal tube that alternated pressure and assisted his breathing. Significant advocacy by Ed, his mother Zona Roberts (nondisabled), and his College of San Mateo guidance counselor Jean Wirth (nondisabled)[13] successfully defeated the

8. "Besides his work on behalf of the blind, he was recognized as a champion of the physically disabled, the poor, immigrant workers, African-Americans, Japanese-Americans interned during World War II, and other disadvantaged minorities. As a scholar of constitutional law, he was a champion of just about every civil rights cause." Source URL: http://www.itodaynews.com/april2008/tenbroek.htm

9. Jacobus tenBroek went to Cal in 1942 as a professor in the Speech Department. In 1963 he moved to the Political Science department where he remained until his death. Source URL: https://nfb.org/images/nfb/publications/bm/bmo6/bmo605/bmo60503.htm

10. The National Federation of the Blind was the first national organization created by and for blind people. URL: http://www.nfb.org

11. University of California Berkeley, Disabled Students Program. *History.* URL: http://www.dsp.berkeley.edu/history

12. "The effects of the polio virus remained throughout Ed's lifetime. He retained some movement of two fingers on his left hand and two toes on his left foot. The rest of his body, including his lungs, remained paralyzed. Unable to breathe on his own for extended periods, he became, in the language of the day, a ventilator-dependent quadriplegic. This meant that both his arms and legs were paralyzed and that he required a machine, such as an iron lung or a ventilator, to assist him with breathing. Although he could not move, feeling remained." from Brown, S.E. (2000). "Zona and Ed Roberts: Twentieth century pioneers." *Disability Studies Quarterly* 20(1). Hosted at *Independent Living Institute.* URL: http://www.independentliving.org/docs3/brown00a.html

13. Zona and Jean are major, but rarely credited, change makers for Ed and the other Cal quadriplegics. See previous note.

Cal administrator who had initially rejected Ed's application stating, "We've tried cripples before and it didn't work."[14]

Since the Cal dormitories were not accessible, Cal administrators designated a wing of the campus Cowell Hospital as a "dormitory" for Ed.[15] The publicity generated by Ed's advocacy and ultimate success brought twelve quadriplegics to live at Cowell Hospital within a few years.[16] They proceeded to live as college students, much to the ongoing aggravation of the hospital staff. The students figured that if the university assigned a hospital wing as their dormitory, they would treat it as such—complete with beer and parties. The students named themselves the "Rolling Quads" in 1969. By then, Ed had left Cal, but his advocacy and approach provided the philosophical basis for them.[17]

The Cowell hospital dormitory allowed students to share resources, such as personal care attendants and spare wheelchair parts. The university created a small space for doing wheelchair repairs and other Cal students came to Cowell to use it.[18] This broadened the physically disabled community beyond the Cowell students and laid the foundation for the Physically Disabled Students Program (PDSP).

As is true of many severely disabled people, their families often provided support well into their adult years. Zona Roberts continued to assist Ed in his advocacy.[19] When the Rolling Quads wanted to create a support base for disabled students, Zona turned to her old ally, and Ed's community college counselor, Jean Wirth.[20] Jean had written successful government grants for the College of San Mateo and she began to investigate possible funding sources for the Rolling Quads.

Jean found a U.S. Department of Health, Education and Welfare grant program targeted towards helping disadvantaged students succeed

---

14. Independent Living USA. *Ed Roberts: The father of independent living.* URL: http://www.ilusa.com/links/022301ed_roberts.htm

15. Edward V. Roberts, "The UC Berkeley Years: First Student Resident at Cowell Hospital, 1962," an oral history conducted in 1994 by Susan O'Hara in *University of California's Cowell Hospital Residence Program for Physically Disabled Students, 1962-1975: Catalyst for Berkeley's Independent Living Movement*, Regional Oral History Office, The Bancroft Library, University of California, Berkeley, 2000. URL: http://content.cdlib.org/ark:/13030/kt9t1nb3t1/

16. Cowell Hospital accepted Ed in 1962. By 1975 when Susan O'Hara became director of the new disabled students' Residence Program she moved it out of the hospital and into the dorms. Her reason? To stop the "needless stigma" attached to living in a hospital. See note 11.

17. See note 11.

18. Johnnie Lacy oral history in the Disability Rights Independent Living Movement (DRILM) Historical Archives. The Regional Oral History Office, The Bancroft Library, University of California, Berkeley. URL: http://bancroft.berkeley.edu/collections/drilm/index.html

19. After her children left home and her husband died, Zona attended the College of San Mateo and then transferred and graduated from Cal in 1969. See note 12

20. Impressed with Jean's successful college retention programs with students of color, the U.S. Department of Education offered her a job in Washington, D.C. See note 12.

at four-year universities. The Rolling Quads decided to apply for the funding, but first they needed to convince the grants managers that disabled people were indeed a "minority," since the grant proposal only designated racial and ethnic minorities in the application. The Rolling Quads, with support from Zona and Jean, argued successfully that disabled students were in fact an underserved minority on college campuses and deserving of funding.[21] In 1970 the Department of Education gave a grant of $80,000 to establish a new Physically Disabled Students Program (PDSP).[22]

The Physically Disabled Students Program rented space one block south of campus. The grant provided funding for a few staff people who would provide these services: referrals to personal care attendants, referrals to off campus housing, wheelchair repair, wheelchair van repair and peer counseling.[23] In addition, PDSP provided free meeting space to local groups if wheelchair access was needed as well as a wheelchair accessible restroom, one of a only a handful near Cal.

Initially, the off-campus disability community welcomed the new Physically Disabled Students Program. Many had written letters and advocated for its creation, believing that while Cal students would be prioritized, the resources would be available for the entire Berkeley disabled community. Although initially envisioned by the community as a community resource, it quickly became apparent that the Physically Disabled Students Program was unable to meet the needs of campus students as well as community members. Soon after it opened, services were restricted to registered Cal students only.

This was a huge issue because in the early 1970s there was no wheelchair accessible public transportation,[24] very few options for wheelchair repair, and no place to get lists of potential attendants or wheelchair accessible apartments.[25] In short, the Physically Disabled

---

21. Charles "Chuck" Grimes, a wheelchair repair technician, documented this history. From Charles A. Grimes oral history in the *Disability Rights Independent Living Movement (DRILM) Historical Archives*. The Regional Oral History Office, The Bancroft Library, University of California, Berkeley. URLs: http://bancroft.berkeley.edu/collections/drilm/index.html; http://bancroft.berkeley.edu/collections/drilm/collection/items/grimes.html

22. See note 14 and Zona Roberts' oral history in the *Disability Rights Independent Living Movement (DRILM) Historical Archives*. The Regional Oral History Office, The Bancroft Library, University of California, Berkeley. URL: http://bancroft.berkeley.edu/collections/drilm/index.html

23. This is discussed in numerous DRILM histories under "Disabled Students Program, University of California, Berkeley." Source URL: http://bancroft.berkeley.edu/collections/drilm/collection/organizations.html#dsp

24. Although public bus service around the Berkeley area began in 1960, the transit company, AC Transit, did not have accessible buses on all lines until 1992. Source URL: http://www.actransit.org. The subway system, BART, did not open until 1972, but it did not have full elevator access until the early 1980s.

25. See note 21.

Students' Program was the only game in town, and yet their services were limited to Cal students.

Many community members felt that this policy was unjust, privileged, and unkind.[26] They, too, had attended meetings with university officials. They, too, had supported the writing of this grant. They, too, were members of a broader disability community.

By 1971 the off-campus disability community had already been meeting for a year to discuss the need for community-based services run by and for disabled people.[27] Using the new term "independent living," they envisioned a Center that supported disabled people in making their own decisions by providing needed services.[28] They agreed with the Physically Disabled Students Program on the key services to be provided, but also envisioned growing to serve other disability communities.

The founders of what would become the Center for Independent Living (CIL) rooted their vision in civil rights work more than in social services models. CIL's founders rejected the PDSP's hierarchical job structures and preferred a collective approach.[29] They did not want job titles such as Executive Director, but wanted all major decisions to come back to the founding collective. The differences in organizational philosophy between CIL's founders and the PDSP's staff could not be more different, although they both subscribed to the principles of disability rights and independent living. The Physically Disabled Students Program embraced a typical organizational structure which CIL's founders rejected. The Physically Disabled Students Program began when they received a large grant. CIL began without any funding and worked out of a rented apartment.[30]

CIL organized cooperatively and was built with a collaborative structure for the first two years. During this time CIL moved from an

26. Guide to the Hale Zukas Papers, 1971-1998. URL: http://oac.cdlib.org/findaid/ark:/13030/tf796nb2t9/

27. Charles Grimes (his wife Ruth was part of this as well), mentioned in note 21; Hale Zukas oral history in the *Disability Rights Independent Living Movement (DRILM) Historical Archives*. The Regional Oral History Office, The Bancroft Library, University of California, Berkeley. URL: http://bancroft.berkeley.edu/collections/drilm/collection/items/zukas.html; and Janet McEwen Brown oral history in the *Disability Rights Independent Living Movement (DRILM) Historical Archives*. The Regional Oral History Office, The Bancroft Library, University of California, Berkeley. URL: http://bancroft.berkeley.edu/collections/drilm/collection/items/brown.html

28. Zona Roberts, oral history in the *Disability Rights Independent Living Movement (DRILM) Historical Archives*. The Regional Oral History Office, The Bancroft Library, University of California, Berkeley. URL: http://bancroft.berkeley.edu/collections/drilm/collection/items/roberts_zona.html

29. Zukas, see note 27.

30. Zona Roberts, see notes 12 & 27.

apartment a few blocks south of Cal to a small office at 2054 University Avenue, a few blocks west of Cal.[31] The office building had a rickety and unreliable elevator, so the wheelchair folks only worked in the office depending on the whim of the elevator.[32] Local coffee shops and members' apartments became impromptu offices to get CIL's work done.

Both the Physically Disabled Students Program and the Center for Independent Living felt content with their separate approaches and lived amicably in Berkeley. The staffs socialized together, shared attendants and wheelchair repair technicians, and often lived together in one of the few wheelchair accessible apartments. The Physically Disabled Students Program embraced the need for a community agency since its workload would lessen if students could get support from other places for off-campus housing and other assistance needs.[33]

Ed Roberts had received his Bachelor's degree in 1964, but he enrolled in Cal's graduate school to study public policy and continued living at Cowell Hospital. John Hessler (disabled), the second quadriplegic housed in the Cowell quadriplegic dormitory, became the first Director of the Physically Disabled Students Program.[34] Even though he was no longer a Cal student, Ed worked closely with John to build the Program and Zona Roberts was on the staff.

Although often quoted as a fact, the oral histories and documents in the Disability Rights and Independent Living Movement collection at Cal's Bancroft Library show that Ed Roberts did not found the Center for Independent Living. He was aligned with the Physically Disabled Students Program's model that was actively rejected by the founders of CIL. There is an undeniable thread of disability rights that goes from the earliest days of Cal and continues through Jacobus tenBroek to the Cowell Hospital dorm program and the Physically Disabled Students Program and finally off-campus to the Center for Independent Living, but that thread is philosophical and involved many different disability-specific communities.

While Ed and the Physically Disabled Students Program had strong parental support to rely on, such as Zona Roberts, Berkeley's CIL was

---

31. Mary Lester oral history in the *Disability Rights Independent Living Movement (DRILM) Historical Archives*. The Regional Oral History Office, The Bancroft Library, University of California, Berkeley. URL: http://bancroft.berkeley.edu/collections/drilm/index.html

32. Ibid. (This means see previous note.)

33. PDSP even offered a desk and meeting space for the unfunded CIL until they got funding to pay for an office. See note 27.

34. See note 14.

built by disabled people and their peers, and nondisabled white allies.[35] Some of these allies were attendants or wheelchair repair technicians who were already connected to the community, while others were just friends of the disabled organizers.

For the first two years after it was incorporated, the Center for Independent Living moved around a lot and finally ended up at 2539 Telegraph Avenue, Berkeley, a former British Motors car dealership located four blocks south of Cal.[36] Largely run in an anarchistic style, with consensus decision-making, the early CIL strove to meet the identified needs of the disability community. The group was almost exclusively white and young, with nearly the whole agency under the age of 30.[37]

A unique challenge of building an organization with severely disabled people is that the government supports they depend on for living outside of institutions—supports such as health care and personal attendant care—require them to remain extremely poor. If they take paid employment, even a minimal amount, they lose their health care and attendant care benefits. In order to compensate them, CIL worked to provide environmental supports such as free rides in CIL's wheelchair accessible van, free office supplies to take home, daytime attendant care for eating and bathroom breaks, and other useful but not wage-oriented compensations.[38] The disabled people on government benefits did not work for CIL for the minimal in-kind exchange, though; they worked there because they believed in the mission of a disability rights organization that provided independent living support.

During the first two years CIL accomplished the near impossible: it survived. A group of severely disabled people, primarily wheelchair users with a few blind folks, set out determined to create community-based services. The fact that within a decade they created an international network, which was nothing short of a social revolution, is amazing, and that makes it even more important to attribute the work to the people that actually built CIL.

Building CIL required money, and the founders worked relentlessly on fundraising. Nondisabled funders had no idea that disabled people were creating a social and political revolution. The concept of

35. See note 27.

36. Started in 1970, the CIL initially rented an apartment, then moved to an upstairs office at 2054 University Avenue in Berkeley, and finally to 2539 Telegraph Avenue in Berkeley. See note 31. CIL remained there until it moved to the newly build Ed Roberts Campus in 2011. From Center for Independent Living, Berkeley. URL: http://www.cilberkeley.org

37. Personal observation. I was staff at CIL from 1974 to 1979.

38. Lester, see note 31.

independent living flew in the face of everything traditional funders knew about disabled people. Unfortunately, these preconceptions consisted of negative societal stereotypes based in ableism. They presumed that we all lived in institutions, perhaps in community ones, and that nondisabled people took care of us. Getting them to grasp the concept of disabled people speaking for ourselves was an uphill battle. Getting CIL funded took several years.

As the money began to flow, CIL faced a new challenge. Funders in the early 1970s wanted to see a traditional nonprofit organization with a strong hierarchical structure. They were dissatisfied with the founders' answer of "all of us" to the question of "Who's in charge?" The disability community needed CIL to succeed and grow, so the founders had a dilemma. Divided over how to proceed, eventually enough people agreed to a hierarchical organizational structure and more funding was secured.

At a minimum, the funding sources wanted a designated Executive Director and bookkeeper. After a lengthy discussion (no one wanted to be the Executive Director), Larry Biscamp (disabled)[39] was selected, specifically because he had no affiliation with Cal or the Physically Disabled Students Program.[40] He was, in the words of one of the founders, "a community person" as opposed to a "student."[41] So in the official record, Larry Biscamp was the first Director of the Center for Independent Living.

Although required by funders to have a traditional organizational structure, CIL just put the titles on papers that the funders saw but kept operating much as it had. Decisions were arrived at collectively and money was spent on community needs, whether or not they matched the funding requirements. John Hessler, Director of the Physically Disabled Students Program, became increasingly concerned about the "lack of leadership" at CIL and enlisted his old friend Ed to take over the organization.[42] While CIL's Board searched for a new Director, Ed Roberts, who had moved to Riverside in southern

---

39. During the early 1970s the Berkeley disability rights community considered Larry Biscamp as one it's most friendly members. A decade later, he was accused of a crime but never convicted. The local disability community discussed this extensively and many people in the community believed that he did commit the crime. Since he was never convicted, few people speak about the charge publicly. With very little paper documentation, nearly all existing accounts of the beginnings of CIL have relied on interviews with early 1970s Berkeley disability rights activists. When these activists omit Larry's contributions to CIL, he slowly becomes erased from the history and the myth that Ed Roberts founded CIL fills in that historical gap.

40. Hale Zukas and Janet M. Brown, see note 27.

41. See note 39.

42. See note 12.

California for a temporary job, wanted to return to Berkeley.[43] He and the Board agreed, and in 1974 Ed became the second Executive Director of CIL, a job he held until 1975 when he became the first disabled person to head the California State Department of Rehabilitation.[44]

1970s Berkeley — A Personal History

I moved to Berkeley from Boston in 1973 with a friend from college who had moved west to attend graduate school at Cal. I'd never been west of Massachusetts and had no idea what to expect. To say that Berkeley shocked me would be a serious understatement. Berkeley in 1973 was like seeing a circus for the first time. People dressed in bright primary colored clothes spent their days living a block from Cal on Telegraph Avenue and sleeping in the adjacent People's Park at night. The Free Speech Movement had been raging at Berkeley for a number of years and loud demonstrations happened nearly every day.[45] People mingled in mixed race groups, something I had never encountered. Posters blasted political slogans. Women held 'consciousness raising' groups and demonstrated for women's rights. There were even discrete flyers advertising gay and lesbian activities.

I felt overwhelmed and disoriented. I felt like Alice; I'd fallen into Wonderland and while it offered many options, many times I wanted fewer choices. I was alone, away from home, with only one friend who was very busy with graduate school. I had never felt more excited or more frightened. I had no idea this would become my adult home, my community.

One of the first things I noticed was people with disabilities, particularly people who used wheelchairs, going up and down Telegraph Avenue, the main south corridor to Cal.[46] Disabled people were out and wandering the streets in a very public way, expecting acceptance. The California State School for the Deaf and the State School for the Blind were both still in Berkeley at that time, and both of

---

43. Ed Roberts: His Life and His Legacy URL: http://www.wid.org/about-wid/booklet%20with %20speech.pdf; also see note 12.

44. In 1984 Ed became the first person from the disability community to receive a MacArthur "genius" award, followed by Ralf Hotchkiss in 1989 and Susan Sygall in 2000. MacArthur Fellows Program URL: http://www.macfound.org/programs/fellows/

45. The Civil Rights Movement. URL: http://www.calisphere.universityofcalifornia.edu/themed_collections/subtopic6a.html

46. The first modern power wheelchair was invented by George Klein in 1950, but useable commercially available chairs were not widespread until the 1960s. *Wheeling Thru Time: The History of the Wheelchair.* URL: https://cocoaandchinwag.wordpress.com/2012/07/29/wheeling-thru-time-the-history-of-the-wheelchair/

them had adults with those disabilities living and socializing both on the campus and in the downtown area. It was not uncommon to be in a restaurant in Berkeley and see someone in a wheelchair, or else a blind person or a deaf person, sitting at different tables with their friends.

The first year that I was in Berkeley I didn't know a soul, so mostly I hung around the Cal Student Union building reading fliers and looking for stuff to do. I had found a job in a small private special education school, but it wasn't particularly exciting and wasn't a good fit for me.

Disabled Women

In 1974 I went to the International Women's Day celebration at the Pauley ballroom in Cal's Student Union. There were lectures inside the ballroom, and different community groups had set up information booths in the hallways. One information table was for the Disabled Women's Coalition. A woman I later learned was Susan Sygall (disabled) was sitting in her manual wheelchair behind the table for the Disabled Women's Coalition. Leaning on my cane, I walked back and forth in front of the table three or four times, trying to look casual, but really trying to get the courage to talk to her. I had no experience connecting with other disabled adults. Finally, I walked up to the table, looked at Susan and said, "I don't know if I'm disabled enough for your group. But I'd like some information."

Susan looked up, smiled, welcomed me, and started talking about what they were doing. She told me that they met once a month and typically had a guest speaker. She was an undergraduate at UC Berkeley and her roommate Deborah Kaplan (disabled) was a law student at Boalt. They'd been assigned to share a wheelchair accessible dorm room, an unusual occurrence since typically undergraduate and graduate students were housed separately.

Susan had transferred to UC Berkeley after starting college in Colorado. Injured in a car accident, she returned to New York for rehabilitation, and when it was time to go to school again, she picked UC Berkeley. Even as an undergraduate, Susan created transformative organizations.[47] The Disabled Women's Coalition sparked decades of disabled feminist work. Susan also created the Bay Area Outreach and Recreation Program (BORP) that continues to thrive today. In 1981, she built Mobility International USA and headquartered it in Eugene, Oregon.

---

47. In 2000 she also received a MacArthur "genius" award. MacArthur Fellows Program URL: http://www.macfound.org/programs/fellows/

Berkeley in the early 70s was a hotbed of feminist activism. There were women's rap groups, women's nontraditional employment training programs, and numerous political organizations that ranged from liberal to progressive to radical. The intersection of disability and feminism really grabbed me and drew me in. I wanted to know where I fit in that world, and Berkeley seemed to be the best place to figure that out.

Susan, sitting at the table, was the first disabled person that I connected with in Berkeley. A few weeks later, I attended my first Disabled Women's Coalition meeting. Debbie Kaplan and Susan Sygall led the meeting. There was a speaker, and about fifty disabled women in the audience. I'd never been in a room with fifty disabled women before. I had never been in a room with five disabled women before. To have fifty disabled women all in the same room focusing on disabled women's issues both excited and awed me. I thought, *these organizers must have some kind of magic powers to find fifty women who wanted to spend an afternoon talking about disabled women.*

I have no memory of the topic or the speaker. I remember sitting in that audience and feeling for the first time since my disabled kids' summer camp that I was 'home.' Other than camp, I had always been in nondisabled environments. I had learned how to navigate that world, but I longed for an alternate reality where I could be seen and appreciated without pretending to be nondisabled. In that room we were all celebrating our disabled female selves. The experience was transformative.

I attended a few more monthly meetings but found myself wanting small groups and a more interactive connection. The structure of being in a room with fifty other people listening to a talk was not really what I was looking for. I began hanging out with Susan and a few women from the group while I looked for ways to make my wish real.

The women's movement in Berkeley provided many options for connecting with other women. One of these was Breakaway, a women's free school.[48.] The premise of a free school is the belief that community members are both teachers and students. Breakaway presumed that there were lots of women in the local community who had skills to share and teach, and other women who wanted to learn new skills. The founders wanted to avoid any of the class barriers such as tuition, application, and acceptance (or rejection), and all of the hoops that you have to jump through to take classes even at the community college level.

Twice a year, Breakaway would put out call to the women's

---

48. Although Breakaway existed for over 5 years, I was unable to find any written documentation, so this information is from my memories.

community. At the New Class meeting, where I volunteered, prospective teachers would fill out a form that identified the teacher, a brief course description, and the class meeting schedule. The volunteer Breakaway collective took those descriptions, published them on newsprint and distributed the course catalog to all the women's spaces around the San Francisco Bay Area.

A month after this meeting, Breakaway held a Student Registration Meeting on a Sunday afternoon. Over a four-hour span women came and signed up for classes. Most classes had a size minimum, so often the teachers hung around to see if enough women signed up for their class. Breakaway classes were so popular that over a hundred women would be lined up outside waiting for us to open the doors on Registration day.

In the spring of 1974 I was going to the Disabled Women's Coalition meetings and volunteering with Breakaway, and I had worked up the courage to offer a Breakaway class for disabled women. I envisioned that it would be a discussion group.[49] I went to the Teachers' Meeting both as a Breakaway volunteer and as a prospective teacher. At the Teachers' Meeting, I saw Lynn Witt (disabled), a woman with a full-length leg cast. I went over and introduced myself.

She had been injured in a motorcycle accident. Her leg had been smashed in many places, so she would be wearing a plaster leg cast for about nine months. She had been a student focusing on lesbian issues at one of the local colleges, but she had been unable to finish her final semester because of the accident. As we talked, she expressed interest in the idea of the disabled women's rap group, so we worked together to create the course description.

During the month between the Teachers' Meeting and Student Registration I was nervous. I wasn't sure that anybody was going to sign up, because typically the disability stuff and the women's stuff were separate, not only in that instance but more or less in every arena. But the next month I was pleasantly surprised when ten women signed up for the disabled women's rap group.

The first session of the group was held in the back room of the Physically Disabled Students Program at UC Berkeley. It was a large sunny room near the back ramp entrance. The initial group of ten women dropped down to eight women and remained the stable group for the entire two years that the group met.[50]

---

49. It was called a "rap" group—a popular way to say "discussion group for feminist women."

50. For historical purposes I am including the names of the group's most stable members: Curtis "Kitty" Cone, who became the strategic leader for the 504 sit-in; Lynn Witt, who co-wrote *Out in All Directions: The Almanac of Gay and Lesbian America*; Ainsley Tedrow, who became an executive with Hewlett-Packard; Susan Shapiro, who became a lawyer.

It became apparent very quickly that Curtis "Kitty" Cone (disabled) was our natural leader. Not that she tried to be, but each week she would come with the story of some injustice that was happening to disabled people by nondisabled people, and she would be in a state of righteous indignation about it. We often followed her lead about the topic she presented. For example, one week she might be complaining about her doctor, and we would all end up in deep discussion of healthcare and disabled women.

Participating in that group taught me a lot about who I am. These disabled women were proud, strong, no-nonsense women, disabled leaders in a nondisabled world that did not even think disabled people could live outside of institutions.

That group also introduced me to the first lesbians that I really got to know, Lynn and Kitty. They both intrigued me. I wanted their confidence; I wanted their bravado; I wanted their surety about their own sexuality. Everyone in the group was sexually active, so there was always intense discussion. We had lots of different viewpoints whenever the topics of relationships or sex came up.

The disabled women's group provided me with my very first adult disability circle. It was the place that I learned that my individual experiences of discrimination were actually part of a larger system of ableism, a bigger system of repressing disabled people.[51] Kitty provided much of the framework for us. She showed us how disability oppression worked.

In her description of trying to get a mammogram, for example, she helped us understand the ways that health care was not designed for disabled people. She taught us to recognize that disabled women have a right to access a mammogram. She talked about the ways in which the assumptions of disabled women as nonsexual beings framed the decision that the clinics made to not make mammograms accessible.

After our meeting we often went out to local coffee shop. When I went out alone, I would usually sit at a table where I could hide my cane, so that while I was sitting down I passed as nondisabled. I avoided at all costs any opportunity to give people a chance to stare at me.

Going out with women from that group ensured that people were staring at us. We entered with power and manual wheelchairs, crutches and walking canes. We were always noticed. I couldn't hide and pass as a nondisabled person. We used to joke that one disabled person in a crowd could sort of hide, especially if they were like me and walked with a cane, but two disabled people together simply could not hide.

---

51. "Ableism – the practices and dominant attitudes in society that devalue and limit the potential of persons with disabilities." *What is Ableism?* URL: http://www.stopableism.org/what.asp

We often got stared at as if the circus was in town, which for me was a lot better than being stared at as if we were runaways from a group home. I would rather be perceived as weird, independent, and employed than weird, helpless, and unemployable.

The disabled women's rap group continued for two years, with eight of us participating the whole time. Before it ended, Kitty, the networking queen, hooked us all up with jobs in disability organizations and projects. She dragged me over to the Center for Independent Living.

Working at CIL

In 1975, my first job at CIL was assisting in the attendant referral department with Wally Whelan and Phil Chavez. It was a part-time job, so in the mornings I would take the bus up into the upper income Berkeley hills and work in a private home childcare center, and then come down the hill, have lunch on Telegraph Avenue, and work at CIL in the afternoons. I recently looked at my records, and discovered that my monthly income was about $600 a month from both jobs.

Wally and Phil were the first spinal cord quadriplegics I had ever known. Typical CIL employees, they were white and in their 20s, living on disability benefits and working at CIL part-time. Wally loved a good party and often hosted social gatherings at his house. Phil was more contemplative and later became a digital artist.

In 1974, after a fire in their office building on University Avenue, CIL took over a former car dealership at 2539 Telegraph Ave. Although the property was huge, only a small portion was usable. The former car showroom was converted into offices. The huge mechanics' area where cars had been serviced had twenty-foot ceilings, garage doors that constantly let in the outside air even when closed, and a cold concrete floor. The parking lot held two large enclosed garage spaces. CIL used one of these to fix wheelchairs and the other one to adapt vans to make them wheelchair accessible. The parking lot was huge too, easily accommodating 30 cars. It was a flat, very large property.

CIL converted the car dealership display and office spaces into wheelchair accessible offices. There were no doors, only six foot high walls. Most desks were flat pieces of plywood positioned about 30 inches off the ground and built into the wall. The plywood was braced with a bracket that went from the front of the plywood to a wall stud. This allowed the desk to be strong but without any legs or other impediments to a wheelchair user.

The front office area consisted of four sections. Along the storefront windows, which ran the width of the building, there were various work cubicle areas. When you first came in the front door of CIL, a receptionist greeted you. The receptionist functioned more as a traffic director than a guard. There were no barriers blocking someone from going to any part of the building. Many people stopped by CIL in those days just to use the wheelchair accessible toilets, something that was extremely rare in 1974.

Directly behind the reception area was the Attendant Referral department. Local disabled people came there to get lists of people, often college students, who wanted attendant work. Phil and Wally interviewed prospective attendants and explained the job. It was my job to enter the screened attendants' information into our database. This was my job partly because I was the newest person in the department, but mostly it was my job because I had the most flexible fingers.[52]

Next to us was the Housing Referral department. Finding wheelchair accessible housing is a challenge in any community, but it is especially tough when you are competing with 35,000 students. In the early 1970s, the wheelchair-riding community in Berkeley was fairly small, so once someone had identified an accessible apartment, people got in line to rent it when they left. Most of the housing referral work at CIL was just keeping a list of where wheelchair folks had already lived. Housing referral staff also made phone calls for deaf people to arrange visits to apartments.

Housing Referral was critically important to the success of CIL, which from the beginning adopted a policy of not participating in housing programs specifically for disabled people, since history showed they inevitably became segregated and that they were rarely under the control of disabled people. CIL's leaders felt very strongly that forcing the open rental market to deal with the access needs of disabled people was critical to creating an accessible city.

Behind the housing referral department was the Deaf Services department. Although they were the newest department and would have been assigned less desirable office space, the Deaf community made sure that we understood the need for deaf people walking by CIL to see the TTY and the people signing so that they knew there were deaf services.[53] CIL's Deaf Services, not part of the original services, was

---

52. Most quadriplegics do not have control of their fingers, so while both Phil and Wally typed, it was a slow hunt-and-peck method.

53. Teletype device (TTY) was a large, heavy machine mostly used in newspaper offices that deaf people had adapted as a primitive but effective form of text communication. Because of the cost and size, the early machines were typically located only in offices and not in people's homes. Soon, however, smaller TTYs were created that could work with any telephone and could fit in any home. Later models were even battery-powered and portable.

created through a collaboration with Deaf adults, the School for the Deaf, and one Deaf man who also used a power wheelchair.[54]

Behind the open office areas were two small rooms with doors, a holdover from the car dealership offices. The larger office was always reserved for the executive director. The other office shifted uses as needed—sometimes peer counseling sessions took place there, and other times it was the bookkeeper's office.

Up a flight of stairs above the director's office was Blind Services. The blind folks volunteered to use that space since none of the wheelchair folks could get there, and eventually they took over the space under the stairs so that blind people who could not go upstairs could still be part of the Blind Services department.[55]

In the outside garages there was a wheelchair repair shop and a van modification shop. Electric wheelchairs were so new that there were few trained technicians to fix them, so nearly all of the existing technicians had been taught hands-on from an experienced technician. We all knew that we could not go anywhere unless our wheelchairs worked, so having an on-site wheelchair shop was critically important to the movement.

Without having any reliable and accessible public transportation, getting around was also extremely difficult. In the 1970s CIL would buy a full size van such as a Ford 150, and the wheelchair modification shop would put on a raised roof, take out all the seats except the driver and front passenger seats, and install a commercial Tommy lift on the back of the van.[56] People who used wheelchairs entered and exited the vans from the rear, rode forward in the empty van, and were tied down in place to tracks on the floor. CIL both maintained its own fleet of vans for disabled community use and modified privately owned vans.

Removing the van seats meant that van bench seats were the primary seating available for the Center's cavernous unfinished back room. The back room was a huge, poorly lit, cold space with an uneven concrete floor. For many years, CIL could not afford to renovate it, so it was used for classes, large meetings, and parties.

Despite significant differences between how people were treated within CIL, the overall atmosphere was festive and supportive. People easily added themselves to the existing social circle and lines between

---

54. OToole, see note 7.

55. Although there were always some blind people who could not walk up the stairs, this population exploded in the early days of the AIDS epidemic when many men went blind early because of the disease and came to CIL for Blind Services.

56. Tommy lift is a brand name for a metal platform on the back of a commercial van that folds up against the back doors when not in use. Folded down, it provides a ramp that allows a person in a wheelchair to ride all the way into the interior of the van.

staff and clients basically never existed.[57.] Staff and clients regularly ate meals together, partied together, shared sexually transmitted diseases and often shared housing, all as part of one big disability community.

Certain houses became de facto party sites. Each subgroup at CIL— the New York City crowd, the Deaf folks, the blind folks, the chair users, the queers, the people of color—had their own party base, but all came together for the raucous CIL parties in the back room, a flat, cold and enormous party space.

Let me describe for you one typical CIL party. First of all, it had to start early, like right around dinnertime, so that we could party hard and people could still get home in time to meet their nightly attendants. That meant there was always a steady supply of food at the parties, but most of it was finger food. The back room at CIL would have simple decorations with the lights low and the music loud. Costumes and other forms of outrageousness were always welcomed.

At one party, the wheelchair repair shop rigged up a remote controlled power chair complete with an outrageously dressed mannequin. Always up for a new adventure, the party guests danced with the dummy in the chair. The wheelchair mechanics showed their extensive talent by having their remote controlled wheelchair move to the beat of the music around the dance floor, and it never hit anyone.

During the parties people could be as much of themselves as they wanted. The queers danced with each other. People could show off their sexy and flamboyant selves and receive a warm welcome. Flirting and kissing mixed with drugs and alcohol to create a libidinous environment. For those of us who'd gone to disabled kids' summer camps, we were living the grown-up version, where we could have sex and alcohol to go with our rock 'n roll.

The Word Spreads

As CIL became more well-known, people began to arrive unexpectedly. They mistakenly believed that it was a residential program, since they'd never known of a community-based non-residential model for disabled people. They presumed CIL had free housing and attendant care. Some people came directly from the airport, and showed up with a joyful expression of "I'm here!" These people were typically housed by an employee until they could decide whether they wanted to stay in Berkeley or go back home.

---

57. For a more nuanced view of how race played into this, see the essay "Race and Disability" in this book.

Most people moved to Berkeley knowing what to expect. Disabled people in the 1950s and 60s were extremely socially isolated. They usually attended special education classes and often disabled kids' summer camps. So the majority of their friendship circle was other disabled kids. These networks continued into their young adult years.

One by one, these disability circles sent representatives (usually just one person) to check Berkeley out. They came not only from across United States but from around the world. The U.S. people stayed about six months and then, once they'd succeeded in community living, their friends started moving out too.

Many people in Berkeley had ties to the same childhood special education classes and summer camps. Most were living away from home for the first time and relied on each other to create the necessary support networks. Some of those networks continue to this day.

People from outside United States often came to the CIL with funding from their home countries to evaluate the Independent Living model and see if they could replicate it back home. CIL received no funding for these visitors, so all the work of helping them was done in addition to the funded projects. Yet staff did it willingly, knowing the incredible isolation of their lives prior to discovering CIL. An entrepreneur in Japan who owned the Mr. Donut chain was so impressed with the CIL's model that he started a fundraising drive to send a few disabled people to Berkeley for a year to learn the Independent Living model and bring it back to Japan.[58] The fundraising consisted of donation jars at the cash registers at his donut shops. So much money was raised during the first fundraising drive that the exchange program was funded for 10 years.[59] The independent living movement is flourishing in Japan, with 130 independent living centers spread across the country, all inspired by the Berkeley CIL.[60]

Sometimes CIL grew through a simple miscommunication. Ed Roberts or Judy Heumann (disabled) would be giving a talk far away from Berkeley and afterwards they would casually say to someone, "You should come to Berkeley." They meant, "You should come and visit, see what we are doing." However some disabled people, desperate for a better life, took that their words as a literal invitation, packed up, and moved to Berkeley.

---

58. Joan Leon oral history in the *Disability Rights Independent Living Movement (DRILM) Historical Archives*. The Regional Oral History Office, The Bancroft Library, University of California, Berkeley. URL: http://bancroft.berkeley.edu/collections/drilm/collection/items/leon.html

59. Ibid.

60. Japan Council on Independent Living Centers. URL: http://www.j-il.jp/jil.files/english/aboutjil.html

Other times the miscommunication happened locally. In 1974 at a local event a disabled man came up and talked to Ed, who encouraged the man to come to CIL.[61] The man assumed that Ed was offering him a job.[62] Since he had never had a job before, he believed that he was just supposed to show up to work one day. The man required a modified desk to work. One day we looked out the windows and a moving van was unloading a large wooden desk. The receptionist asked them why and the man said he was here to start his first day of work. Ed was quickly consulted and figured, "why not?", so after some shuffling a space was made for the man's desk. He continued to work at CIL for many years.

Perhaps surprisingly, the CIL staff agreed with this open-arms approach. We had all experienced the loneliness of being in restrictive environments, unable to make our own choices. We had found freedom in living independently and were willing to make a lot of compromises so that other disabled people could have that opportunity too. The overriding unwritten philosophy was that community comes first, that the funding was simply a guideline for how to spend the money. There would always be work that needed to be done but for which there was no funding. One simple illustration of this is what happened with Ralf Hotchkiss.

In the late 1970s Marilyn Golden (disabled), a wheelchair user, went to Nicaragua during the revolution. She came back very disturbed by the lack of wheelchairs available for all the newly disabled people in Nicaragua. She began to search for resources. One of the local resources she found was Ralf Hotchkiss (disabled). Prior to his spinal cord injury Ralf had been a skilled bicycle mechanic. After his injury he switched his focus to manual wheelchair design.

The first time I met Ralf, in the mid-1970s, he was riding in an adapted 1955 Everett and Jennings wheelchair. He had reconfigured the armrests so that they could pivot and brace his knees when he needed to stand up. He was relatively unknown in California, since he worked in Washington, D.C., but a recent marriage had brought him back to the west coast.

In 1980 Marilyn and Ralf approached CIL to ask for money to send

---

61. Kenneth Stein oral history in the *Disability Rights Independent Living Movement (DRILM) Historical Archives*. The Regional Oral History Office, The Bancroft Library, University of California, Berkeley. URL:
http://bancroft.berkeley.edu/collections/drilm/collection/items/stein.html

62. Disabled people understood that having a "job" at CIL did not mean getting a salary. Few severely disabled people could afford to lose their health care and attendant benefits, which would happen if they took a paying job. So people worked at the CIL for the job experience and camaraderie.

Ralf to Nicaragua, where he would assess the wheelchair needs.[63.] People at CIL understood the importance of the work, so CIL bought a plane ticket for Ralf. There was no budget, no line item, no official way to fund a trip to Nicaragua. But true to the philosophy of CIL, a plane ticket was purchased and the accounting department was left trying to figure out how to deal with the problem.

Ralf's work in Nicaragua not only changed the lives of many Nicaraguans, but also changed the trajectory of Ralf's work. He realized the international need was enormous for wheelchairs that could roll across muddy roads, gravelly surfaces and be placed on the top of the buses, which are the most common transportation in most poor countries. He also realized that the wheelchairs needed to be made from steel so that they could be easily welded in any country, and use bicycle parts, since they are also widely available throughout the world.[64.] Ralf went on to establish Whirlwind Wheelchairs, an organization dedicated to building and providing wheelchairs for people throughout the world.[65.]

Judy Heumann Comes to Berkeley

Even before Ed became the CIL director in 1974, he realized he needed a disabled work partner, and he heavily recruited Judy Heumann (disabled). Judy had become famous when her application to get a teaching license was denied because she was disabled. She sued the New York City Board of Education and won out of court. The discrimination against Judy catalyzed the New York disability community to form Disabled in Action.[66.]

Working with Disabled in Action and using her media attention, Judy highlighted various forms of discrimination against disabled people. Her work brought her to the attention of U.S. Congressionl staffers, and she was brought in to work on burgeoning legislation, specifically Public Law 94–142: The Education For All Handicapped Children Act, as well

---

63. See note 31.

64. In 1989 he got a MacArthur 'genius' award for his work. MacArthur Fellows Program URL: http://www.macfound.org/programs/fellows/

65. Whirlwind Wheelchairs. URL: http://www.whirlwindwheelchair.org/

66. "Disabled in Action was organized in 1970 by Judy Heumann, a young militant disabled woman, and other disabled activists at Long Island University, Brooklyn Campus. Ms. Heumann sued the New York City Board of Education when her application to obtain a teaching license was rejected because of her disability. Although the suit was settled out of court, the publicity it received served as the impetus for founding DIA." Source URL: http://www.disabledinaction.org

as Section 504 of the 1973 Rehabilitation Act.[67.] Ed realized she would be in an enormous asset in Berkeley. Like many east coast people, though, Judy was reluctant to leave the power centers of New York and Washington, D.C.

When Judy finally came to Berkeley, many things changed at CIL. While Ed was rather quiet, Judy's enthusiasm bubbled throughout the agency. She brought fresh ideas, helped heal the wounds with the founders and connected CIL with the national disability rights movement, which up until then was primarily focused on the east coast. Judy's presence made CIL a player in that national disability rights movement.

While Judy, like Ed, had survived polio and used a power wheelchair, she grew up in community with other disabled people. When she was finally allowed to attend public school, her classroom was with other physically disabled children. She also attended summer camps designed for physically disabled children. So she grew up with a very strong sense of herself and her place in various physical disability communities.

While Ed and Judy brought very different strengths to CIL, they shared a joint vision of an agency run by and for disabled people that supported people living independently as decision-makers in the community. CIL refused to provide or collaborate with anyone creating disabled housing, nor did they work in environments that prioritized non-disabled people in the helping professions making decisions. They both felt very comfortable talking with the media and soon became the identified voices of the west coast disability community.

I often joke that Ed Roberts and Judy Heumann are well-known not because they were the most articulate or most informed of the Berkeley disabled people, but because they were the least afraid of being interviewed. Media often contacted CIL. At staff meetings the opportunities to do the interviews were often thrown wide. But nearly all the staff shook our heads adamantly "no," so the responsibility of talking to the media fell to Ed and Judy who worked together as a team, replacing each other if a scheduling conflict arose.[68.]

The more they worked with the media, the easier it was for the

67. Judy Heumann oral history in the *Disability Rights Independent Living Movement (DRILM) Historical Archives*. The Regional Oral History Office, The Bancroft Library, University of California, Berkeley. URL:
http://bancroft.berkeley.edu/collections/drilm/collection/items/heumann.html

68. Corbett O'Toole oral history in the *Disability Rights Independent Living Movement (DRILM) Historical Archives*. The Regional Oral History Office, The Bancroft Library, University of California, Berkeley. URL:
http://bancroft.berkeley.edu/collections/drilm/collection/items/otoole.html

rest of us to not do it. This is not in any way to minimize their substantial accomplishments, but it is to acknowledge that what they were saying to the media reflected a group perspective, something they always stated in their interviews, and not any individual self-aggrandizement on their part. Their self-selection greatly benefited the disability community in the U.S. and the world. Many people's lives were changed because of their articulate and thoughtful public speaking.

In order to do the political advocacy work necessary, Judy needed to find people who understood political systems. At CIL, Judy found a natural ally in Kitty Cone. Kitty had gone to the University of Illinois Urbana-Champaign,[69] which for many decades had been the sole U.S. university willing to accept students who used wheelchairs. After college she moved to Chicago and worked with the Student Nonviolent Coordinating Committee (SNCC),[70] an organization focused on African American civil rights in the American South. Kitty learned political strategies, planning protests and creating coalitions while she was in Chicago. When she came to Berkeley, she worked with other leftist groups, but it was not until Judy came to CIL that Kitty was able to use her skills on behalf of the disability rights movement. Perhaps their greatest joint accomplishment was the phenomenally successful 504 sit-in in San Francisco during the month of April 1977 (see "Flexing Power" in this book).

Deaf Services

In the mid-1970s when Dale Dahl came to CIL, I was excited to use my limited fingerspelling, but I also wanted to learn American Sign Language. This was a strong desire for me. One of my most vivid memories of the CIL's back room was when it became the classroom for Dale Dahl's American Sign Language classes.

The Deaf leadership in Berkeley, many of whom were associated with the California School for the Deaf, saw CIL as a potentially important community resource and reached out to create Deaf-focused services. But the most significant turning point in creating Deaf Services was the arrival of Dale Dahl.

---

69. "Facts 2013-2014." *Illinois By the Numbers.* URL:
    http://illinois.edu/about/overview/facts/facts.html

70. Student Nonviolent Coordinating Committee (SNCC) is best known for the Freedom Rides and voting registration campaigns in the American South. Source URL: http://mlk-kppo1.stanford.edu/index.php/encyclopedia/encyclopedia/enc_student_nonviolent_coordinating_committee_sncc/

Dale came to CIL having been referred by the CIL's Computer Training Program.[71] Dale was from a multigenerational Deaf family and grew up using American Sign Language (ASL) at home. He attended schools for the deaf where American Sign Language was valued and taught. Prior to arriving in Berkeley, he had an accident, become hemiplegic, and used a power wheelchair.[72] After that, he adapted his signs to allow for one-handed signing. His deep commitment to teaching American Sign Language infiltrated CIL and brought many ASL-using Deaf people into the agency.

To understand the importance of Dale's contribution and his reliance on American Sign Language, you need to understand a little bit of the history of deaf people in the United States. Nearly all deaf children are born into hearing families. Those families rarely choose to learn American Sign Language, so deaf children often grow up without any access to language until they enter a school situation. Obviously, this leads to an enormous language deficit.[73] Prior to the 1980s many deaf children attended schools for the deaf, which in some communities were run by and for deaf people. The children arrived at school without any language and needed to be taught their first language, American Sign Language, as well as learning a second language, English.[74]

Most of the children had to catch up on language, which was very challenging after five or six or seven years without any. A few very lucky children were born into families with deaf parents or had family members who were hearing but decided to learn American Sign Language. In those families, the children acquired language early, and they learned a second language much more easily. Their brains developed more fully, and their language skills were high.[75]

Unfortunately, a much more typical scenario was the deaf child who had no access to American Sign Language, who went to a school for the deaf that was run by and for hearing people, and who never really acquired adequate language skills. They would rely on lip reading and English, both of which are extremely difficult to master without a strong linguistic base.[76]

---

71. Computer Technologies Program URL: https://www.ctpberk.org/

72. Dale often said that he missed the social connections with Deaf people because so many of the Deaf spaces, such as Deaf clubs, were not wheelchair accessible.

73. Humphries, T.; Ushalnagar, P.; Mathur, G.; Napoli, D.; Padden, C. & Rathmann, C. (2014). "Ensuring language acquisition for Deaf children." *Language and Public Policy*, 90(2). URL: http://www.linguisticsociety.org/files/archived-documents/Humphries%20LaPP.pdf

74. *Sign Language.* URL: http://wfdeaf.org/human-rights/crpd/sign-language

75. *Education Rights for Deaf Children.* URL: http://wfdeaf.org/databank/policies/education-rights-for-deaf-children

76. *Lipreading as an Imperfect Skill.* URL:

Having Dale come to CIL as both a culturally Deaf man and a wheelchair user provided a rare and extremely important opportunity for networking across communities. Not only did Dale work with Judy Heumann and the Deaf community to create services at CIL, but he also worked to create the first American Sign Language classes in the San Francisco Bay Area. Dale and his friends taught ASL classes in the cavernous, and frequently cold, back room of CIL.[77] When the Deaf community saw the large response to Dale's informal classes, they created a more formal program at Vista College.[78]

Intersectionality at CIL

While the disabled community is often viewed as one group there were, and are, many tensions among the various communities that intersect with disability, such as disabled people of color, disabled women, and disabled queers. These communities all existed at CIL but have largely been written out of the historical accounts.

There was an interesting tension at the Center during the 1970s. The disability rights movement leaders felt a huge urgency to create as much physical accessibility as they could, as quickly as possible. They focused on gaining entrance to public services such as libraries and medical centers, while pushing for legislative efforts to ensure more permanent access. At the same time they were building a national and international disability rights network and independent living centers. Though it went largely unnoticed by the leaders, these efforts provided greater opportunities primarily for white, physically disabled males.

The disabled leadership, almost entirely white, agreed to work on physical accessibility. They included disability-specific needs such as interpreters for deaf people and Braille for blind people, but the vast majority of the access efforts were focused on people with mobility disabilities. The leaders widely believed that all disabled people would benefit from this approach. To a large extent, they were right at a basic level. All people who need a wheelchair ramp will benefit when one is provided.

This focus tended to be myopic, however, when looking at the

http://www.boston.com/bostonglobe/ideas/brainiac/2013/03/lipreading_as_a.html

Also, *Seeing at the Speed of Sound.* URL:
http://alumni.stanford.edu/get/page/magazine/article/?article_id=59977

77. OToole, see note 7.

78. In 1982, deaf professionals began an American Sign Language program at Vista College in Berkeley (now called Berkeley City College). Their curriculum became the widely used *Signing Naturally* by Ella Mae Lenz, Ken Mikos and Cheri Smith.

needs of the broader disability community. While the local independent living center fought hard for access to the library, they rarely fought for access to a battered women's shelter or for interpreters for the Gay Pride Parade and English-as-a-second-language classes. Many disabled people of color and disabled queers were left on their own to fight for their access rights.

Very few disabled people of color had leadership positions in disability rights organizations.[79] Efforts to build networks for disabled people of color were often ignored or thwarted by the white leadership.[80] Disabled people of color were rarely promoted into staff positions, even when they were more qualified than a white disabled person.[81] So neither their contributions as "volunteers" nor their work in communities of color, such as the work by Brad Lomax (disabled)[82] and the Black Panther Party[83] to establish independent living services in Oakland's communities of color, are preserved in the historical accounts of the 1970s disability rights movement.

White disabled leaders often told the disabled people of color, "We just need a little more time to make the world accessible before we can deal with the intersections of race and disability." While they might have believed it, forty years later the white leaders are still saying essentially the same thing. Outside of a few rare instances, the white disability rights community has made no institutional commitments to addressing the intersections of race and disability. Looking back over 40 years of disability rights history shows the scarcity of disabled people of color in leadership positions within disability rights organizations, the ongoing silence by disability organizations about issues critical to racial justice, and the widespread retelling of disability history as a white-led and white-focused movement.

Disabled queers had a different trajectory, largely because of Kitty Cone, an "out" lesbian.[84] Although she avoided media attention, Kitty's community organizing skills played a critical role in the success of the

---

79. The National Council on Disability has numerous reports over the past decade documenting the barriers for disabled people of color. Reports on Cultural Diversitiy. Source URL: http://www.ncd.gov/policy/cultural_diversity

80. Donald Galloway and Johnnie Lacy oral histories in the *Disability Rights Independent Living Movement (DRILM) Historical Archives*. The Regional Oral History Office, The Bancroft Library, University of California, Berkeley. URL: http://bancroft.berkeley.edu/collections/drilm/index.html

81. Ibid.

82. Schweik, S. (2011). "Lomax's matrix: Disability, solidarity, and the Black power of 504." *Disability Studies Quarterly* 31(1). URL: http://dsq-sds.org/article/view/1371/1539

83. An interview with Elaine Brown by the Paul K. Longmore Institute on Disability, *Patient No More* Exhibit, conducted July 26, 2014.

84. "Out" means that a person is known as queer at work and in the community.

1970s CIL and especially the historic 504 sit-in at San Francisco's Federal Building. Kitty was a consummate political strategist, and her advice was highly valued by CIL's leaders.

In the 1970s in Berkeley there was no wheelchair accessible transportation, few accessible public venues, and almost no accessible housing. Kitty bought and renovated a house in north Oakland, about a mile south of the CIL. She put a pool table in the living room, a large table in the dining room, and a hot tub in the backyard. Her house quickly became the hangout for disabled and nondisabled lesbians.

Largely because of Kitty, queers were always part of CIL. Nondisabled queers worked in the van modification shop, wheelchair repair, various administrative offices and drove the CIL vans. People were open about their same sex partners and their queer lives. In many ways disabled people in the 1970s at CIL were welcome to be who they were in the office, but were discouraged from talking about their differences in any media related to disability rights.

While a number of staff people at the Center participated in local gay communities,[85] CIL had had no official relationship with them. For example, in the years when there was no seating area for disabled people at the San Francisco Gay Pride Parade, CIL's queer employees had to work on those issues on their own time and without any institutional support.

The disconnect between the gay and disabled communities came into clear focus with the AIDS crisis in the early 1980s. Early cases of AIDS rapidly caused severe disabilities, often blindness. CIL had requested and received significant support from gay community groups during the 1970s, particularly during the April 1977 San Francisco 504 sit-in. The disability community leaders openly accepted help from gay groups and promised to be allies together. When men with AIDS started needing disability services, they came to CIL in Berkeley.[86] Unfortunately, the disability rights community did not embrace this opportunity, and soon the AIDS activists realized they needed to create their own services and support networks.[87]

While disabled people of color, disabled women and disabled queers were welcomed to state publicly how these created additional barriers, they were actively discouraged from publicly naming any concerns about the biases within the disability community and

---

85. I am using "gay" as the preferred 1970s term.

86. Although by this time there was an independent living center in San Francisco, I got the impression that because there were openly gay staff at CIL in Berkeley, the AIDS men preferred to go there.

87. See "Disability Queered" in this book.

organizations.[88.] Discussions of racism, homophobia and sexism took place privately, but never institutionally.

Institutional bias towards people who are white and physically disabled can be seen clearly in the narrow scope of the archived histories of the Berkeley Disability Rights and Independent Living Movement oral histories at the Bancroft Library at Cal. Out of 109 oral histories, there are 64 people with physical disabilities but only 7 people of color and 3 queers.

Even without the benefit of historical documentation, people of color, disabled women and disabled queers collaborated across communities. The Black Panther Party actively committed itself to providing disability services and creating resources in poor communities that were unserved by disability organizations. Disabled women found allies at the local Planned Parenthood, resulting in staff trainings and the 1981 publication of Kathy Simpson (disabled) and Kathleen Lanasky (disabled)'s "Table Manners and Beyond," which graphically demonstrated many different gynecology examination positions.

1980s and Beyond

During the 1970s, CIL grew with increased funding and visibility, bringing more people to Berkeley. Each person brought with them dreams and aspirations that had been denied them in the nondisabled world. Believing that anything was possible and that the arc of history was on our side created an intoxicating environment. For the first time, people believed in and lived with self-determination and personal freedom of choice. Watching the transformation from despair to hope fueled many a long day of fighting for disability rights.

Coming to CIL meant that people temporarily suspended their personal goals in order to build the organization. The 1977 sit-in at the San Francisco federal building created an historic turning point both personally and for the disability rights movement. For the first time, disabled people won a major concession from the United States government, that is, the passing of the 504 regulations.[89.]

After the 504 victory, people began to turn back towards their individual dreams. Robert Funk (disabled), who came to the Center as a VISTA legal volunteer, turned his attention to creating a national

---

88. Donald Galloway oral history in the *Disability Rights Independent Living Movement (DRILM) Historical Archives*. The Regional Oral History Office, The Bancroft Library, University of California, Berkeley. URL:
http://bancroft.berkeley.edu/collections/drilm/collection/items/galloway.html

89. For more on this see "Flexing Power" in this book.

disability rights center in 1980, the Disability Rights Education and Defense Fund (DREDF). In 1982 Hal Kirshbaum (disabled), with his wife Megan Kirshbaum (disabled), turned their attention to serving parents with disabilities by creating a new agency, Through the Looking Glass. Other CIL employees went on to create new independent living centers throughout California and across the nation. In 1983 Jacqueline and Steve Brand founded the Disabled Children's Computer Group (DCCG), which later morphed into the Center for Accessible Technology (CforAT). In 1983 Ed Roberts, Joan Leon and Judy Heumann created the World Institute on Disability.

Each person who passed through the Center for Independent Living has an important story to tell. In this essay, I can only share mine. Although it might seem silly to talk about parties, those dances increased my self-confidence more than the political rhetoric. Surviving the daily aggressions of ableism requires not only strong political communities but also spaces where we can celebrate our diverse bodyminds. Participating in those celebrations transformed my internal beliefs about disabled people, and dancing with disabled people has continued to be, for me, the strongest inoculation against ableism.

There are hundreds more stories that need to be preserved. The disability rights movement cannot only tolerate, but absolutely needs, multiple stories told from multiple perspectives in order to create a more realistic and more historically useful documentation of these important early days.

JUST THE FACTS MA'AM

1970 — Disabled people and their friends create the Center for Independent Living in Berkeley, California.

1972 — CIL opens an office in an old car dealership at 2539 Telegraph Avenue, four blocks south of the University of California Berkeley.

1972 — Larry Biscamp is the first Director of the CIL.

1974 — Ed Roberts becomes the second Director of the CIL.

RESOURCES

DRILM Interviews, especially Judy Heumann, Jan McEwen Brown and Hale Lukas for beginnings of CIL; Zona Roberts for PDSP; and Ed Roberts, Johnnie Lacy and Donald Galloway for CIL. Collection URL: http://bancroft.berkeley.edu/collections/drilm/collection/collection.html

A full bibliography is available at my website: www.corbettotoole.com

4.

1975 Disability Studies: Hal Kirshbaum's Grand Experiment

"I've learned that you should not go through life with a catcher's mitt on both hands;

You need to be able to throw something back."[1] — Maya Angelou[2]

Summary

In 1975, Hal Kirshbaum created the first Disability Studies Master's program in the world at Antioch University West. The classrooms were located in a prefabricated building at the Center for Independent Living in Berkeley. The teachers were all people who were connected in some way to the disability community and who understood and appreciated the experience of disabled people. The students were mostly disabled people. The program was new and exciting. It lasted for a year, and then Antioch wanted to use their own teachers, who did not understand disability, and they wanted to have the classes in San Francisco. The program ended, but it became a model for all the Disability Studies

---

1. Source URL: http://www.usatoday.com/story/news/nation-now/2014/05/28/maya-angelou-quotes/9663257/

2. "Dr. Maya Angelou (her preferred title) wrote six memoirs about her life up to the age of 40, the most celebrated of which was *I Know Why the Caged Bird Sings*, published in 1969. An inspirational and influential woman, she was also a poet, novelist, dramatist, dancer, actor, film-maker and Civil Rights activist." Source URL:
http://www.independent.co.uk/news/obituaries/maya-angelou-obituary-inspirational-writer-and-activist-whose-remarkable-series-of-memoirs-charted--a-troubled-eventful-life-9455303.html

programs that exist today.

❖ ❖ ❖

The history of Disability Studies is typically told as starting with the founding of the Society for Disability Studies in the mid-1980s, but a decade earlier an innovative Disability Studies program had a short life in Berkeley, California. Although that program began in 1975 and continued for two years, its history has almost been completely lost. To my knowledge, it was the first Disability Studies program in the United States, if not the world.

The Antioch University West program was the brainchild of Hal Kirshbaum (disabled), a scholar who wanted to create an environment for vigorous academic engagements with both the existing concepts of disability and the new ideas from the emerging disability rights movement.[3.]

Hal (disabled) and Megan (disabled) Kirshbaum are best known as innovative researchers who transformed the negative cultural assumptions towards disabled people as parents and documented the resources that disabled people bring to the job of parenting. In the early 1970s Hal took on the challenge of creating a supportive and innovative environment to investigate the issues raised by the independent living and the disability rights movements in an academic context.

Hal Kirshbaum had an idea. What if graduate school classes presumed that disabled people were capable, resourceful, and interesting? What if scholars were encouraged to view us this way instead of the existing 1970s presumptions of people with disabilities as incompetent, incapable and definitely uninteresting. What if teachers taught about people like Hal? What if people like Hal were the teachers? And the students?

In the early 1970s, Hal worked at the Center for Independent Living (CIL) in Berkeley, California. As an agency founded by disabled people, CIL proposed an entirely new approach to serving disabled people. Believing that disabled adults were competent to make their own decisions, CIL created organizational resources to support them. CIL offered resources for finding housing, personal assistants, and wheelchair repair, as well as readers for blind people and a teletype machines (TTY) and interpreters for deaf people. Hal contributed his considerable expertise to creating mental health support networks at

---

3. Ph.D in Philosophy.

CIL using both peer counselors and professional therapists.

While the disabled community developed and trained disabled people from other disciplines, especially social services, in this model of assuming the competence of disabled people, the academic and professional communities remained unchanged. Hal sought to bridge this gap and began to integrate this new understanding of independent living into the classes he taught at local universities. He yearned for the opportunity to provide students with a more thorough academic grounding in the reality of disability. He approached the schools where he taught about setting up such a program, but they were not interested.

Finally, when he brought together the Center for Independent Living[4] with Antioch University West,[5] the spark finally caught. In 1975 the first Disability Studies program in the United States was created. It was designed as a Master's program awarded by Antioch, but the program did accept a few undergraduate students. Antioch's 'campus without walls' philosophy honored community-based learning and self-directed proof of mastery of the class material. The few undergraduate students merged well with the graduate students in the program, since they were all part of the Berkeley disabled community.

In some ways, Hal was an unlikely Pied Piper. A quiet man, he often focused on getting the job done and not on promoting himself. Though he was well liked, he was easy to miss in the boisterous and somewhat self-promoting atmosphere at CIL, yet his accomplishments are vast. He created the Antioch Master's degree in Disability, and he co-founded Through the Looking Glass, an international research and training center of and for parents with disabilities.

Hal's vision was to create a challenging academic environment where the principles of independent living and disability rights could be examined. Instead of the traditional approach of nondisabled people, that of using a negative (ableist) understanding of disability, Hal wondered how a positive measurement of disability might ask new questions, challenge old assumptions and lead to new areas of research. Instead of looking at what's wrong with disabled people, what if we investigate what is right with disabled people? How would that shift the existing research? What new areas of academia would open?

Although he had already spent two years knocking down barriers just to get an academic home for the program, Hal soon encountered new impediments. Antioch depended on students coming to its campus

---

4. Center for Independent Living. URL: www.cilberkeley.org

5. Antioch University. URL: www.antioch.edu

in San Francisco for classes. Hal knew that would not work for the students in his new program. The student base would come from people affiliated with the Center for Independent Living. Most of the students would have significant disabilities, and many used wheelchairs. In 1975, few buildings had wheelchair access, so finding accessible classrooms would be challenging. Accessible public transportation was more an idea than a reality. Getting people from Berkeley across the bay to San Francisco at night would be a daunting task. At that time public transit had infrequent and undependable accessibility.[6]

Hal argued that it was impossible for potential students to get across the bay to San Francisco reliably. He convinced Antioch to rent a two-classroom trailer instead. At that time, CIL was housed on a former car dealership lot. There was a lot of empty space in the parking lot, so the trailer was put there. Ramps were built to make it accessible. Because both the students and the space were busy with CIL during the day, classes were held in the evenings and on weekends.

Hal's other big problem was to find professors. Hal knew that the students would be smart and politically sophisticated about disability. His challenge was to find teachers who could lead the students academically. Traditionally-trained academics had not yet examined their ableist assumptions that being nondisabled was inherently better than being disabled, so that eliminated most of the existing pool of teachers.

Hal's challenge was that the group of people who understood disability and had the right academic credentials were also primarily the people that were already working with the local disability rights organizations. The most appropriate teachers for his program were the friends and colleagues of his potential students. However, since Antioch always hired professors on a one-class contract, Hal was able to seek out instructors willing to use nontraditional approaches. Using his extensive academic and community networks, he created and staffed a series of courses for the Master's program.

Because the potential teachers were already inside of the social networks of the potential students, there was no clean separation

6. The main Berkeley to San Francisco transit was the BART subway system. Although BART had elevators, they were added on after the main construction and were often outside the paid areas, so BART kept them locked. In order to use an elevator, a person had to contact the station agent over the intercom. The elevator was only controllable from the station agent's booth in the station. If the agent was not available, then the elevator was inoperable. During the mid-1970s, BART station agents were assigned to 10-hour shifts. During that time they were told to take two 30-minute breaks and a one-hour lunch/dinner break. That meant that out of 10 hours the elevators would only be operable for 8 hours. But there was no consistent schedule. Each agent took their breaks on their own preferred schedules. And if an agent went home sick, then Bart rarely replaced them. Instead they just waited until the next shift started.

between the students and teachers in this program. While this strategy meant that the students got the most experienced teachers, people who thought deeply about the intersections of disability with their professions, it also meant that the students felt very free to challenge the teachers' authority.

The new teachers were the leading thinkers in the country on the intersections of disability in their academic areas. In developing community programs, they'd examined the traditional medical models of "helping the handicapped" and rejected them. They'd been forced to develop new approaches. At the growing CIL, they had an incubator in which to try their new ideas. Successes and failures became apparent very quickly. They geared their program ideas to white, college educated, physically disabled people, because that was the group that mostly (or most visibly) populated CIL, both as staff and clients. Although CIL had only officially opened a few years earlier, the constant activism pushed these professionals to develop new approaches and train other professionals in how to use them.

Students benefited from the teachers' extensive knowledge. All the teachers had been trained in traditional paternalistic approaches to providing services for disabled people. Through their personal interests and work with the disabled community they had forced themselves to re-evaluate the traditionally ableist approaches and create new models that presumed the competence of disabled adults to manage their own lives. The dual knowledge base, traditional and activist, of the teachers made them invaluable to the students.

The students were drawn from the disability community, mostly disabled people, but also a few nondisabled attendants and lovers. Most of the disabled students had Bachelor's degrees, because in the 1960s and 1970s State Departments of Rehabilitation typically provided free tuition and room and board for white disabled people, to increase their likelihood of employment.

Hal's dream came true after a lot of work. For three academic semesters, faculty and students engaged in rigorous thinking about disability. The program offered classes in philosophy, sexuality, psychology, physiology, health care delivery systems, and families. Teachers had degrees in Occupational Therapy, Philosophy, Psychology, Medicine, Social Work, and Sociology.

Working with his new faculty, Hal helped them create course curricula. They incorporated Antioch's flexibility by allowing oral as well as written proof showing student mastery of the course materials. Staff understood the significance of this new academic approach and encouraged creativity in selecting research topics. Since none of the new disability community work was documented, the professors encouraged students to bring their community-originated questions for academic examination. Students enthusiastically embraced the opportunity to put their community experiences under an academic microscope. Students researched topics as diverse as disabled male expressions of masculinity and masturbatory techniques of spinal cord injured quadriplegics.

One student in the program wrote, "[t]he classes were tailored toward people with disabilities, so that was one of the things that appealed me. I'd always hated traditional school structure anyway, all the way back as far as I can remember, so this is what really appealed to me about this program. It was always called 'school without walls' and that really appealed to me. A lot of my evaluations of the classes that I either documented or I took were done by people I really liked or knew personally. I had some just great classes, some incredible classes."[7]

Class sizes were intentionally small to provide opportunities for in-depth discussions and to pace the class to accommodate disabled students.[8] Students, particularly undergraduates, noticed a big difference between the Antioch program and their previous universities. One student who had attended the University of California Berkeley noted, "It was totally the opposite of what UC Berkeley was. UC Berkeley was so impersonal—classes would be 300 and 400 people in some of the lecture halls—whereas here usually the biggest classes may be ten people, and usually six or eight, with a teacher that you knew intimately. If you wanted time from him or her, you know, you'd just ask for it. It wasn't like you had to schedule a time during study time once a week; you'd just say, 'Hey, do you have a minute?' And talk about whatever it was you were trying to learn. So that was a really positive experience."[9]

Classes

All the teachers worked in disability rights organizations or projects. Some worked at CIL while others worked on disability projects at local universities. There were so few professionals working on disability rights projects that everyone knew each other. The students, if they were employed, had jobs at CIL. Students and teachers often worked side by side in their day jobs. Many times a conversation that started in

7.   Phil Chavez oral history in the *Disability Rights Independent Living Movement (DRILM) Historical Archives*. The Regional Oral History Office, The Bancroft Library, University of California, Berkeley. URL: http://bancroft.berkeley.edu/collections/drilm/index.html

8.   With only two wheelchair accessible bathrooms, students needed more time for breaks.

9.   Chavez, see note 7.

a classroom spilled over into the job the next day, pulling non-Antioch folks into the discussion.

I was lucky enough to be a part of all of this. Being in a room full of disability rights activists and talking about theories made my head dance and my heart happy. It was the first time in my life that I had gotten a taste of Disability Studies. Up until that point, my life in Berkeley had been grunt office work with a little bit of protesting. With the Antioch program, though, I was sitting in rooms full of very smart disabled people, and having nuanced conversations about disability.

Teachers pushed students to move beyond the political rhetoric of disability rights and to explore how their new perspectives challenged existing academic work. The teachers also pushed the students toward high academic standards, knowing that they would be presumed to be inferior scholars because they were disabled and they were studying disability.[10.] Being the first scholars to examine new issues sometimes has a down side. There are few resources to lean on. Here is one example:

Carla Thornton (nondisabled) and Susan Knight (disabled) ran the prestigious sexuality and disability training program at the University of California San Francisco. They came and taught a class for the Antioch program on sexuality and disability. Two of the students, CeCe Weeks (disabled) and Jack Rowan (disabled), shared a house and were both spinal cord injured quadriplegics. CeCe had been trained at the University of Minnesota Sexuality and Disability program, the pioneer curriculum on which the UCSF program was based, so CeCe knew all the literature that was available on the subject of sexuality and disability.

She and Jack proposed that their paper for the class would be on masturbation by spinal cord injured quadriplegics. When they proposed the outline for their paper, Carla pointed out that they did not include a literature review. CeCe responded that since she knew there was no available literature on masturbation and people with spinal cord injuries, or on the sexuality of spinal cord injury quadriplegics, that there was no need for a literature review. Carla insisted that Master's level work required a through literature review, even if the finding was that there was no literature. This disagreement happened in the classroom during class time. The tension between academic rigor and lived experience created conflicts that at times were increased by the

---

10. In 1992, at the Society For Disability Studies annual meeting, Ph.D candidate Kirk McGugan reported that her dissertation proposal on the history of disabled people from 1909 to 1945 was rejected because, according to the history department at her university, "people with disabilities have no history." [I attended the event and heard this statement.]

fact that students and teachers lived, worked and socialized together in the disability rights community.

Although that tension existed for many of the professors and students, the majority of the classes provided rich opportunities for developing nuanced thinking on existing academic presumptions. For example, if all philosophies presume a nondisabled bodymind, how does the disabled bodymind challenge that thinking? Can a philosophy embrace the disabled bodymind as a norm and not a variation on abnormal? What kinds of new questions get asked when the disabled bodymind is brought into the discussion?

Although all the classes were interesting and challenging, numerous remembrances by former students talk about one class as the best of the program. The fact that this praise is given to a medical doctor is nothing short of miraculous. All disabled people have had numerous negative encounters with medical professionals. Many disabled people see doctors as little more than inconveniences to be managed in order to get the medication and treatment that is needed. CIL had a few medical professionals on staff, mostly occupational therapists, but their disabilities trumped their professional credentials and they were widely accepted as disabled people with special skills.

Medical doctors were in a whole other category. In the 1970s the medical doctor was the ultimate gatekeeper. His (it was nearly always a man)[11] decisions either made the disabled person's life easier or harder. The relationship between most disabled people and doctors was full of control (on the doctor's side) and manipulation (on the disabled person's side). So it was surprising when Sheldon Berrol (nondisabled), a medical doctor, began to come to CIL.

Sheldon "call me Shelly" Berrol was the head of Rehabilitation for the Santa Clara Valley Medical Center, the northern California trauma center. He also trained students in Physical Medicine and Rehabilitation at Stanford University Medical School and other local medical schools. He understood how important family and community supports were for people recovering from traumatic injuries. He also knew that with appropriate community support many, if not all, of his patients could live successfully and have good lives in their home communities. In the 1970s it was typical for people to remain at a rehabilitation hospital for six months post-injury, but Shelly knew that each year, insurance companies were paying for shorter and shorter periods of rehabilitation time and more of the work of rehabilitation was happening at the

---

11. 8% of doctors were women in 1978. Patterson, E.C. (1978). "Review of *DOCTORS WANTED: NO WOMEN NEED APPLY: Sexual Barriers in the Medical Profession, 1835–1975* by Mary Roth Walsh." *American Scientist* 66(4).

community level. He actively sought out community-based solutions and had discovered the Center for Independent Living.

Although the disabled folks at CIL were initially very leery of him, Shelly soon won them over with his open-heartedness, his respect for the lived knowledge of disabled people, and his willingness to freely share his knowledge. Once he checked out CIL, he realized it was an invaluable resource for his patients, and he spoke with CIL management to see how we could make use of his medical credentials. He wrote letters of support to funders, went to meetings with funders, and publicly talked about the importance of the independent living model in his professional circles.

His positive impact cannot be underestimated.[12] When the new Antioch program began, Hal asked him to teach a class. Shelly was a very busy man. He was the head of rehabilitation for major trauma center, a medical school professor, and a parent of five children. None of this gave him much free time, but he made time to teach that class for an entire semester.

People liked Shelly so much that the class had double the normal enrollment. Twelve disabled students sat in a small windowless alcove under the stairs at CIL for his class. Under the best of circumstances, putting a doctor in front of a group of disability rights activists would create a lot of tension. Shelly diffused it by acknowledging that his role was to share information, facilitate discussions and guide the academic work. He stated that the students were full partners in the endeavor to create new ideas that challenged existing beliefs about disabled people.

The class focused more on the function of the body then on learning the names of the parts of the body. The class was very emotionally difficult for many students, particularly those of us who had grown up with disabilities and had interacted extensively with medical systems. Many of our experiences were negative, and sometimes abusive. Taking the class with Shelly was a huge leap of faith.

In one particularly poignant moment, a student with cerebral palsy talked about the pain of wearing rigid metal leg braces throughout his childhood. Many of us had experienced wearing leg braces and shared memories of our distress being ignored by medical professionals. We looked up at Shelly who in that moment was a stand-in for all of the medical professionals who had made those decisions about equipment

---

12. We were a bunch of scruffy young disabled people who liked to party. We were not people that funders ever gave money to. Shelly was our de facto professional cosigner, meaning that his presence on our letterhead and on our Board told funders that there was a grownup in the room. Even though Shelley would laugh at being portrayed that way to the funders, he very much served that role.

for our bodies that caused us pain.

Shelly compassionately looked at the student and said that bracing is never an effective long-term solution for people with cerebral palsy. "The cerebral palsy always wins," he said, "so while bracing maybe may have short-term effectiveness there is no long-term benefit." The room hushed. None of us had ever heard a medical professional acknowledge our reality. Shelly took a breath and then said, "I'm very sorry that happened to you." Shelly did more healing about our medical trauma in that one exchange then most of us ever experience in a lifetime.

That was the power of the Antioch program. Disabled people's experiences were validated and documented. Students were encouraged to delve into academic theories and challenge the presumptions of the dominance of the nondisabled body and mind. Surrounded by others who shared the disability rights perspective, students could dive deeply into topics and discuss them for hours until new thinking emerged. It was, as one student said, a dream-like environment. Like all dreams, it had to end, and much too early.

How it all Ended

For two semesters in 1975, Antioch tolerated paying for off-site classrooms and teachers that they did not control. Then they started to pressure Hal and the department to bring the disabled students into the existing Master's programs in San Francisco. Hal knew that this would not work because of transportation barriers, so they compromised. The portable classrooms would stay, but Antioch's existing teaching staff would start to teach the classes.

Unfortunately, those teachers had no knowledge of the disability community or disability etiquette. The Antioch staff's classroom practices created enormous access barriers. They would stand between the interpreter and the deaf person. They would not make their materials available for the blind students. They did not know how to set up the classroom chairs so that folks who use wheelchairs were able to get around. They basically had no knowledge of, or really much interest in, disabled people. Because the teachers were white and the students were mostly white, the teachers just imposed a medical model of disability on us without any understanding of the ways in which we were culturally diverse from them.

Although we were all sorely disappointed with the new disability-ignorant teachers, we were trying to make this work because none of us wanted to go to San Francisco for classes, since those of us with mobility disabilities knew that we could never we get reliable enough transportation to be successful in the program.

For me the tipping point came in a class on child psychology. The teacher was covering the well-known theories of early childhood development. This was familiar territory to me, as I had a degree in Early Childhood as well as Special Education. A critical component in all of the theories at the time was that bladder continence is required for emotional maturation. (We now know this to be nonsense.)

The students looked around the room. We knew there were a number of adults in our class who were disabled as children and had never achieved bladder continence. So we teased out the question to the teacher by asking, "Are there any studies that separate bladder continence from emotional maturation?" The teacher's response was "Gee, I never thought about that." After we posed the question, we fully expected that the teacher would have thought about the question, possibly done some research, possibly talked to other colleagues, but at a minimum that she would take our question seriously. When we asked her again the following week, however, she answered that she had not thought about it because it didn't seem very important.

That was the moment I knew that, as the program was structured, it could never succeed, and I could not succeed in it. I had no interest in being an outsider and alone in an academic program about disability. Within a month, Hal was told that he had lost the fight and all of the students were going to be required to attend classes in San Francisco with Antioch's existing teaching staff, teachers like our psychology professor. Nearly all the students left the program when Antioch required us to go to San Francisco for classes.

A few students persisted, and they found many challenges. "You'd get all the way over there and, you know, it's at night and you're trying to take a class in like something maybe you weren't that interested in. Like I was doing a hospital administration minor, so you're taking these health care administration classes, which to me is really like ugh. I wanted to focus on the nitty gritty counseling stuff of working with people with disabilities, and so that was hard. Yes, it was."[13]

Closing

Although it lasted less than two years, Hal Kirshbaum created a grand experiment. He provided the first environment where academic knowledge joined with disability community knowledge to ask new

---

13. Chavez, see note 7.

questions, explore new ideas, and create new intellectual lines of inquiry. Hal moved onto his next project, which was starting Through the Looking Glass, an international research and training organization that examines how disability and families interact and creates support networks for families to be successful, with his wife Megan Kirshbaum. (see "Disabled Parents" in this book).

Hal Kirshbaum's visionary program encountered substantial resistance, but it laid the groundwork for disabled people to get interested in the academic side of disability and encouraged disabled people to pursue advanced degrees. As participants in that early program have died, much of this history is permanently lost, but it is my sincere hope that scholarly interest emerges to document this important history before all of its participants are gone.

JUST THE FACTS MA'AM

1972 — Hal Kirshbaum begins working at the Center for Independent Living in Berkeley, California.

1975 — Hal Kirshbaum creates the first Disability Studies program, a Master's program, through Antioch University West.

1977 — Antioch University West decides that all students must be in their San Francisco classes even though there is no wheelchair accessible public transportation. Most of the students drop out and the program ends.

RESOURCES

Academic Programs in Disability Studies in North America. URL:
    http://disabilitystudies.syr.edu/resources/programsinds.aspx
Disability Studies Quarterly. URL: http://www.dsq-sds.org/
Society for Disability Studies. URL: http://www.disstudies.org

A full bibliography is available at my website: www.corbettotoole.com

5.

Race and Disability

"…it is not difference which immobilizes us, but silence. And there are so many silences to be broken." — Audre Lorde[1]

Summary

People of color were an important part of the history of the American disability rights movement. Disabled people of color were living and working in Berkeley in the early 1970s when the Center for Independent Living (CIL) was being founded. The 1977 San Francisco sit-in for disability rights succeeded because the Black Panthers brought the protesters food every day. But even though there were many disabled people of color, the stories about disability history do not include them. I believe this must be changed. I tell the story of Johnnie Lacy, a black woman who used a wheelchair. She was a project director and community organizer, but her important contributions are ignored in disability history.

There are not many disabled people of color running disability organizations, even though many of them are qualified. I believe that disability organizations need to deal with the racism in their organizations and support and promote the projects and leadership of disabled people of color.

❖ ❖ ❖

---

1. Audre Lorde, *The Transformation of Silence into Language and Action.* Originally delivered at the Lesbian and Literature panel of the Modern Language Association's December 28, 1977 meeting. It was then published in many of Lorde's books, including *The Cancer Journals* and *Sister Outsider.* It also contains a poem that was originally published in *The Black Unicorn* (1978).

As long as my worldview is tied to racial and disability hierarchies, I will never know the wisdom and skills of people different from myself.

This essay is, in many ways, a letter to the contemporary white American disability rights movement. I love and take pride in the work that has been accomplished under the banner of the "disability rights movement." I love the ways we have challenged nondisabled society, fighting for our rights and gaining some important concessions. In forty years, we have accomplished many great things. In my youth I worked in the disability rights movement, but now as an elder I devote my limited energy to supporting and fostering the academic work done in Disability Studies, which also struggles with committing to diversity.[2] Yet I am fully aware that I am able to do this work because, as a white woman with a physical disability, a college education, and fluent, articulate speech, I am automatically accepted and validated as part of the movement, part of who is supposed to be doing this work.

For me, the "disability rights movement" consists of organizations run by and for disabled people.[3] They might be an independent living center, a state disability-specific association, a legal rights center, or a national cross-disability association. They state that their mission is tied to either independent living or disability rights (or both), and they believe in the right of disabled people to make their own decisions. Most of these organizations also see themselves as tied to the original principles of 'disability rights' and 'independent living' as defined by the work of disabled activists in the 1970s in Berkeley, California.[4]

In many places in the U.S., the current disability rights movement evolved from 1970s grassroots, action-oriented activists, to 2000s office workers who are service providers. We've gone from protesting on the streets to writing letters to legislators as the extent of our advocacy. We

2. While the problem of racial exclusion did not originate in the field of Disability Studies, their decision to accept the 1970s American disability rights and independent living perspectives meant that they also inherited those movements' exclusion of disabled people of color. Disabled scholars of color make up a tiny percentage of Disability Studies graduate students and professionals. Most of the scholarly work by disabled people of color is being done without any academic support—often published online, by such scholars as Leroy Moore, Naomi Ortiz, Eddie Ndopo, and others.

    "Of the ninety nine dissertations published in the past five years that include "disability studies" in the title, abstract, or as a key term, only twenty four include analyses of race or ethnicity." from Ferri, B.A. (2010). "A dialogue we've yet to have: Race and disability studies." In C. Dudley-Marling & A. Gurn (eds). *The Myth of the Normal Curve* (Ch.10). Peter Lang, New York, NY.

3. While I wish that all disability rights organizations were run by disabled people, increasingly they are not. As many disability activists have noted, many disability organizations that were founded by disabled people are now being run by nondisabled people, in some cases by people who ran organizations actively opposed by disability rights groups. For more, see Caitlin Wood at Criptiques. URL: http://criptiques.com/

4. I discuss this in more depth in the introductory essay "Celebrating Crip Bodyminds."

have had many opportunities to become more racially and disability diverse organizations, to take to the streets in protest of discrimination, but the mainstream disability rights organizations have not done so. Disconnected from the impoverished lives of the vast majority of disabled people, the movement must either face the challenges of these structural inequalities or fade away from relevance.

I love the quote that starts this essay. Audre Lorde (disabled) was a black lesbian who got cancer and told the world about it in her writings. She is widely appropriated by white disability scholars and activists, without any consideration for what she said about race, queers, or social justice. So I use her words here for two reasons. One, because her wisdom shines through her writing so deeply and so clearly. We need to break silences in order to change. Second, throughout her work she kept reminding us of people's intersectionalities—how we all live in multiple communities—and how some of those communities are privileged and others are very disenfranchised. This essay directly addresses intersections of race and disability, and sometimes also class and disability hierarcharies.

This essay has had many titles. I wanted to call it "differences," to talk about it as "diversity," to talk about it as anything other than what it is, which is a white girl sitting down to talk about racial and disability hierarchies.

It is easy to make this essay self-flagellation for all my mistakes as a white person. It is easy to make this chapter be about explaining away the hierarchies and privileges at the intersection of race and disability. I'm more interested in doing the deeper work of telling a story of privilege, mistakes, and learning from those mistakes and breaking the silences.

I do this with great reluctance. White people often undertake this work to congratulate ourselves for how much we have grown, how cool we are, how much other people should look up to us, but I undertake this chapter to say I don't have a clue. I really wish I did because I would feel a whole lot better if I did.

I have practiced my privilege in so many different ways with so many different people over the years that, like all unconscious white people, I have left a trail of harm everywhere and every time I have unconsciously used that privilege. For that I am truly sorry.

Johnnie Lacy (disabled), a Black professional woman, taught me about my own prejudices when we worked in the same building at the Center for Independent Living in Berkeley[5] in 1979. At that time I was

---

5. For clarity, when I say "Berkeley" I mean the City of Berkeley. When I say "Cal" I mean the University of California, Berkeley.

high on my own ego from many years of successful disability rights activism. I believed that the Berkeley disability rights organizations were not prejudiced, and that as a part of those organizations, I was justly an insider and Johnnie was an interloper. Neither my work life nor my personal life included people of color. As you can imagine, I did not make Johnnie welcome. Yet, as she told me many years later, I was often one of the "better" people to deal with in the disability rights movement. In the nearly two decades that we knew each other, she provided me with many opportunities to learn about my white privilege.

I want to tell her story because it illustrates the patterns and practices of how the white-based disability rights movement has focused on white people while pretending it has not. The story I tell below is based on her oral history that is part of the Disability Rights and Independent Living Movement oral history collection in the Bancroft Library at the University of California Berkeley.[6]

More personally, I want to tell her story because I have just discovered, in researching this book, parts of her experience within the disability rights movement that completely reshape my thinking about the 1970s disability community in Berkeley. Even though I am a long time disability activist, I had no idea of her role in disability history as the first Black project manger at the Center for Independent Living and one of the very few Black leaders in the U.S. disability rights movement. No existing disability history even mentions her name.[7]

The ways in which the histories of disabled people of color have been ignored and discounted in disability historical accounts is both pathetic and frightening.[8] In the past two decades, nearly all the works written about the American disability rights movement focus on white

6. Johnnie Lacy oral history in the *Disability Rights Independent Living Movement (DRILM) Historical Archives*. The Regional Oral History Office, The Bancroft Library, University of California, Berkeley. URL: http://bancroft.berkeley.edu/collections/drilm/index.html

7. A DRILM search on her name shows it only appears in her oral history.

8. Chris Bell's posthumously published anthology *Blackness and Disability: Critical Examinations and Cultural Interventions* is the latest and in some respects the most ambitious contribution to date in the study of race and disability. This field of study was first brought to widespread visibility by Bell himself, with the essay "Introducing White Disability Studies: A Modest Proposal," which appeared in the second edition of the *Disability Studies Reader*.

    In that essay, Bell posits that disability studies (DS) has historically failed "to engage issues of race and ethnicity in a substantive capacity, thereby entrenching whiteness as its constitutive underpinning" (275). According to Bell, this failure has both severely limited the relevance of much Disability Studies scholarship, and further disenfranchised people of color with disabilities. As a first step toward rectifying this disciplinary oversight and its grave impacts, Bell suggests that we as a field need to acknowledge the oversight, acerbically suggesting that we even rename the field, as currently practiced, "White Disability Studies." From Bell, C. (2011). *Blackness and Disability: Critical Examinations and Cultural Interventions*. Reviewed by Adam P. Newman in *Disability Studies Quarterly*, Vol. 32. No. 3 (2012).

disabled people and white-led disability organizations. Finding the disabled people of color in any historical accounts is difficult. Even the extensive Disability Rights and Independent Living Movement's 109 oral histories only include seven people of color.[9]

Like all dominant culture people, white disabled people in the disability rights movement are leaving a record behind that tells the story of how great we were, while pretending that everybody else was not there.

If you only looked at photographs of the disability rights movement over the past four decades, you would believe that we were a multiracial community. In advertising, the Disability Rights and Independent Living Movement oral history collection shows photographs of 100% disabled people, of whom 25% are people of color. Yet only 1/15th of the collection is people of color. Images of people of color often accompany online disability materials written by, and intended for, white disabled people. The practice is widespread and unchallenged. This I take note of, as a form of systemic racism—the images of people of color are appropriated, but their voices are not welcomed. Many times, images of international disabled people are inserted without noting that the image is of a person who lives outside the United States, and in their country they are a dominant culture person. So the article's readers see an image of a person of color, whom they assume to be an American person of color, and often mistakenly assume that the writer is including the perspectives and input of American disabled people of color when that is almost never the case.

While people of all races participated in the hard work of fighting for disability rights, the rewards of that work—employment opportunities, leadership, speaking opportunities—have not been shared equally. One needs only to glance at the statistics of who is employed in disability rights organizations to take note of this. They are by and large white people.[10]

The presence of disabled people of color, particularly in leadership positions, continues to be abysmally small. If you follow even a few

9. This collection heavily favors white people, as 102 of the 109 individual interviews are white people. This collection also heavily favors people with physical disabilities (64), the vast majority of whom are people who use wheelchairs. Nondisabled people (29) are the next largest group. And there are token numbers of people from other disability communities (21), queer people (7), and parents of disabled children (4). Even with these limitations, the oral histories are enormously valuable, particularly as they capture a number of people who have since died, but who provide critical historical information.

10. National Council on Disability (1999). *Lift every voice: Modernizing disability policies and programs to serve a diverse nation.* URL: http://www.ncd.gov/publications/1999/Dec11999

historical threads by disabled people of color,[11.] the struggles of disabled people of color have been marked with incredible resistance from white disabled people and disability organizations. Like poverty, disability disproportionately impacts communities of color.[12.]

The disability rights movement, like many white-run middle class aspiring movements, promotes an educational message that "disabled people are just like you." This approach presumes that, with a small change in awareness by nondisabled people, disabled people will be accepted and welcomed. This approach makes us seem friendly and unthreatening. For the past 40 years, the disability rights movement has sent this message out, rebranding it for different issues and needs.

Not only is this an incredibly simplistic worldview, it completely ignores the underlying social mandate that disabled bodyminds are undesirable in the nondisabled world and are only tolerated under very specific conditions.[13.] (If you don't believe me about this just read the essay on violence.) This approach leaves unchallenged the insidious ableism that defines disabled people as having lesser value than nondisabled people.

In this essay I am giving you some facts and a lot of opinions. At the end of this I hope that you will have learned a little something, know a little bit more history, and have a reason to have a conversation with someone else about hierarchies and privileges.

Perspective

I'm writing this on a dark and stormy night in 2014 in Richmond, California, a poor working class community a few towns north of Berkeley. There's Christmas music playing quietly in the background and my newsfeed is full of stories of my friends and colleagues protesting yet again about the violence against black people in America. Coordinated through #BlackLivesMatter, people across America and

---

11. Examples: the DRILM interviews with Galloway (see note 30), Lacy (see note 6) and the work of Bell (see note 8).

12. I changed "people of Hispanic origin" to Latinos: "When disability rates are computed for men only, racial and ethnic differences become even more pronounced. Again, the highest rate of disability is among Native Americans (21.9%), followed by whites (19.1%), blacks (18.0%), people of Hispanic origin (14.3%), and Asians and Pacific Islanders (9.1%)." Bradsher, J.E. (1996). *Disability Among Racial and Ethnic Groups.* Published by U.S. Department of Education, in *National Institute on Disability and Rehabilitation Research (NIDRR) 10.*

13. Instead of saying "bodies and minds" I am using Margaret Price's phrase "bodymind." Price states, "mental and physical processes not only affect each other but also give rise to each other—that is, because they tend to act as one, even though they are conventionally understood as two—it makes more sense to refer to them together, in a single term." from Price, M. (2015) "The bodymind problem and the possibilities of pain." *Hypatia* 30(1), 268–284.

around the world are taking to the streets to raise awareness of the fact that every 28 hours a black man, woman or child in America is murdered by police or vigilante law enforcement.[14] That's a fact that black people have known for years but that white people are just discovering.

During these months of protesting, discussions and engagement led by black people, white people have struggled to not be center stage through signs and campaigns to that speak to white experiences more directly, such as the alternative #AllLivesMatter. While most people would agree that all lives do matter, black people have to continually remind white people that, right now, the conversation is about black life mattering. It's about the reality that every 28 hours a black person is killed.

When it comes to valuing the lives of disabled people of color, the disability rights movement has never done well. In the past 40 years there were a handful of disabled leaders of color in disability rights organizations, but frequently they're asked to leave their quest for racial justice outside the door and just focus on disability rights issues.[15] It's a tragedy of epic proportions that four decades into the current disability rights movement in the U.S., we are still limiting ourselves to a very narrow range of disabled people to shape our visions, our leadership, and be our spokespeople—people who are white people and are blind or physically disabled. Implementing the tenets of "we're just like you," they are people who look good on camera, who speak fluently, and who are able to make the imaginary white nondisabled audience believe that white disabled people are not threatening, that if they would just let us in, we would be well behaved and not be a bother.

When the hell did we decide that being nice was our goal? I never signed onto that. I signed onto fighting for social justice. I didn't sit in a federal building for 28 days at the 504 sit-in because I wanted to build a movement that maintains white disabled privileges. I sat there because I wanted civil rights. I never signed up to be nice and people who know me would argue that I'm constitutionally incapable of that. I signed up for justice. And that's what I want.

All white disabled people, particularly those who are physically disabled or blind, have benefited from the work and the opportunities of the disability rights movement organizations. White people with fluent speech, non-shaking bodies, who can dress and speak in white

---

14. #BlackLivesMatter. URL: http://blacklivesmatter.com/

15. See Lacy, note 6; Galloway, note 30; and National Council on Disability (1999). *Lift every voice: Modernizing disability policies and programs to serve a diverse nation.* URL: http://www.ncd.gov/publications/1999/Dec11999

middle-class ways, know that we will always be in the consideration for jobs, for public speaking, for the limited opportunities offered to disabled people. We do not have to think about these privileges because we did not earn them. They came to us because we look like the people who started the disability rights and independent living movements in the U.S. in the 1970s.

One Story: Johnnie Lacy

I want give you a little historical context. To do that I'm going to use the often repeated shorthand of how the 1970s Berkeley disability rights movement came into being. In the shorthand version, Ed Roberts, a disabled man who used a power wheelchair and an iron lung, fought his way into Cal (the University of California, Berkeley). There he was joined by other students who also used wheelchairs, and they created a group called the "Rolling Quads." They also created the Physically Disabled Students Program at Cal, a service organization providing support for disabled students. Ed became director of the Center for Independent Living, also in Berkeley. (He was actually not the first director, nor did he have any direct role in creating CIL—facts that are almost always misrepresented. See "Center for Independent Living, Berkeley" in this book.) This simple, if very incomplete, narrative is used as a framework to teach American disability history. But Ed was not at Cal when the Rolling Quads were formed, nor did he create the Physically Disabled Student Program although he, Zona Roberts (his mother) and Jean Wirth (his community college counselor) lobbied hard for the initial funding. Ed was not even living in Berkeley for the first two years of the Center for Independent Living.

When you read historical accounts of the people who were in the Rolling Quads, or even the people who worked in Physically Disabled Students Program or Center for Independent Living, you get the impression that all disabled people who came into their circles were welcomed and included.[16] You also get the impression that the only people who were there, with the notable exception of Billy Barner, were white.[17] There are many stories of people wandering into the

16. The best source for Cal post 1960 disability history is the *Disability Rights Independent Living Movement (DRILM) Historical Archives*. The Regional Oral History Office, The Bancroft Library, University of California, Berkeley. URL:
http://bancroft.berkeley.edu/collections/drilm/index.html

17. Billy Barner oral history in the *Disability Rights Independent Living Movement (DRILM) Historical Archives*. The Regional Oral History Office, The Bancroft Library, University of California, Berkeley. URL: http://bancroft.berkeley.edu/collections/drilm/index.html

world of the Rolling Quads and getting swept up and included in this new social justice movement for disability rights. You see this information spread throughout the oral histories at the Bancroft library, the largest archive of oral histories of the disability rights movement in the United States.[18]

I've read quite a bit about the 1970-2010 disability rights history, particularly the Berkeley area history. I have even examined it in depth in order to correct the myth that Ed Roberts created the Center for Independent Living. When I was doing research for this book, I was completely astounded to read the transcript of Johnnie Lacy's oral history.[19] From 1969 to 1978, extremely formative years for the disability rights movement, the time when the Physically Disabled Students Program was created at Cal, the time when the Center for Independent Living was created, Johnnie Lacy was hanging around with the disabled people who were credited with founding the disability rights movement.

From 1969 to 1972 Johnnie was a graduate student at Cal, the location of the Rolling Quads and the Physically Disabled Students Program. She talks about visiting the wheelchair repair shop at Cowell Hospital, the "dormitory" for the physically disabled students on the Cal campus. She talks about hanging out and chatting with the different folks who were there. She talks about doing the same thing at the Physically Disabled Students Program after 1970. Once the Center for Independent Living was up and running in 1972, she started getting her wheelchair and van repairs done there as well.

During this time there were only a handful of people with electric wheelchairs in Berkeley. I could drive down the street with my friends and if we passed a wheelchair-modified van, we could name whose it was. So for example, if we passed a van near a restaurant we would say to each other "Oh, Greg's eating pizza tonight." Often we would verify that the next day with Greg, who indeed would say "Oh yeah I went to the pizza place last night." The community was so small and the resources, such as having your own wheelchair van, so rare, that we were a very interdependent and well-networked community. When new disabled people, particularly if they were wheelchair users or blind, appeared at Cal or at CIL, they were nearly always immediately welcomed and embraced. In the Bancroft Library's oral histories of disabled people from the 1970s, you constantly read stories that say basically, "so-and-so appeared one day and pretty soon they were

18. *Disability Rights Independent Living Movement (DRILM) Historical Archives.* URL: http://bancroft.berkeley.edu/collections/drilm/index.html

19. Lacy, see note 6.

integral to the disability organization." In short, new people were noticed and welcomed and brought deeper into the disability rights community.

So it's extremely aberrant when Johnnie Lacy says that she was at Cowell Hospital, the Physically Disabled Student Program, and the Center for Independent Living, and yet somehow escaped anyone's attention. It's not like there were hundreds of black women in power chairs running around Berkeley. In fact, she was probably the only black disabled female wheelchair user that most of these folks had met. There were a handful of black disabled men, such as Ron Washington and Gary Gray, who also are also rarely mentioned in historical accounts and who also were not given leadership or speaking opportunities.

In Johnnie's history she talked about getting her wheelchair repaired at all these different locations at the time that I was in Berkeley and I was at CIL, and I realized that I didn't remember her, nor do I remember anyone talking about her, although as a black power chair user in the late 1960s and 1970s she would definitely have been noticed.

Getting her wheelchair fixed would have involved multiple visits and lots of waiting around in the repair shop. In her oral history, Johnnie talks about hanging out at the repair shop in Cowell Hospital and getting to know the other Cal students. She also knew the wheelchair technicians well, since they possessed a rare skill and often participated in disability community events. It was very common, if your wheelchair broke at night or on a weekend, to call the wheelchair repair technician at home ask him[20.] to help you out. If he could, he would.

In the decade before Johnnie was hired at CIL in 1979, she knew many key disabled leaders and knew their wheelchair technicians. Through her anti-poverty programs she also knew Alan Kalmanoff (nondisabled), who became the master trainer for all the 504 trainers, the job that Johnnie was eventually recruited to do. To summarize, many disabled people and nondisabled people attached to disability work at Cal and CIL knew Johnnie in various capacities. Yet when the funder required that disabled people of color were hired for the 504 Training program grant, no one suggested Johnnie.

Johnnie was ultimately recruited by the famous disability rights and Berkeley Center for Independent Living leader Judy Heumann (disabled) while shopping at a local mall. Judy went up to Johnnie and said that she was required to hire people of color for the 504 Training project and she asked Johnnie to apply.

---

20. Wheelchair techs were always men in those days—especially if they were employed.

We are fortunate to have Johnnie's oral history where she related this encounter:

> [I was in the Hallmark store in the mall and] I realized that she [Judy Heumann] was really focusing on me for some reason or another, and I thought, She doesn't know me, does she? [chuckling] … [S]he approached me, and she introduced herself… And being the very abrupt and straight-to-the-point kind of person, she asked me if I was interested in being in the 504 training. She explained that they had been basically ordered to get more people of color involved and that they were really having a hard time recruiting people of color. And this was always a problem at CIL anyway.
>
> And she asked me if I was interested, and I told her, "Well, yeah, I might be." So she asked me for my phone number, and she said, "Well, somebody will get in touch with you and send you an application."[21]

This story is extremely troubling for a number of reasons. As Johnnie recounts in a separate part of the interview, Alan Kalmanoff, the main trainer for the 504 training program, had not only met Johnnie earlier but had worked with her on a project where she was the project leader. The second troubling aspect of the story is the fact that by 1979 Johnnie had spent ten years in conversations with key leaders in the disability community and yet had somehow failed to register on the radar of any of the white disabled people who she had met over the years. Remember that at this point there were very few skilled disabled people. We had very little access to professional training, although because of Department of Rehabilitation policies, many of us had college educations. A person like Johnnie, with extensive work experience, deep community resources and professional management experience was an extremely valuable resource to the newly forming disability rights movement. Yet, somehow, she failed to be noticed and brought into the disability rights work.

A third troubling aspect of this story is the fact that in 1979 the leadership of the disability rights movement had no idea how to find disabled people of color for jobs. Even though the photographs most commonly used for the 504 sit-in clearly show a number of disabled people of color, and even though Brad Lomax (disabled), a Black

---

21. Lacy, see note 6.

Panther, and Elaine Brown (nondisabled), the leader of the Black Panther Party, had ongoing conversations with CIL, and Ed Roberts specifically, for over five years, the presence of disabled people of color was neither registering on the consciousness of the white disabled leaders, nor was it considered valuable enough to be recorded when they recounted their histories of the 1970s.

The final troubling aspect to the story is that Judy was blatantly saying that she was seeking out a complete stranger in a public place because she looked visibly disabled and had a skin color that marked her as a person of color. As my friends would say, "face-palm," meaning "I am flabbergasted."

I was incredibly sad when I read Johnnie's history, not in small part because I was part of the problem. We cannot ask her any more questions, because Johnnie died in 2010. Her oral history was conducted by a white man in a wheelchair, recorded for posterity as part of the history of the disability rights movement. The oral history demonstrates that Johnnie, above all else, was a kind and gracious human being. Horrified as I was reading her story and the racism she experienced, I want to note that the outrage is mine. Johnnie told her story as simple and straightforward facts, without rancor or judgment.

By 1979, the Center for Independent Living had received a number of grants, some of them under "minority" programs, but the funders had seen the Center appoint exclusively white staff to these "minority" funded programs. They made it a condition of a new grant for the Community Services Administration (CSA) program that it be run by a person of color.[22] Although Johnnie had come to the Center to work on the 504 Training project, she disliked the "I talk, you listen" approach to the trainings. Instead, since the Center needed a person of color to administer the grant, she became the director of the CSA program at the Center, as she'd already run a CSA-funded program at a different agency.

Johnnie was already working at the Center, one of the only disabled people of color employed there, and since she had extensive experience with CSA programs outside of the Center she was the natural choice to run that program. As she recalls, "The CSA liaison had insisted that he hire someone of color because at this time the [legal program] had either no people of color or they weren't that familiar with the issues

---

22. Often funders, particularly for government programs designated for "minorities," were the only people requiring the Berkeley disability rights organizations to include disabled people of color. From Charles Grimes's oral history in the *Disability Rights Independent Living Movement (DRILM) Historical Archives*. The Regional Oral History Office, The Bancroft Library, University of California, Berkeley. URL: http://bancroft.berkeley.edu/collections/drilm/index.html

around the CSA programs."[23]

Johnnie's program trained people in CSA-funded anti-poverty organizations on disability rights. Her previous years of work in CSA-funded organizations provided her with valuable insights into their needs and the gaps in their services for disabled people.

Johnnie Lacy at CIL

The reception Johnnie received at the Center's Disability Law Resource Center was less than welcoming, even though she was a respected program director for previous non-disabled-focused CSA programs:

> [T]he people at CSA knew me well. They knew my reputation, from the anti-poverty program. And since I was going to be in charge of this program, I would be able to set the tone and the direction because that's what I was hired to do, and it didn't really matter to me that people like Bob [Bob Funk (disabled), her white disabled boss], who didn't know me, didn't know what my background was, had this [negative] attitude because I had experienced this before, you know, on many occasions. I knew that I was qualified. I knew that I had administrative experience. I knew that I had organizing experience. I knew that I had training experience. And for me, I think he recognized what I thought were the lesser qualifications. I can remember him saying, sarcastically, "Well, you have community organizing experience, and that's what we need, so we'll hire you." Well, I had that, but I had a great deal more, and I think I was able to show it in many ways at CIL.[24]

Johnnie's program at the Center provided training that the CSA organizations were mandated to receive. The 504 regulations passed in 1977 required that any agency that received federal money, directly or indirectly, did not discriminate against people with disabilities. So CSA contracted with CIL to provide these trainings. But even the materials required for the training embedded white presumptions into them.

> Nobody in the project really had a full understanding and knowledge around the issues of disability in minority communities, and the training was basically a training for white

---

23. Lacy, see note 6.

24. Ibid. (This means see previous note.)

disabled activists that could not—there just wasn't the ability to incorporate minority disabled issues in this training outline.[25.]

Despite the limitations of the training materials, Johnnie brought in three interns who were all disabled people of color. Her heavy recruitment for the training brought 150 disabled people of color together. "We had Hispanic, we had Filipino, we had Asian, we had African Americans, Hawaiian, Korean. The mix was just astounding for that group of folks."[26.] Given that she had no institutional resources from the disability rights movement, who had largely ignored organizations in communities of color, getting this diverse audience for her training was an astounding accomplishment.

But even with all her networking, the training participants were keenly aware of the disconnect between the white-run disability rights movement and the people of color run community organizations.

> Well, I think the—one of the most important issues was around the fact that everybody in charge was white and that somehow or other this again came over, came across as a kind of condescending thing, that there was no empowerment being provided in terms of taking charge of minority individuals' lives when that's what the training was supposed to be all about... [agency leaders of color felt the] lack of sincerity that was taking place, the question of whether or not minorities were really, really welcomed into the CIL world or whether this was just something that was foisted upon them because they were getting paid, getting funded to do it.[27.]

Johnnie Lacy was a very accomplished Black disabled woman. She became disabled with polio as a young adult and used a wheelchair. Even though being Black and disabled were major impediments to her employment and education, Johnnie worked her entire adult life. By the time she came to the Center for Independent Living in 1979, she had already had three jobs. After she left CIL she went to Community Resources for Independent Living a few towns south of Berkeley. She trained disabled people of color to be mentors, created deep and powerful support networks, and created an agency[28.] that supported a

---

25. Lacy, see note 6.

26. Ibid.

27. Ibid.

28. "She went to Community Resources for Independent Living in Hayward, CA, in March 1981— becoming the second Executive Director in one year—ran it for 14 years [until 1994] till she died

wide variety of disabled people.

Johnnie's experiences at CIL were not isolated incidents. Donald (Don) Galloway (disabled), a Black blind man, also worked at CIL in the 1970s. He went onto the CIL Board of Directors and attempted to create a Black Caucus, but his efforts were thwarted by the CIL leadership. After he left CIL he attempted to create a Minority Caucus at the National Council on Independent Living where he met resistance as well. As Don recounts:

> So we first started off with the minority caucus of citizens with disabilities, as minorities with the national office. But we changed it to a cultural thing, caucus for cultural affairs, or caucus for people with different cultures and that was a struggle... They were very opposed to it initially because they felt that it would splinter our organization. They didn't see the logic that it would strengthen, they thought it would weaken... Always in the IL [Independent Living] movement, they talk about inclusion of minorities, but when minorities get together to create a mechanism to include themselves, with us having some sort of control on it, they seem to be opposed to it. Especially when it comes to funding.[29]

The exclusion of disabled people of color from leadership positions continues throughout our 40-year history. Even with multiple American conferences and research reports over the past two decades documenting the problems of exclusion, showing the disparity gap between who is excluded from disability rights organizations, the exclusionary practices are seemingly intractable. Disabled people of color continue to need to create their own organizations, find their own funding, and build up their own communities, even while disability organizations claim to serve them and use their images in marketing materials.

The National Council on Disability has held meetings and created numerous documents discussing these barriers and possible solutions. They published reports in 1999 and 2002 about "Minorities with Disabilities" and published reports specific to American Indians and

---

in 2010. She was named woman of the year by the California State Senate in 1988." Cobb, P. (November 10, 2010). "Johnnie Ann Lacy: Ably led the disabled." *The Post News Online*. URL: http://content.postnewsgroup.com/tag/paul-cobb/

29. Donald Galloway oral history in the *Disability Rights Independent Living Movement (DRILM) Historical Archives*. The Regional Oral History Office, The Bancroft Library, University of California, Berkeley. URL: http://bancroft.berkeley.edu/collections/drilm/index.html

Alaskan natives with disabilities in 2003 and 2004. Although these reports reflect the best thinking of disabled people committed to racial equality in disability communities, very little change has occurred.

Disabled people of color have built online and offline networks, cultural organizations, and professional associations.[30] Yet they receive no funding and very little support from white-led disability organizations. The intersectional work of disabled people of color, often captured under the term "disability justice," continues to grow and engage multiple communities simultaneously. Their work addresses the intersections of ableism and racism and usually includes other disenfranchised communities.

There have always been disabled people inside and outside the disability rights movement that have raised the issues of racial privilege. Some have worked inside the movement and others have created interracial organizations and networks outside the disability movement.

For many years I was supporting white privileges while at the same time I was speaking about need for more racial diversity. In spite of the many learning opportunities offered by other disabled people, I did this without either self-awareness or any willingness to address the barriers. I am saddened that the organizations that cling most tightly to white disability privileges are the most professionalized and separated from grassroots disabled communities, for it foreshadows their demise and irrelevance. I am heartened by the pioneering work of disabled people of color in creating new models of disability community and social justice.[31]

JUST THE FACTS MA'AM

22% of Native Americans are disabled
19% of white Americans are disabled
18% of African-Americans are disabled
14% of Latinos are disabled
9% of Asians and Pacific Islanders are disabled

---

30. Some examples:

   National Black Disability Coalition. URL: http://www.blackdisability.org/

   Black Disabled Peoples Association. URL: http://brent.gov.uk/your-community/community-directory/black-disabled-peoples-association/

   Asian People's Disability Alliance. URL: http://www.patient.co.uk/support/apda-asian-peoples-disability-alliance

   Native American Disability Law Center. URL: http://nativedisabilitylaw.org/

31. A more thorough discussion of this is in the essay "Dancing Forward."

RESOURCES

Bell, C. (2011). *Blackness and Disability: Critical Examinations and Cultural Interventions.* Reviewed by A. Newman (2012) in *Disability Studies Quarterly* 32(3).

Cultural Diversity Reports, National Council On Disability. URL: http://www.ncd.gov/policy/cultural_diversity

DRILM Interviews, especially Johnnie Lacy and Donald Galloway. URL: http://bancroft.berkeley.edu/collections/drilm/collection/collection.html

A full bibliography is available at my website: www.corbettotoole.com

6.

Dancing Through Life

"Woes are fleeting/ When you're dancing/ Through life."
— From the musical *Wicked*. Music and
lyrics by Stephen Schwartz

Summary

This essay wanders around the world of disability culture. I look at the ways that disability culture provides a mirror to disabled lives, showing us our humor and struggles. Disability artists tell stories in words and images of disability pride, resilience and humor. In the words and images in nondisabled media, like television and newspapers, disabled people are shown as helpless and "special." Disabled artists provide disabled people with words and images that show disabled people as powerful and interesting. Disability culture is an important part of creating and building a community of proud disabled people.

Axis Dance Company is an internationally famous group of disabled and nondisabled dancers (called "physically integrated dance"). Patty Overland (disabled), Cheryl Marie Wade (disabled), Thais Mazur (nondisabled) and I began Axis. I tell the story of how Patty wanted to create just one short dance piece but when we all came together we realized that we could create an ongoing dance group. I end this essay by writing about why I love to dance.

❖ ❖ ❖

Why disability culture?
Why not?

Disabled people know ourselves better when we see ourselves reflected in the world around us.[1] As people who have largely been kept out of the light, hidden in back rooms, disabled people see very few images of ourselves. The kid with cerebral palsy who uses a power chair and a communication board is not going to see herself in a department store ad or in the latest television teenage sitcom. She is not going to see herself in the posters and photos on the walls of her school.

People with disabilities live surrounded by nondisabled people, nondisabled culture, and nondisabled stereotypes about who they are and who they can be. Disabled people are not reflected in the world around them.

Disabled people need reflections of ourselves, because in a capitalist society we know that what is shown is what is valued. If a sitcom character has a particular look and identity, it means that the people who control the money, the advertisers, believe that that character's identity is worthwhile and can be associated with their product.

Disabled people are almost never associated with the product. We are always presented as an aberration, an inspiration, or a villain. The aberration, the singularity of one, gives us a single narrative of Helen Keller (disabled) who is frozen in time as a young child. Her graduating from Radcliffe, her writings, her socialist work, all of her adult life is a meaningless distraction from her role as the blind/deaf/mute child who learned to speak,[2] taught by the long-suffering special education teacher. How does knowing that Anne Sullivan was also disabled change both their images?

Often disabled people are presented as "inspiring." We in the disability community mockingly call this, "inspiration porn."[3] Stella Young (disabled), a brilliant comedian, described "inspiration porn" as "an image of a person with a disability, often a kid, doing something completely ordinary—like playing, or talking, or running, or drawing a

---

1.   This reminds me of Junot Diaz:

     "If you want to make a human being into a monster, deny them, at the cultural level, any
     reflection of themselves. And growing up, I felt like a monster in some ways. I didn't see myself
     reflected at all. I was like, "Yo, is something wrong with me? That the whole society seems to
     think that people like me don't exist?" And part of what inspired me, was this deep desire that
     before I died, I would make a couple of mirrors. That I would make some mirrors so that kids
     like me might see themselves reflected back and might not feel so monstrous for it." from
     Donohue, B. (October 21, 2009). "Pulitzer Prize-winning author Junot Diaz tells students his
     story." *The Star-Ledger*. URL:
     http://www.nj.com/ledgerlive/index.ssf/2009/10/junot_diazs_new_jersey.html

2.   Shattuck, R. (July-August 2004). "Helen Keller: Brief life of a woman who found her own way."
     Harvard Magazine. URL: http://harvardmagazine.com/2004/07/helen-keller.html

3.   Young, S. (2012). "We're not here for your inspiration." *Ramp Up*. URL:
     http://www.abc.net.au/rampup/articles/2012/07/02/3537035.htm

picture, or hitting a tennis ball—carrying a caption like 'your excuse is invalid' or 'before you quit, try.'"

In inspirational porn we the disabled people are all interchangeable. This week the "inspiration" is a deaf child who now has good hearing aids and can finally hear a noise which they are told is the voice of their mother speaking "I love you." This, of course, ignores the fact that the child's first language is sign language. If the parents had chosen to learn that language, because in America it is a choice and not a requirement for parents and children to have the same language, the parent and child could have said "I love you" to each other since the child's infancy. The deaf child must learn to perform "hearing," because in nondisabled society only hearing connections account. We are all supposed to feel inspired by that moment of auditory contact, even though many deaf educators say that denying a deaf child access to American Sign Language is like putting a hearing child in a soundproof room and denying them opportunities to learn oral language.[4]

If disabled people are not an oddity and not an inspiration, then they must be a malicious aberration. Nearly every time there is an act of horrific violence committed by an individual, the U.S. news media immediately begins to discuss the probability of mental illness. It happens with such regularity that one almost imagines that these news people believe they have medical degrees and have thoroughly assessed the perpetrator of the crime. In fact, all they're doing is relying on the stereotyped monster images where disabled people who are not compliant, are not inspiring, must be terrifying monsters with mental disabilities.

Disability culture smashes these approaches in a very direct and gut-level way. When I sit in my wheelchair and listen to a disabled comic talk about how he does not want people to touch the handles of his wheelchair because it is an intimate act to him, I feel validated. Using humor he explains to nondisabled people: "I need you to imagine that the handles of my wheelchair are like a woman's breasts. You would not touch them without permission or invitation. Therefore please don't touch my wheelchair handles without my permission or invitation." That simple reframing of a small and common act of aggression takes it, turns it on its head, and makes it both instructional and humorous.[5] His humorous example connects me to him.

There can be no disability pride without disability community. There can be no disability pride without disability culture.

4. Cochlear War. *The battle between deaf pro-implant and Deaf community advocates.* URL: http://www.cochlearwar.com/

5. Michael O'Connell. Blog URL: https://oconnellmd.wordpress.com/

There is almost no place where disabled people's creative strategies, our hard learned lifelines, are captured and preserved. Disability culture is where we celebrate and educate. Our ways of moving are rarely celebrated, but they are often recorded without our permission for "medical education." Our dancing throws off that medical gaze and invites a sexy gaze, full of joy and appreciation. Our ways of thinking are often framed as "sick." Our writing shows our image-rich minds full of inventions of new language and novel concepts. We see the averted stares, the denigrating looks full of pity and confusion. We paint eyes gazing back in defiance.

Our thousand ways of knowing come back to us in our arts. Disability culture provides a context for sharing visual history information. It might come in a painting, a comedy routine, a novel, or a dance. Each time we see a disabled person's work or performance, our internal idea of what is possible expands.

The arts have always served to help socially excluded groups validate their experiences and reflect back to themselves. When I watch a quadriplegic dancer thrust her power chair forcefully towards the audience, I am in awe of her power while mesmerized by her outstretched arm, never quite straight, and her quadriplegic fingers where the fingertips permanently touch her palm. The power and grace in those moments up on the stage shows me the beauty of our bodyminds, the depth of our talents.

Leroy Moore (disabled) is a black poet, historian, community activist and scholar. His cerebral palsied body tightens at knees, hips and elbows, presenting him as always ready to spring forward to engage. His rhythmic breathing forces the audience to pay attention to his rapid fire insights delivered in the hip hop staccato. His *Krip Hop Nation* shows the black side of disability culture or the disability side of black culture.[6]

Someone like Leroy will never be on television, because too many people in the disabled community want our public image to be a good looking white guy with a perfect body, other than the fact he doesn't walk, sitting in a slick expensive manual wheelchair. They have no room for the shakers, the droolers and the ugly. The ones who look like what they are—poor outsiders. I reject our community's investment in having our media spokespeople all be "disability pretty" and unthreatening to the ableist stereotypes of disabled people. I embrace our inventive bodyminds. Although he will never be embraced as a public speaker for the disability rights movement because he is too

---

6. Sins Invalid. *Who we are.* URL: http://www.sinsinvalid.org/artistic_core.html

black, too committed to speaking about oppression, too spastic, Leroy is my preferred media spokesperson.

We look exactly likely Leroy. He is our real poster child.[7]

Eli Claire (disabled) tells stories of violence that are so sad I am moved beyond tears. He rewrites his words until the distillation contains deep sadness, deep anger, survival, and eventual release. He is willing to sit with horror until he can communicate it without traumatizing his reader. He teaches me how to sit with the pain in my heart and have hope.

Two very different disabled men, Leroy and Eli, offer gazes that empower and heal. They show us possibilities where the world offers restrictions. They invite us to face that which harms us, embrace its lessons, and release it from ourselves, to sing our truths, to dance our pain in communion with each other.

I love the way crippled bodyminds move. I love the way my daughter's double jointed hands open backwards so widely that they appear to form the number seven. I love noticing how differently my oldest goddaughter (disabled) taps her white cane, the arc, the rhythm as she walks down the street, and how her dance is so different from that of my other friend, Jesse (disabled), who barrels forward, her white cane challenging the environment to resist her.

I love the way my Autistic friends expand language, embedding novel nuances. They trade the learned compliance from strict childhood behavioral programs for the subversion of stillness. Instead of swearing with traditional words they talk about the "asshat" and the "nozzlebox" and exclaim saying, "dafuq", "truedat" and "glargh!"

There is so much beauty in disabled people's bodyminds. So many ways our expressions illuminate creating new patterns. Our cultural artists reflect our beauty and our joy back to us. For this I am profoundly grateful.

Axis Dance — A Story Told In Two Voices

The year is 1984. I am sitting in the back of a large crowded room with about 100 people, a third of them in wheelchairs, at the Women's Building in the San Francisco Mission District. The disabled women's

---

7.   The term *poster child* originally referred to a child afflicted by some disease or deformity whose picture was used on posters or other media as part of a campaign to raise money or enlist volunteers for a cause or organization. The definition of "poster child" has since been expanded to a person of any age whose attributes or behavior are emblematic of a known cause, movement, circumstance or ideal.

performing group Wry Crips[8] is about to start. Because the stage has no ramp, the performers are seated in one corner of the room, but only the people closest to them can see them. I'm far in the back and all I see are the backs of the people.

The emcee opens with the usual introductory information. I laugh when she points out the fire exits, since there's no way any of us is getting out of this room quickly or safely in an emergency. The first few performers do an adequate job, but nothing earth shattering. I've started to space out, expecting more mediocrity, when this honeyed voice leaps across the room, singing of trickster coyotes, gnarly bodies and women with juice. I am transfixed. I am in the presence of genius. I have no idea who she is but I will gladly follow wherever she leads.

Cheryl Marie Wade (disabled) is probably the most famous poet you have never heard of. In large part she's obscure because her topic is the disabled body, not a topic that most people want to think or talk about. Cheryl was the first disabled artistic genius I had ever met, but luckily not the last. Although she had a distinguished solo career, in this essay I am going to talk about the work she and I did as midwives to the Axis Dance Company, a physically integrated professional performing group.

I'm telling the story of the founding of the Axis Dance Company in two voices—mine and Cheryl Marie Wade's. She's no longer here so her words come to you from her oral history.[9] Our words blend together so that it is hard to show you where her words end and mine begin. I encourage you to go and read her oral history, which covers so much more than just this one small story.

I want to start with a contradiction. I started Axis Dance Company but I did not build it, so I have nothing to do with their fabulous success. Patty Overland (disabled), Cheryl Marie Wade (disabled) and I shepherded Patty's idea of one short dance piece, which later grew into Axis, but at no point did any of us envision creating a professional, world-class, physically integrated dance company. Cheryl and I just wanted to assist Patty in creating her dance.

Axis has very humble beginnings. In 1987 Patty was in a day treatment program for people with mental disabilities. Patty was one of the founding mothers of Wry Crips. She had joined a dance class at her day program. The class was taught by Thais Mazur (nondisabled).

Earlier in her life, Patty had attempted suicide by jumping out a

---

8.   Wry Crips: Writers' Theater for Disabled Women. URL: http://wrycrips.blogspot.com/

9.   Cheryl Wade oral history in the *Disability Rights Independent Living Movement (DRILM) Historical Archives*. The Regional Oral History Office, The Bancroft Library, University of California, Berkeley. URL: http://bancroft.berkeley.edu/collections/drilm/index.html

window. The fall broke her back, which made her a wheelchair user. Patty had written a number of powerful poems about becoming physically disabled. In 1986 she decided that she would like to develop a dance piece around her poem of the experience, so she talked to Thais and they rented a dance studio.

The arc of Patty's story was that she walked into an office building in New York City, went up to the fifth floor, opened the window and jumped. She landed in such a way that she did not die but her back was broken. After that she used a wheelchair and canes to get around.

Patty envisioned the dance to be the story of how she found community and connection and the will to live by connecting with other disabled women. She initially just worked with Thais and Thais' nondisabled boyfriend.

As they worked on the piece, Thais saw an opportunity for herself to be in the starring role as the pre-injury Patty. When the tensions between their differing artistic visions got too contentious, Patty called me in. She did not recruit me because I had any knowledge of dance. She just figured I was big and bad enough to help her win the fights with Thais.

The dance slowly started coming together. Patty wanted her hospital bed to be front and center during the first half of the dance, so we created a translucent screen behind the bed that extended across the stage, so that any nondisabled dancing would be in silhouette.

Patty wanted the first half to be somber, with the only dancer on stage being Patty, sitting in one spot in her wheelchair, with nondisabled dancers in silhouette showing the suicide attempt behind the screen. Patty even envisioned this being done with paper silhouettes and not dancers, since she wanted the presence of the wheelchair dancers to dominate. But in those pre-digital technology days, to accomplish Patty's vision took more resources than we had, so she allowed Thais to dance behind the screen.

As we developed the second half of the dance we needed disabled women dancers to join Patty on stage, so I became Patty's dance partner. Thais quickly attempted to fill the void as I left my director role, and she attempted to take over the choreography, so it was necessary for us to bring in a disabled artist as the director.

Enter Cheryl Marie Wade (disabled), the original gnarly woman and a seriously kickass arts activist. Cheryl was an accomplished poet, playwright and performer/director with Wry Crips, a disabled women's theater group. She had a strong artistic vision and wrestled us all into creating a polished, professional piece. One of our biggest challenges came from the lack of disabled professional dancers. In those pre-

YouTube days there was no way for people to see the work that was being created, by us and other disabled artists. So we relied heavily on Cheryl to create that which was not yet imagined, a job she did beautifully.

The work was overwhelming for Patty, which we could understand. It's an incredibly difficult story to dance repeatedly, so Cheryl and I worked hard to support Patty. We loved the idea of doing this kind of theatrical dance that would combine story, movement and emotion.

While Cheryl's vision of the work got clearer, Patty's ability to perform it declined. Seeing her story enacted, reliving it with each rehearsal, became increasingly difficult for Patty. After all of the major elements of the dance were settled, Patty announced that she could no longer participate in the project. After some discussion she allowed us to continue to develop the story. This left us with a gap for our main dancer.

Cheryl and I beat the bushes to find a female wheelchair dancer or two, because as the dance developed we realized having a trio for the second half was better than having a duo. After a lot of networking and a little bit of begging, Bonnie Lewkowicz (disabled) and Judith Smith (disabled) came onto the project. Bonnie had danced before her spinal cord injury, and Judy's athleticism came from riding and training horses.

Cheryl created the narrative for the piece, a sort of poem that would go with some of the movement. Everything was done collaboratively. People created the piece out of Patty's framework, but we came up with different ideas as we improvised and improved.

In a duet between Bonnie and me, Bonnie held her body in a closed position as we showed the accident, then as she found disability community she opened up into freedom and broad movement. It became a really beautiful piece called *In This Body*.

As the director of the piece, Cheryl would come up with an idea. Then, together as a group, we would create the piece. As a director, she would set the piece, and then stand back from it and say, "This is how it now goes." But in the end, the choreography was created collaboratively, always. That was always our experience of the dance group right from day one.

Cheryl guided us through the next few months, developing the piece until it was good enough to be on stage. Along the way we added yet another nondisabled friend of Thais', so the piece developed with three nondisabled dancers, along with three disabled dancers and Cheryl as the director.

While we worked on Patty's piece we wondered how and where to stage it. We needed to be part of someone else's dance performance, since we only had a three minute dance. For the past few years, disabled artists had encouraged the local arts groups to include more disability artists, and the Dance Brigade, a feminist dance company, took up the challenge. The main impetus for continuing the project after Patty left was that Thais had secured us a three minute slot in the Dance Brigade's 1988 *Furious Feet III* festival in Oakland, California. Our dance got a very positive response from the audience, although to be honest it was hard to tell if they were reacting to the quality work itself or to the presence of wheelchair dancers on the stage, something almost no one in the audience had seen before.

The success of the performance created new tensions. Thais, who had not been a star as a nondisabled dancer, was suddenly thrust into a leading dance role with us. We had a hard dilemma. The only person with dance experience was nondisabled and wanted to be the Artistic Director of a disabled dance troupe. But she was not part of the disability community. She was a teacher of disabled people, which is a huge difference.

Bonnie, Judy, Cheryl and I had taken on the project as a favor to Patty and we were unsure whether we wanted to continue. We had a series of meetings to discuss what we wanted to do next. I facilitated the brainstorming meeting, and suggested the word Axis as a name for the company if we wanted to continue. I liked the way that Axis was a homonym for access and how it implied intersections.

The Dance Brigade offered us a spot in their December show, *Revolutionary Nutcracker Sweetie*, a humorous alternative dance version of *The Nutcracker*. Accepting that opportunity kept the group working together for a while.

Cheryl and I continued with Axis Dance for another year or so, but Cheryl wanted to get back to her poetry and performing, and I was getting ready to move 40 miles away. Bonnie, Judy and Thais then built the Axis Dance Company. It is now over 25 years old and one of the leading "physically integrated" dance companies in the world.

In her 2003 oral history Cheryl talked about Axis.

> They are now not just recognized as an integrated dance troupe [within] the disability scene, but they are recognized internationally as a modern dance troupe of importance. I think you can only do that when you get people who don't have ideas already about what you can and cannot do. They got people like Joe Goode in, and Bill T. Jones, who did a brilliant piece, won every dance award locally, just began to get legitimate reviews in dance magazines, instead of as 'the handicapped group,' it was

as 'this very fine dance troupe that is doing very innovative choreography.' The group has gone on, and I think they do incredible work. Although I don't work with them anymore, I'm still a big fan and cheerleader of them. I'm very proud of the association I had in the beginning with them, and feel sort of motherly about the group, if that's the right way to put it. I sort of feel kind of motherly towards the group in the sense of, I was there in the beginning when it got born. I think it's thrilling, even though it has nothing to do with me anymore.[10]

As the Los Angeles Times noted recently while reviewing the 25-year impact of Axis:

> Altering perceptions of disability through the medium of dance has been a central tenet for Lewkowicz and her colleagues at Axis Dance Company, one of the best-known practitioners of physically integrated dance, which uses performers with and without disabilities. Founded in 1987, the Oakland-based repertory ensemble has distinguished itself for its collaborations with top contemporary dance choreographers and comprehensive education programs for adults and children of all movement abilities. "We realized early on that rather than being a limitation, disability can radically expand what's possible with choreography," says Judith Smith, Axis' artistic director since 1997. "People that move differently, whether it's in motorized wheelchairs, on crutches or with prosthetics, create all these partnering and ensemble possibilities that wouldn't exist with dancers who can all move the same way." "What dance companies like Axis are challenging is the idea that being in a wheelchair or losing a limb makes you compromised as an individual," says Marks, who found the experience of working with the dancers to be a "feast of movement possibilities. What they're doing is reframing what it means to be a fully functioning human being."[11]

The Dance

It's always about THE DANCE. No matter what else is happening in

---

10. Wade, see note 9.

11. Josephs, S. (July 3, 2011). "Axis Dance Company revels in its abilities." *Los Angeles Times.* URL: http://articles.latimes.com/2011/jul/03/entertainment/la-ca-disabled-dancing-20110703

my life. No matter where the Dance is happening. Being in a room full of people that love disabled bodyminds, that welcome stimming, spazzing, twisting, sliding, jumping and lurching is exactly the best place for me.

There is nothing more beautiful to me than our freaky bodyminds moving. I love the simplicity, how the slightest movements telegraph our bodymind differences. In crip dancing, those who wish to allow their bodyminds to expand can take up space, often tottering unevenly across the dance floor. There is no 'ease' in this—no 'normal'—for these bodyminds do not match the nondisabled body's rules. We do not move with smooth balance. We jerk, lurch, tilt and gimp. We stretch ourselves out, uncertain that our balance will hold us. We revel in the ways our bodyminds display our unevenness, digress from the expected. We can extend digits bending in unexpected directions. Our bodyminds offer questions—What is movement? What is dance? What is beauty?

For those of us with mental disabilities, our bodyminds inhabit and take up spaces differently than nondisabled folks. Like people with physical disabilities, we are taught to contain our bodyminds, to hide our disabilities. On the crip-loving dance floor we can share how our bodyminds enact our disabilities. We can unconfine ourselves.

Judi Rogers (disabled) taught me the concept of visual history, the idea that each of us internally records what we have observed as we wander through life. For people who process visually, this is visual history. But whether or not people access this visually, we all learn the 'expected' ways of the bodymind. We learn that there is a 'right' way to diaper a baby—with fingers and not elbows, feet or teeth. (See the essay on disabled parents in this book.) We learn that 'dance' is smooth multi-step movements with interpersonal interactions.

We have not been shown the glorious ways that disabled bodyminds create movement, move through space, choose self-directed ways of being in a space in relation to other bodyminds. We have all been taught, and often shamed, for the ways our bodyminds prefer to work. We have learned that our natural ways of moving through space are often so non-normative that they are rejected in nondisabled spaces. When we have a very rare opportunity to be in a nonjudgmental space, where we can let our bodyminds throw off the shackles of nondisabled normativity, we fling ourselves into our natural movements.

On the crip dance floors, I am always awed by our collective disabled beauty, by the strength of our belief in our own wondrousness, by our trust that others will allow us to show ourselves without pretending conformity. I love the way disabled bodyminds distend, unravel, extend, lurch. I celebrate the variety of digital configurations—

the fingers contracted into fists, the spaghetti dancing digits of the spasticity, the disjointedness of the loosey-goosey finger joints. I want to make close-up videos of these delicate dances, these celebrations of joy and empowerment. Hands incapable of lifting a literal middle finger express themselves with joyful glee and rebellion.

Crip dancing does not require verticality, the upright postures we associate with grace. We inhabit horizontal spaces—writhing on floors, bending over laps, flying on the backs of wheelchairs. Our movements are not limited in directions either—we take up small circular spaces, we circle the dance floor, we wander seemingly without purpose—in short, we go where our bodyminds lead us. We move to the down beat, the up beat, the beats of our hearts, syncopating beats, dissonant beats.

To see a gathering of crippled bodyminds flowing in dance space is to witness the beauty of the disability universe in microcosm. The rarity of opportunity for this beauty makes it precious and sad. Many disabled folks say that being at a crip dance was one of the most transformative experiences of their life. Dancing in crip spaces opens us to ourselves. We dive deeper into our bodyminds, unfurl our deep freakishness, and in so doing we explode with joy. We are the people our mothers warned us about—the untamed, the uncontrollable, the unacceptable.

Each dance offers new adventures. When John Kelly dances, his long, sensuous tongue shows his joy. We gather around him, tall in his high-backed wheelchair and extend our much-more-limited tongues in joyful collaboration with him. At crip dances there are no outliers. We bring our A game, our excellence, and those who wish company will find ready dance partners. We show each other how we prefer to move so they can join us. If we want to be touched, how to touch us. We embolden each other with boob dancing and booty shaking and sexy touching. We have all been rejected before, so we hold each other's needs carefully—working hard not to overstep, not to create less safety. Our joy comes from being free to show ourselves—our freaky crippled selves.

Many of us come to the dance to watch. We seek to develop a visual history of ways of moving, to learn that the permission to move as we wish is built into the environment, to feel safe enough to allow our bodyminds to move. In crip dance spaces we lean into each other, offer support, share space, acknowledge and mirror our unique movements. Our only rule is to keep the space physically safe—so while we might dance sexily it's always kid-friendly, at least until the kids go off to bed. We might hurl ourselves across the dance floor, but always ensuring that we do not collide with others. If someone seems overheated or overwhelmed, we might offer to take a break with them.

To move in public without restrictions is a gift rarely offered to disabled bodyminds. At crip dances we are not the freak on the dance floor—we are one of many freaks on the dance floor. We are celebrated for our inventive ways of moving.

These moments of being seen, of being deeply acknowledged just as we are—no attempts at passing or fitting in—these moments are so rare that they only occur in crip-controlled spaces and rarely more than once a year. These moments liberate us, feed us for another year of discrimination, hold us in collective support until we can come together again.

JUST THE FACTS MA'AM

1987 — Patty Overland gathers dancers to create *In This Body*.

1988 — The dancers create Axis Dance Troupe (now called Axis Dance Company) and perform *In This Body* at the Dance Brigade's *Furious Feet III*

RESOURCES

Axis Dance Company. URL: http://www.axisdance.org
Cheryl Marie Wade, *Disability Culture Rap*. URL:
    https://www.youtube.com/watch?v=j75aRfLsH2Y
Leroy Moore. Personal URL:
    https://leroymoore.wordpress.com/about/
Sins Invalid. URL: http://www.sinsinvalid.org

A full bibliography is available at my website: www.corbettotoole.com

7.

Court Crips

"Sports is where everybody counts, effort is rewarded, and there are no barriers."   — Loretta Claiborne (disabled)[1.]

Summary

Some disabled people are athletes. We love the feeling of pushing ourselves, taking on new challenges, learning new skills. Being an athlete really makes me happy. I played wheelchair basketball on a women's team for many years. But eventually my body was not strong enough, and now I play power soccer in my electric wheelchair. When I am playing sports I feel powerful and I really like the teamwork and skills of sports.

Even in 2015, people like me, people with significant physical disabilities, are not supposed to play sports. In nursing homes and rehabilitation centers, we are sometimes allowed to participate in pale

---

1.   Black and female, raised in Pittsburgh, Special Olympian, inductee in the Women in Sports Hall of Fame, Loretta is a world-class runner and gifted motivational speaker who happens to also be a person who has an intellectual disability. Loretta's accolades are too many to account, but a few of her most impressive awards include: receiving two honorary doctorate degrees (Quinnipiac University in 1995 and Villanova University in 2003); completing 26 marathons with her best time being 3:03, finishing in the top 100 women of the Boston Marathon; the 1996 ESPY Award-Arthur Ashe Award for Courage recipient; a Walt Disney Productions Movie titled *The Loretta Claiborne Story*; WorldScapes publishing company producing *In Her Stride – the biography of Loretta Claiborne*; a 4th degree black belt in karate; communicating in 4 languages and fluency in American Sign Language; induction into the Women in Sports Hall of Fame and Special Olympics Pennsylvania Hall of Fame. Source URLs: www.ydr.com/local/ci_24242266/loretta-claiborne-at-60-yorks-world-renowned-special and http://lorettaclaiborne.com/

imitations of "real" sports—the ones played by nondisabled people. Instead of playing volleyball, we are offered a balloon and the "net" is a string tied between two chairs. No chance of injury there. Or we are offered "buddies" to lead us or push our wheelchairs in an attempt to have us approximate the real sport. There is nothing wrong with adaptive activities, but it's important not to confuse recreational adaptations with playing competitive sports. [2]

Some disabled people like to play sports hard, to face an opponent with the full intention of beating them. I am one of those disabled people. I like my sports challenging, fast-paced, requiring both teamwork and lots of strategizing. As an adult, I have been lucky enough to play two competitive sports: wheelchair basketball and power soccer. Both have challenged my bodymind, engaged my competitive instincts, and taught me a lot. I am lucky to live in the San Francisco Bay Area that regularly offers sports opportunities including sailing, goal ball, biking, swimming, rafting, rugby, boccia, hockey, basketball, and soccer.

Although many disabled sports emerged from rehabilitation programs for war-injured veterans, the various sports developed their own organizations as they transitioned away from rehabilitation centers and into the wider community.

By the early 1970s, most competitive disabled sports held national tournaments and competed in international competitions such as the Paralympics and the Pan American games. [3] In some sports there are also junior divisions. In the United States there are eleven Paralympic training sites for disabled athletes in sports as diverse as cycling and shooting. [4] Most sports for physically disabled athletes like myself have separate men's and women's divisions, although a few, such as rugby and power soccer, have only one division that is open to everyone. [5]

I love disabled sports. I love the total immersion of my bodymind, the way that time seems suspended, the intense focus that is required. I love hurling myself down a court, not knowing what new opportunity will emerge, paying attention to the nearest opposing player at the same time as the flow of the whole court. I love sharing this with other

2. Although the Special Olympics is offered throughout the world, the focus of this piece is on physically disabled athletes, so the Special Olympics athletes and programs are not discussed in detail.

3. Paralympic Games. *History of the Movement.* URL: http://www.paralympic.org/the-ipc/history-of-the-movement

4. U.S. Olympic and Paralympic Training Sites. URL: http://www.teamusa.org/USA-Canoe-Kayak/For-USACK-Athletes/Olympic-Training-Centers-and-Sites/Olympic-and-Paralympic-Certified-Training-Sites

5. Power soccer allows any power wheelchair athlete to play starting at age 5.

wheelchair athletes, admiring their specific skills, slyly learning their moves so I can use them against my next opponent. When I am on the court I feel invincible. That's a feeling I don't get anywhere else.

Athletics asks disabled people to break through a million assumptions of weakness, incompetence, and powerlessness. Many disabled people shy away from this once-in-a-lifetime offer to be public and proud of our gnarly bodyminds. But a few take up this freak flag and smash through those stereotypes.[6.]

When competitive sports is offered to disabled people, it's nearly always focused on recruiting disabled males. Females are rarely seen as athletes. This bias is apparent when looking at large sports, such as wheelchair basketball, which has over 100 men's teams and only a dozen women's teams. It's not that disabled females don't want to participate, but rather that they are not offered the opportunities and support.[7.]

Modern Paralympic sports have a long history. Deaf communities in Berlin, Germany, had sports clubs as early as 1888.[8.] Modern international deaf sports began with the 1924 Silent Games in Paris, France. The 2013 Summer Deaflympics in Sofia, Bulgaria attracted 2,711 deaf athletes from 83 nations who competed in 16 sports.[9.]

In the 1960s Eunice Kennedy Shriver coordinated efforts to create the Special Olympics, which is geared to athletes with intellectual disabilities. The first International Special Olympics took place in 1968 in Chicago, Illinois, where over a thousand athletes from the U.S. and Canada competed in track and field, floor hockey and swimming. At the 2011 Special Olympics World Summer Games in Athens, Greece, 6,000 athletes competed from 170 nations. At the 2013 Special Olympics World Winter Games 2,300 athletes from 100 countries competed in PyeongChang, Republic of Korea.[10.]

Most modern physically disabled sports, particularly wheelchair sports, emerged from the post-World War II disabled veterans in England. Stoke Manville Hospital began to treat disabled veterans in 1944. Timed to occur on the Opening Day of the 1948 Olympics in

---

6. "Freak" here connects the present to the 1932 film *Freaks* that demonstrated disabled people organizing, creating a supportive community and meting out justice to those that harm disabled people. Some disabled people have reclaimed the word "freak" to express disability-based pride.

7. The official interpretation of Title IX for intercollegiate athletics says that no public or private institution which receives federal money (including federal student loans) may discriminate on the basis of sex. Source URL: http://www2.ed.gov/about/offices/list/ocr/docs/t9interp.html

8. *Brief history of the Paralympic movement.* URL: http://www.paralympic.org/the-ipc/history-of-the-movement

9. *Sofia 2013.* URL: http://www.deaflympics.com/games.asp?2013-s

10. *History of Special Olympics.* URL: http://www.specialolympics.org/history.aspx

London, Stoke Manville hosted the first modern competition for wheelchair athletes, with 16 archers. By 1952 Dutch athletes competed. By 2012, Summer Paralympic Games took place in London, England, with 4,200 athletes from 160 countries. The 2010 Winter Paralympic Games in Vancouver, Canada, had 502 athletes from 44 countries.[11.]

Disabled sports in the United States begin with the first wheelchair basketball game in 1946.[12.] Since wheelchair sports emerged from rehabilitation efforts for male veterans, women have a hard time breaking in—even in sports like power soccer where muscle strength is pretty irrelevant. If you can tilt a three-inch rod forward and back, and side to side, you can drive a power chair. Yet females are a very small part of the power soccer athlete numbers. In fact while there are currently 271 male players, there are only 82 female players.[13.]

I am eternally grateful to the veterans whose new disabilities created these opportunities. Smashing balls on a power soccer court with other disabled people makes me enormously happy. When we are on the court, our opponent is just another athlete. If he's out there, he's fair game for all kinds of shoving and chair-jockeying. We all have a 'take no prisoners' approach to that soccer ball and will use every advantage we can get. Got an opposing player who cannot turn her head? Best place to pass is behind her. Got an opposing player with poor trunk balance and no chest strap? Run him in circles.

If you think this sounds heartless, realize we're just being athletes. When we are on the court, we give it our all. We are not sick or injured or weak. We are athletes who try to outmaneuver and outsmart each other and get as many goals as we can. We do it because we love the sport, we love being physical and sometimes, as one MVP athlete says, "I just need to hit something."[14.]

Basketball

As a child with polio in a Catholic school without a gym, and therefore no physical education school requirements, I escaped all formal sports instructions. Walking with a heavy limp meant that I was never

---

11. *Paralympic Games – Facts and Figures*. URL:
    http://www.paralympic.org/sites/default/files/document/120209104749033_2012_02+facts+and+figures.pdf

12. *History of Wheelchair Basketball*. URL:
    http://www.wheelchairbasketball.ca/History_of_Wheelchair_Basketball.aspx

13. This is a count based on the roster of the United States Power Soccer Association. The 57 players with ambiguous names were excluded. URL: http://www.powersoccerusa.net/

14. MVP means most valuable player. This quote is from a private conversation with Karyn Hernandez, an early star athlete in power soccer.

included in the informal team sports on our street. I loved watching sports, and Boston in the 1950s and 60s provided a fabulous training ground to learn the rules of different sports and to admire athletic skills. I learned baseball from watching Ted Williams and the Boston Red Sox, hockey from Bobby Orr and the Boston Bruins and, most importantly to me, basketball from Larry Bird and the Boston Celtics. Football did not arrive in Boston until I was going off to college, so I spent my youth cheering for the Green Bay Packers. (It was the Vince Lombardi years so the training was fabulous.) While I knew the rules and admired the athleticism, I never believed that I would be an athlete. So as I approached my 30th year I had no experience with team sports.

In my late 20s, when my legs weakened and I needed to use a manual wheelchair, I decided to explore wheelchair sports. I wanted some positive reasons for using a wheelchair, not just the medical limitations of my legs. Searching for a wheelchair sport, I discovered the only one in the San Francisco Bay Area open to adult females was the women's basketball team, the Bay Area Meteorites. Not an ideal athletic candidate, I was greatly relieved to find that the team took all comers, no auditions or previous skill required. I gleefully joined the team, glad of my first opportunity to be an athlete.

Women's wheelchair basketball provided me with an experience I never had before. I got to fly across a room much faster than my legs could ever carry me. Exhilarated by the sensations and proud of my hard-earned skills, the wheelchair became a symbol of my athleticism, which helped fight off the drowning feelings that came with the new social stigma and the oppression of using a wheelchair in public for the first time.

I came to the team during its third season. The players were largely uncommitted to the team and the sport, resulting in high turnover. The serious players came to practice regularly, but a lack of conditioning on the part of the casual players meant the overall team was very weak.

The national rules for wheelchair basketball require a variety of ability levels on the court. Wheelchair basketball employs a classification system. Teams of five players can field up to twelve 'player points' on the court at any one time. Quadriplegic players who have impairments in both legs and arms are assigned one point. Paraplegic players who have leg impairments but full use of their arms count for two points. All other players are worth three points. [15]

In order to get five players on the court, a team can have a maximum of three players worth three points, plus one paraplegic and

---

15. Note: international rules vary slightly.

one quadriplegic player. Obviously, teams wanted the strongest, most able players in each category on the court, but since in the 1980s there were only twelve women's teams in the United States playing competitively, there were few available players to recruit.

The heart and soul of our team at the time was Debbie Dillon. Barely thirty years old, Debbie had brown hair that framed her face and wide open smile. She was slight, with the typical quadriplegic abdominal bulge, but she pushed her manual wheelchair with calloused hands and knuckles. With fingers that bent back towards her palms, the surface area of her hands for holding the basketball wound up being two inches shorter than other players.

I joined the team with a lot of bravado but an absolutely weak body. I pushed my wheelchair slowly, labored during even the simplest drills, and could not anticipate what would happen on the court because I mostly looked down at the floor in front of me. Debbie's quiet voice instructed me as we moved around the court, and I slowly became more skilled. She would remind me to look up and see the whole court, to notice how a player relied on a specific shooting spot, to anticipate the opposing team's next move. She took me from an unskilled player to a valuable member of the team.

Often, even though I was a three point player, I was the second slowest player on the court after Debbie. By watching her I learned to use my lack of speed, and the assumptions the other team made about my skills because of it, to create good defensive opportunities. During my first two, possibly three, seasons I fouled out of every game. It took me a long time to hit the opposing wheelchair quietly enough not to get caught, to wait until the referee looked elsewhere before I moved an opposing player's wheelchair, and to learn enough of the rules to be an asset and not a liability on the court. Through it all Debbie provided quiet encouragement.

We relied on Debbie to read the opposing team's offense and to guide our defense. Although slow, she always had great strategies. She often stopped the opposing team's offense by placing her chair directly in their path. She blocked out players and provided scoring opportunities that enabled our team to slowly build skills, and with winning we built confidence.

Debbie Dillon's quiet ways belied a fierce competitive streak, a deep compassion, and an unwavering commitment to team excellence. She had learned the sport on the University of Illinois at Urbana-Champaign's women's basketball team, the Ms. Kids, during college. The university pioneered non-veterans disabled sports, started a wheelchair basketball team in 1948, and for many decades produced the most talented disabled athletes in the world. Debbie benefited from their extensive expertise, and when she moved to the San Francisco Bay Area she co-founded the Bay Area Meteorites.

During the late 80s, when I played with the Meteorites, there were nearly 180 men's wheelchair basketball teams and only 12 women's teams in the country. Debbie was the representative of the women's teams to the National Wheelchair Basketball Association Board of Directors. In a sport typically shown in the media to be about strong-armed men, Debbie epitomized the crippled bodies that the sport was made for—actual paraplegics and quadriplegics.

The Meteorites rarely had consistent coaching, so Debbie provided our ongoing training. She could read the court with experienced eyes trained by the best college coaches. Her quiet manner gave instruction to players with gentleness informed by deep knowledge. Under her tutelage, players' skills grew.

With Debbie's support we played together for about five years before we found a coach who committed herself to our team. By that time we had a respectable set of skills, had won a few games, and two of our players had qualified for international competition and played on Team USA in the Paralympics. Even though I was still slow, my chair skills improved, and I became a fierce defensive player.

Our first truly committed Coach (nondisabled) had played college basketball and now played in a recreational league. She loved the sport and saw us as athletes, something that rarely occurred. She pulled us together, focused our training, and committed to the improvement of each player on the team. She particularly wanted to help Debbie, since during her five years of playing at Urbana-Champaign Debbie had never shot a basket. In assessing Debbie, Coach challenged the belief that Debbie could not shoot a basket. They devised a training program to find a shot for her.

Shooting the ball forward would be impossible because Debbie lacked the necessary arm muscles, so some version of a hook shot became the focus. Debbie worked on improving her right arm strength, and at practice she would pass the ball to us with hook shots until her range and height improved. Then she began to aim for the basket. Trying various spots on the court, her sweet spot became just outside the key (the boxed area under the basketball hoop), on the right side of the basket. Nearly two seasons of practicing built the needed skills until Debbie could do the shot reliably. She needed just the right conditions: to have her chair stopped, the ball balanced carefully and no defender on her right side. Coach developed a few plays to create these conditions, and the team enthusiastically practiced them.

Debbie's decision to try to learn to shoot a basket was layered with the negative assumptions that see disabled bodyminds as broken, never as competitive athletes. We all knew that she might try and never succeed. Like my futile attempts to go faster, her hard work might not result in a shot. Yet she took the challenge like any determined athlete. We all invested in her attempt, as she had always invested in ours.

The twelve women's teams came together once a year to establish the national standings, and that year we met in Balboa Park in San Diego. The gym had three basketball courts next to each other, a noisy and distracting environment. Debbie's former college team, the Fighting Illini, always ranked in the top two teams nationally. As an alumnus of that team, as well as our division's representative, Debbie was well known and respected throughout the league, but everyone knew she could not shoot. Although she had made a few baskets in practice, she had not yet made one in a game. Our team was determined to change that. Coach planned for Debbie's shooting debut at the Nationals.

On the court the other teams never defended against Debbie, because everyone knew she could not shoot. That assumption gave us the opportunity we needed to get Debbie the ball. That day, all the other games were finished so the other ten teams surrounded our court as we played, making the audience for our game huge.

The ball had gone out of bounds behind our basket. We set up, as we always did, around the key. Susie Grimes (disabled), our strongest player, took the ball out on the baseline on the left side of the basket. The other forward and I moved around on the left side of the key, while our guard moved back and forth, shaking off their defender at the top of the key.[16.] Debbie quietly moved to the right side of the key. As we expected, the defense players ignored her. Susie looked around at her passing opportunities. She saw Debbie and gave her a head nod. We noticed and moved around more, asking for the ball so the defense would keep their eyes on us.

Susie faked to me on the left side of the key then gave a soft bounce pass over to Debbie who pulled the ball onto her lap. As she had practiced hundreds of times, she moved the ball onto her foreshortened right hand, put her left hand onto her left wheel's handrim for counterbalance, and then she pulled her left arm down hard while thrusting her right hand up quickly. As her chest sped from right to left, the ball soared off her hand. The entire gym went silent. Every single eye followed that ball as it flew upwards. With just a gliding touch on the backboard, the ball swished into the net. After

---

16. In basketball there are three main positions: forward, guard and center.

thirteen years of playing wheelchair basketball, Debbie had scored her first basket in a game.

The gym exploded with cheers and more than a few tears. An historic moment had occurred, and we all witnessed it together. We applauded her determination, her commitment, her skill but most of all we applauded because she had done what the best coaches in the country had deemed impossible all those years ago—she became a shooter, a player against whom you had to defend.

In her typically unassuming way, Debbie demurely accepted the accolades which, if I remember rightly, made her player of the year that year. And if that is not correct, she certainly should have been. In my ten years of playing basketball, that moment is the most meaningful to me. Not because some woman in a wheelchair made a basket, but because an athlete took on impossible odds and beat them. And she did it surrounded by people who understood the depth of that accomplishment.

Debbie went on to marry the love of her life a few years later and moved away to live with him. She developed breast cancer and died a decade later, one of the many disabled women who are diagnosed too late because most diagnostic equipment is not accessible. She, like many disabled athletes, is an invisible part of American athletic history. But for me, she is the best part of it.

I soon became too disabled to play manual wheelchair sports and retired once again to watching games from the sidelines. I missed the fast pace of the games, the strategies, the quick decision making, the camaraderie of teammates. My next venture into athletics came when I was inquiring about sports options for my daughter, Joy (disabled), who uses a power wheelchair.

Power Soccer

In 2003 I discovered the sport of power soccer. Played indoors on a basketball court, power wheelchairs have steel footguards attached around the players' footplates.[17] This provides a solid surface for pushing and striking the 13 inch soccer ball around the court. In 2003

---

17. "[F]ootguards must consist of unbreakable material and be securely attached to the powerchair—bottom of the footguards should be no more than 10 cm (5 in) (and not less than 5 cm (2 in) from the floor – front of footguards should be at least 20 cm (8 in) high but no more than 45 cm (20 in) from the ground – footguard surfaces shall be solid and not angled to hit the ball upwards – all surfaces must be flat or convex. Concave surfaces are not allowed. No part of the footguard shall be constructed so as to be able to trap or hold the ball." from the United States Power Soccer Association. URL: http://www.powersoccerusa.net/our-sport

each country had its own rules for the sport.[18.] Some countries did not allow players to back up, other countries kept the wheelchair speeds very slow.

The desire to build an international sport grew until the Federation International de Powerchair Football Association was created in 2006. This change standardized play across countries, allowing for international tournaments. The sport has grown exponentially since the rules changed, and now includes 21 countries.[19.] The Federation has hosted two Power Soccer World Cups, in Tokyo and Paris.

While power soccer is played on an indoor basketball court, the similarities to wheelchair basketball end there. Power soccer is a sport of brute force. As wheelchair technology gets increasingly sophisticated, the ability to hit the ball with greater force has changed the nature of the game. While speed is capped at 6.2 mph (10km), a strong team can move the ball down the court in two or three passes. Players are tested for speed and equipment before each game, and one player from each team is selected by the head referee for testing at the end of the game to check that the player did not increase their speed during the game.

There are four players on each team, with one designated as the goalkeeper. All players are allowed to move freely on the court, but the goalkeeper can go out of bounds to stop a goal. Teams typically set up with one center and two wings, one on either side of the center. Since the wheelchair is providing the power, teams with greater funding can afford higher-end equipment and the technicians to keep it working optimally. This is a huge advantage for teams, since increased funding provides stronger equipment that overpowers teams with less funding and weaker wheelchairs. The current, state of the art, power soccer wheelchair costs around $8,000, depending on the options. With up to 8 players, a nationally competitive team can expect to spend nearly $70,000 to outfit the team with new wheelchairs and have parts for spares. These wheelchairs are not covered by any medical insurers since their purpose is for sports, so teams must raise all the funds themselves.

This shift to newer, stronger equipment has occurred over the past two years, and there is an increasing divide between teams with older wheelchairs, which are significantly weaker, and teams with the newer designs. At this point the United States Power Soccer Association has not divided the 60 teams by equipment, but the need for it to occur seems inevitable. The difference, to use a car analogy, is between a Formula 1 racing car and a used Volkswagen Beetle.

18. See note 17.

19. Six countries play power football but do not follow the Federation International de Powerchair Football Association rules.

The vast majority of players and coaches in the sport are male. Players can start as young as age 5, and there is no upper limit age limit. Coaches are often parents of players, usually a father. Although a few teams are connected with recreation programs for disabled people, the vast majority of teams are loose affiliations of families who create a team to support their children. A few universities have also started providing sports options for disabled students and are fielding Power Soccer teams.[20]

One of the biggest differences between power soccer and wheelchair basketball is that in basketball all of the athletes are adults, and in power soccer most of the athletes still live with their parents. An even deeper difference is the types of disabilities. The vast majority of power soccer athletes either have a form of muscular dystrophy or have cerebral palsy. While cerebral palsy is stable, most people with muscular dystrophy have progressive conditions. In power soccer we watch fellow athletes change functional levels and sometimes even die.

I play soccer with children who are living, but who are widely treated as if they were dying. Not in the "here today, dead tomorrow" sense. More in the tone of: "We're all dying one day at a time, but some of us will get there more quickly than others." We all know their bodyminds are changing, becoming weaker, and they know we know. But we silently agree not to mention it. Sometimes because we don't want to upset the families. Sometimes because no one wants to talk about their mortality. But mostly because we just want to play ball. We are focusing on living, on being kickass athletes, on competing.

The children are diagnosed with various forms of Muscular Dystrophy. If they have Duchenne's, many are not expected to live to age 30; the rest will most likely not live past age 40.[21] Although unspoken, this is common knowledge. The parents often seem sad, which is a heavy burden for the kids, who just want to be cool.

Power wheelchair soccer requires using an electric wheelchair, an expensive piece of equipment reserved for folks with significant body

---

20. Rick Spittler (disabled) is leading a national effort to establish sports programs for disabled students: "Rick is currently focusing his efforts on a new project to create a Title IX inspired law for individuals with disabilities. The goal of the project is to establish national guidelines to open the door for students with physical disabilities throughout the United States." from KQED. *Disability culture heroes.* URL:
http://www.kqed.org/community/heritage/disability/heroes/2007.jsp

21. In early studies, most patients with DMD died in their late teens or twenties as a result of respiratory infections or cardiomyopathy. However, later studies have reported a median survival to age 35 years. Thus, survival appears to be improving with advances in respiratory care and cardiac care. Again, these ages represent the average for all patients with DMD; individual patients may have complications earlier or later in life. Source: UpToDate. *Overview of muscular dystrophies.* URL: http://www.uptodate.com/contents/overview-of-muscular-dystrophies-beyond-the-basics

impairment, often weakness. Outside our chairs, most of us cannot sit up independently, but in our chairs we fly around the indoor basketball court, spinning to hit the 13 inch (32cm) soccer ball with maximum torque. Steel footguards smack the ball across the court where, hopefully, our teammate catches it and kicks it farther down the court. When we are in sync, three good kicks get us within goal range. We train hard to be in sync. We want to win.

At the United States Power Soccer National Tournament in 2010, my team played a team of young men from the Midwest. Halfway through the first half, a player on the opposing team was in a chair-to-chair fight for possession of the ball. During the struggle, his tracheotomy tube popped out of his neck attachment.[22] This meant that until it was reattached, a quick and simple thing, he would be gasping for breath.

The players on both teams spotted this right away, and the nearest player kicked the ball out of bounds so the referee would pause the game. But the referee didn't notice until an opposing player loudly called out, "Equipment, Ref," and the referee came and called a time-out. The player's coach came onto the court and reattached the tube and we resumed play.

For some members of the crowd, seeing this kind of vulnerability seemed to disturb them. They saw us as broken bodies in need of constant protection to prevent us from harm. But what we want is to live with freedom and face the challenges of living. Yes, with support, but not with paternalistic restrictions. We want the freedom to fail as well as succeed.

From the outside, off the court, many people only see a bunch of sick people pretending to play a ball game. They do not see our athleticism, our finely honed skills practiced over many hours and even years. They do not see us. They see their own stereotypical fragments of who they believed we were even before they saw us. We are weak, suffering, sad. We deserve "special" treatment, "special" events, "special" opportunities. They wonder why anyone would allow a kid with a tracheotomy onto an athletic field. "Don't people realize he could get hurt?" they say to each other.

Yes we all know that any player can get hurt. That's the point. We show them the vulnerability of the bodymind, the ways it does not work, the fragility of life. They question whether players who have

---

22. A hole in the base of his neck created a permanent opening (tracheotomy). A long 2 inch wide tube connects the tracheotomy to a machine that rhythmically pumps air into his lungs. When the tube popped out, he had to cover the hole with his hand and gulp air (called "frog breathing").

tracheotomies should play sports. Because they do not see our awesome skills or our athletic prowess, they also miss our deep joy at making the perfect play, our pride at mastering a new skill, our passion to practice week after week. Essentially, they see only their assumptions of our brokenness and entirely miss our kickassness. They never really see us and that is their loss.

Even the player with the tracheotomy, and perhaps most especially him, wants to be full of himself, living in his potential. He wants to kick an opponent's ass because he is the smarter player. He does not want to always be the sick boy that people whisper about when they think he cannot hear them. He wants to live—right here, right now, on this court, kicking ass. So if his trach tube falls out, he'll get someone to put it back in. And he will gulp air, as he's practiced many times, until it's reattached. He's trained for tubes popping out; he knows exactly what to do. No fear for him. Lots of folks around to reattach it. He knows that whether we are teammates or opponents, we have his back. Just as he has ours. We are athletes.

I will gladly endure a flipped over wheelchair any day over the "special" pity train. When my wheelchair flips sideways, it's because I am running my driving tire up and over the opposing player's driving tire. I am not paying attention to my chair because my entire focus is on getting that damn ball to my teammate. If I fall in the attempt, so be it. It's my own fault for keeping my focus too narrow. I will learn to steal that ball sooner, before I tip over, so the other player cannot even get that close to me.

We are athletes. We will fall, get hurt, over-extend ourselves. We will take no prisoners on the court and take no crap off the court. We will support each other regardless of teams or skill levels. We treat each other as athletes because that is what we are, whether the people watching us play can see that or not.

Playing sports took my disability activism to a different level. Sports require me to inhabit my bodymind, to address its limitations, and to challenge myself physically. I am required to leave my comfort zone and engage on a gut level. On the court, flying around in my wheelchair, I move faster, take up more space, and challenge myself in always surprising new ways. It's a journey of living the contradiction of being in a disabled bodymind and performing feats of great athleticism. It's the best high in the world.

JUST THE FACTS MA'AM

1946 — Stoke Mandeville Sports Centre in Ashbury England hosts the first international wheelchair competition.

1975 — First woman's wheelchair basketball tournament.

2006 — Creation of Federation International de Powerchair Football Association.

RESOURCES

Claiborne, Loretta. URL: http://lorettaclaiborne,com/
Deaflympics. URL: http://www.deaflympics.com/games.asp?2013-s
International Paralympic Committee. URL: http://www.paralympic.org
Special Olympics. URL: http://www.specialolympics.org/history.aspx

A full bibliography is available at my website: www.corbettotoole.com

8.

Violence Against Disabled People

"Violence against individuals with disabilities appears to have been a fact of life throughout history although it was rarely discussed until the 19th century."[1]   — Dick Sobsey (nondisabled)

Summary

Disabled people experience abuse and violence at home, in the community, at school, in hospitals and doctors' offices, and in many other situations. The abusers can be family, caregivers, doctors or nurses, teachers or aides, bus drivers, police, or strangers. If people with disabilities report the abuse, they are often not believed, or even ignored or punished.

Sometimes disabled people are murdered by their caregivers, but usually the murderers receive little or no punishment. Often, other people feel sorry for the murderers because they think it is so hard to take care of a disabled person. Or they feel that the disabled person's life was too hard, and killing them was a kindness. The murder of disabled people is not treated the same way it would be if the victim was nondisabled.

At the end of the chapter, I list some of the disabled people who have been murdered, so that they are honored and remembered.

❖ ❖ ❖

1. Sobsey, R. (1994). *Violence and abuse in the lives of people with disabilities: The end of silent acceptance?* Paul H Brookes Publishing, Baltimore, MD.

Introduction

This essay is about violence against disabled people in the United States. Even if you just follow one thread of violence—whether it be crime, sterilization, bullying, or murder—you find very little public discussion. In 1994 Canadian researcher Dick Sobsey (nondisabled)[2] published the pivotal book *Violence and Abuse in the Lives of People With Disabilities: The End of Silent Acceptance?* Twenty years later we have many more reports, but the violence continues and in some cases is increasing. Throughout this essay, research reports repeatedly state the key to ending violence against disabled people is addressing the prejudice and ableism that allows the abuse to continue.[3] The data is there. We've known for decades that nearly all disabled people get abused, yet few organizations are willing to tackle the problem. Regardless of the decade, over the past forty years I have seen small, isolated abuse prevention projects come and go without any national will to stare down the institutional biases that allow violence to continue. Without creating accountability on both the community and systemic level, in another forty years this essay will still be current.

As numerous studies have documented, disabled people are unexpected and unwelcome in the world of nondisabled people.[4] We're often portrayed as burdens,[5] the causes of our parents' stress,[6]

---

2. Dick Sobsey (nondisabled) has tracked and documented violence and abuse against disabled people for over 30 years. He does the hard work of finding the data and making it accessible to people at the community level. He also conducts research that yields often heartbreaking new data, such as when his review of the death records of people with cerebral palsy's autopsies revealed that 25% of them had been murdered. For me, he is the best kind of ally. He is committed to ending the ableism that creates these abusive conditions. He provides activist scholars like myself with invaluable information and analysis.

3. "Current research clearly and consistently shows a strong relationship between violence and disability for both children and adults." Sobsey, see notes 1 & 2.

4. Disabled people's second-class status is reflected in abled-bodied bias in the development of architecture, access and societal representation. On a deeper level, however, disabled people share an insidious history of eugenics and societal maltreatment, most recently witnessed in Nazi Germany, which reflects a willingness, on a societal level, to make disabled people expendable. From Roguski, M. (2013). *The hidden abuse of disabled people residing in the community: An exploratory study.*

5. Wright, Suzanne. (2013). *Point of View.* Published on the website Autism Speaks. URL: http://www.autismspeaks.org/news/news-item/autism-speaks-washington-call-action

6. O'Brien, J. (2004). *UCSF-led study suggests link between psychological stress and cell aging.* UCSF URL: http://www.ucsf.edu

useless eaters,[7] expensive,[8] taking up too many resources[9] and generally unworthy of life.[10] These beliefs are shown in the inferior educational options given to disabled children,[11] the persistent unemployment and underemployment of disabled people[12] and the physical harms disabled people experience. There is no safe space in which to be a disabled person—not at home, not in the community and certainly not in any type of "special" facility,[13] whether it be a school, hospital, group home or nursing home.

Abuse and ableism are intricately tied together.[14] Whether it's because disabled people are seen as weak and therefore easy victims, because abusers know that when disabled people report the abuse they don't get believed,[15] or whether it's just that a disabled person's life does not seem valuable, abuse happens to disabled people across the life spectrum from babies to elders.

In the Resources section you can find reports that tell you this information with numbers and charts, and for some folks that might be

---

7. *Nutlos Esser.* Literally, "useless eaters," a term used by the Nazis to refer to the mentally and physically handicapped. From the Center for Holocaust and Genocidal Studies. *Holocaust terms.* URL: http://www.chgs.umn.edu/educational/edResource/holoTerms.html

8. "In 2006, disability-associated health care expenditures accounted for 26.7% of all health care expenditures for adults residing in the United States and totaled $397.8 billion" from the CDC. *Health care data and statistics.* URL: http://www.cdc.gov/ncbddd/disabilityandhealth/healthcare-data.html

9. "Arguments are sometimes made for the deserving disabled and against those who may use up too many resources." From Chaterjee, D. K., (ed.) (2011). *Encyclopedia of Global Justice.* University of Utah. Salt Lake City, UT

10. "Between 70 and 85 percent of women in the U.S. confronted with a prenatal diagnosis of Down syndrome choose abortion...." from Becker, A.J. (February 21, 2013). "Better prenatal testing does not mean more abortion." *The Atlantic.*

11. "Despite clear legal rights and numerous judicial rulings affirming the rights of students with disabilities, they far too frequently remain isolated and separately educated within our education system, and are often provided a diluted, inferior education and denied meaningful opportunities to learn." From TASH. *Inclusive education.* URL: http://tash.org/advocacy-issues/inclusive-education/

12. "By severity, 27.5 percent of adults with severe disabilities were employed compared with 71.2 percent of adults with non-severe disabilities," from the U.S. Census Bureau. URL: http://www.census.gov/prod/2012pubs/p70-131.pdf

13. People with disabilities have to live in institutional or residential settings away from public scrutiny and with little or no access to police, support services, or advocates. More abuse occurs "behind locked doors." From Crossmaker, M. (1991). "Behind locked doors – Institutional sexual abuse." *Sexuality and Disability.* URL: http://link.springer.com/article/10.1007%2FBF01102393

14. In this essay, I use 'violence' to mean all forms, such as institutionalization, and 'abuse' to mean person-to-person violence, such as assault.

15. The most common reasons that were given for not reporting disability hate crime incidents were that: the police could not have done anything (36 per cent); the police would not have been interested (31 per cent); or the incident was too trivial to report (17 per cent). From Coleman, N.; Sykes, W. & Walker, A. (2013). "Crime and disabled people: Baseline statistical analysis of measures from the formal inquiry into disability related harassment. *Equality and Human Rights Commission.* URL: http://dhcn.info/dhcn/wp-content/uploads/2014/01/rr90_pdf_final.pdf

an easier way to digest it. But I just want to tell you my truth, even if it makes me cry to tell you and it makes you cry to read it. We have not shed enough tears for the disabled people who are abused. Part of why people are not crying about the abuse of disabled people is because we're not noticing it. Instead, we're being blasted with inspiration porn.[16] The inspiration comes in the form of stories that present disabled people's everyday lives as "inspiring," full of "courage" and "grit." The porn comes in the form of the objectification of people. Inspiration porn always distracts us from the hard realities of disabled life.

Across our lifespans, disabled people are controlled, manipulated, and always devalued. Disability, like race and gender, makes us an automatic "other." Society has a long history of treating the "other" very badly, with neglect, abuse, and institutionalization. Fortunately these very threats create resilience in those who survive, giving disabled people the opportunity to both name the violence and offer solutions.

Disabled people are in an interesting double bind. If one only looks at the official reporting of abuse, one might think there's not a lot, because much of it is not reported. If disabled people report the abuse that's occurring, we're seen as vulnerable victims who need intervention, which often means even more restrictions on our lives. But if we don't report the abuse that we're experiencing, we're not challenging the ableist environment that allows the abuser to continue. It's a no-win situation.

In 1985 a disabled woman told me about how, as a teenager, the paratransit[17] driver for her afterschool program regularly abused her. When I asked her if she reported it or even told her parents she said "No." I asked why. She replied, "If I tell my mom what happened, she's just going to take me off the bus. Then all I'll have is sitting home watching TV all day." This is often the situation for disabled people, the conflict of trading minimal freedoms for remaining in abusive situations. The abusers, who are nearly always nondisabled people, know this very

---

16. "You might have seen the little girl with no hands, drawing a picture with a pencil held in her mouth. You might have seen a child running on carbon-fiber prosthetic legs. And these images, there are lots of them out there, they are what we call "inspiration porn." And I use the term porn deliberately, because they objectify one group of people for the benefit of another group of people. So in this case, we're objectifying disabled people for the benefit of nondisabled people. The purpose of these images is to inspire you, to motivate you, so that we can look at them and think, 'Well, however bad my life is, it could be worse. I could be that person.'" Young, S. (April, 2014). "I am not your inspiration, thank you very much." Delivered at TEDxSydney.

17. Paratransit is a specialized, door-to-door transport service for people with disabilities who are not able to ride fixed-route public transportation. This may be due to an inability to: board, ride, or disembark independently from any readily accessible vehicle on the regular fixed-route system. Fact Sheet: Paratransit Services - Amputee Coalition. URL: www.amputee-coalition.org/fact_sheets/paratransit.html

well.[18.] The abuser targets the disabled person, because they know we have very few options and that they are unlikely to face any consequences.

In a report for UNICEF,[19.] Disability Studies scholar Nora Groce presented a useful overview of the problem. She is discussing disabled children here, but her points are just as valid for disabled adults:

> According to researchers, children with a physical, sensory, intellectual or mental health impairment are at increased risk of becoming victims of violence. Current research indicates that violence against disabled children occurs at annual rates at least 1.7 times greater than their non-disabled peers. For example, one group of researchers report that 90% of individuals with intellectual impairments will experience sexual abuse at some point in their life, and a national survey of deaf adults in Norway found 80% of all deaf individuals surveyed report sexual abuse at some point in their childhood. There are however, several key issues that appear time and again when such violence occurs. Most striking is the issue of reoccurring stigma and prejudice.[20.]

There are different statistics about abuse and disability depending on the focus of the questions and the data used. But there are consistent trends that show that disabled people are most often abused in the environments where they sleep, that their abusers are nearly always people they know well, and that the more restrictive their living environment is, the more abuse they will experience.

Understanding the data is confusing because while we, as non-researchers, understand "disability" to be a category of people with permanent impairments, the people collecting the data often count people with temporary impairments under the term "disabled." For this essay I only use data related to people with permanent disabilities, often categorized as "severely disabled."

The ableism that creates conditions for abuse also creates systemic survival issues for disabled people. Only 26% of severely disabled people in the U.S. are in the workforce.[21.] People with severe disabilities

18. There are, however, definitely disabled abusers.

19. United Nations International Children's Emergency Fund.

20. Groce, N.E. (2005). *Summary report: Violence against disabled children.* UNICEF, United Nations, NY

21. U.S. Census, see note 12.

had median monthly earnings of \$1,577 and family income of \$2,376. [22.] According to the 2010 report on housing by the National Council on Disability, "Currently, about 35.1 million households have one or more people with a disability—nearly one-third of all U.S. households in 2007. In addition, about 1.6 million people live in nursing homes and another half million in group homes."[23.]

Social Environment

If you are new to the topic of abuse and disability, then the conditions that enable abuse might not be obvious to you. I am including some examples of the ways that societally-embedded stigma and prejudice are enacted. The examples below are a distillation of common requests for services from disabled people and their families. The answers are composites, sadly accurate and widespread, from the typical responders, often an anonymous voice at the end of a very long waiting time on the phone.

I include these scenarios in a chapter on violence because the lack of community support and institutional resources produces stressed environments and leaves disabled people and their families functioning with extremely limited resources and support. This in turn creates the environments where abuse can and does occur.

> **Parent of disabled child:** My child needs to be in the regular classes.
> **Answer by school district:** Denied. Disabled children in our school district all attend special education classes.

> **Disabled student:** I need a high school diploma.
> **Answer by school district:** Denied. Disabled children receive a Certificate of Completion. A high school diploma is for children who have spent most of their school time in regular classes. Since you did not, no high school diploma for you.

> **Disabled adult:** I need job training.
> **Answer by Director of Job Training:** Denied. Our job training opportunities are limited. We prioritize those applicants most likely to be employable. Disabled people are not employable.

22. This is compared to \$2,724 for nondisabled individuals and \$4,771 for nondisabled households. See note 12.

23. National Council on Disability. (2010). *The State of Housing in America in the 21st Century: A Disability Perspective.* URL: http://www.ncd.gov/publications/2010/Jan192010

Disabled adult: I need a job.
Answer by potential employer: Denied. Without a high school diploma, company policy prohibits me from hiring you.

Disabled adult: I want to handle my own life.
Answer by parent: Denied. Other parents have told us to place you in our guardianship as soon as you turn 18 years old.

Disabled adult: I want to have children.
Answer by parents and medical professionals: Denied. Disabled people are incapable of safely caring for children. If we didn't sterilize you before, we will try to do it now. If you succeed in getting pregnant, we will encourage you to abort. If you continue the pregnancy, we will encourage you to give the baby up for adoption. If you still keep the baby, we will file Child Protective Services claims against you. They are very successful at removing children from disabled parents.

Disabled elder: I want to stay in my own home.
Answer by social worker: Denied. Now that you have become disabled as you've aged, we've decided that you are not safe at home. So your options are to find nondisabled people to live with you or to be sent to a nursing home. No, we do not offer the option of having paid help in your home. That would be too unwieldy for us. So we prefer to just pay a few large corporations to run nearly all the nursing homes across the country.

These examples are extremely common.[24] Each one was selected for inclusion only if I'd heard it 30 or more times. Restricted options at every age level puts enormous burdens on disabled people and their support systems. Nearly all disabled people are one frighteningly short step away from institutionalization. Lack of support, plus societal indifference and no consequences for abusers, equals an environment ripe for abuse to occur.

---

24. *Restraint and Seclusion: Hear Our Stories.* Video by Dan Habib. URL: https://www.youtube.com/watch?v=pD4UomQL2uI

Violence Data — General

The rest of this essay talks about abuse directly. If you want to continue reading please take a deep breath and give yourself a little emotional protection. Thank you for reading this far. I hope that as we all build awareness around these issues, we can fight against abuse together.

The numbers below are provided to give a bit of context. Remember that nearly all cases of abuse experienced by disabled people are never reported. In those cases that are reported the data shows that disabled people are experiencing abuse at rates three times higher than persons without disabilities.[25] Disturbingly, from 2009 to 2012, violent crimes decreased in the U.S. for nondisabled people but increased for disabled people.[26] In 2012 there were reported cases of 1.3 million nonfatal violent crimes against disabled people. This includes 233,000 robberies, 195,200 aggravated assaults, 838,600 simple assaults and 80,100 rapes or other sexual assaults.[27]

In a large 2013 U.S. survey of 7,200 disabled people and the people in their lives, researchers found that over 70% of people with disabilities said they had been victims of abuse. More than 50% of these victims had experienced physical abuse, with some 41% having been victims of sexual abuse. Nearly 9 of 10 respondents with disabilities had suffered verbal or emotional abuse. Most victims said they had experienced abuse on more than 20 occasions.[28] These numbers are a very small fraction of the actual cases of abuse.

Yet almost none are framed as hate crimes, even though they typically meet the criteria. As Mark Sherry (disabled) points out, "Notice how crimes against disabled people are rarely phrased in terms of bias or hate crimes, even though they fit all the criteria (non-random selection of victims, targeting this person because of their disability identity, large number of perpetrators vs. Isolated [sic] victim, etc.)."[29]

You may have noticed that I am not saying that nondisabled people are the abusers and disabled people are the survivors. This is intentional.

25. Bureau of Justice Statistics. *1.3 Million Nonfatal Violent Crimes Against Persons With Disabilities in 2012, Unchanged From 2011.* URL: http://www.bjs.gov/content/pub/press/capd0912stpr.cfm

26. "Disturbingly while the age adjusted rate of violent victimization decreased from 22.4 to 22.3 per 1,000 [people] between 2009 and 2012 for Americans without disabilities, the rate rose substantially for persons with disabilities from 50.1 to 60.4 per 1,000 [people]." Sobsey, see notes 1 & 2.

27. See note 38.

28. Disability Abuse Project. (2013). *Report Finds Rampant Abuse, Flawed Response Systems.* URL: http://disability-abuse.com/survey/media-release.htm

29. Sherry, M. "Notice how crimes against disabled people…." *Facebook,* November 6, 2014.

Abusers come in all forms, including people with disabilities. In my circles, I have met disabled people who sexually abused children, physically abused a partner, kidnapped and abused a sex worker, and numerous accounts of stealing other disabled people's money. Both disabled and nondisabled people have the capacity to abuse.

Having a strong support network, staying out of institutions, and being a resourceful person certainly helps to reduce the chances of being abused. Yet there are numerous accounts of resourceful disabled people with strong support being abused. Numerous friends of mine, some of whom were employed at a high paying jobs, have had their money and identity stolen. I consider myself pretty savvy, yet two disabled women succeeded in stealing my life savings. The systematic deprivation of support insures that abuse can happen to anyone.

Risk Factors

Although all disabled people are at risk for abuse, the levels of abuse vary by types of disability, perpetrator's role, the relationship to the disabled person and the overall environment. One study on the abuse of disabled seniors found that risk factors contributing to the abuse include: when the senior has an intellectual or mental disability, needs personal care assistance, is poor or was previously abused. Caregivers without their own strong support systems are more likely to become abusive.

Even though my focus is on the U.S., I am including the following report from New Zealand for a number of reasons. First it's a report on an indigenous community, which is a population rarely included in disability and violence data. Second, the research is being directed by indigenous people in a research institute, Community Research, that they created and control. Third, because the researchers are part of the community of the interviewees they have a unique ability to both identify the problems and enact solutions. I can only summarize a few of their points here but I strongly recommend reading their full reports, because they tease out nuances only reported by interviewees who trust their interviewers.

Community Research[30] found that people did not report abuse because of pressure from the abuser, negative experiences from past reporting, fear of retribution, fear of loss of caregiving support, expectation of increased abuse if they reported and increased threats of violence by abusers and their supporters after abuse was reported.

---

30. Formerly called Tangata Whenua, Community & Voluntary Sector Research Centre.

Numerous interviewees reported that the close proximity of abuser and disabled survivor deeply complicated the ability of the survivor to escape repeated abuse.[31] "In a survey of individuals with disabilities who had been abused, 96% of the cases involved perpetrators who were known to their victim. The largest group of offenders (44%) were individuals who had a relationship with the victim specifically because of their disability (27.7% disability service providers, 5.4% specialized transportation, 4.3% specialized foster parents and 6.5% other disabled individuals)."[32]

Barriers to reporting abuse are pervasive and deeply systemic. When abuse occurs, disabled people are not believed nor are they deemed as reliable reporters, so legal action is deferred. In his groundbreaking 1994 book, Dick Sobsey found that

> Social practices go beyond mere attitudes and beliefs. For example, people with intellectual disabilities have often been denied the right to testify in court about the abuse they experience, even when they have been quite capable of communicating what happened to them. Institutions housing people with psychiatric or developmental disabilities commonly kept telephones locked away from residents and censored all incoming and outgoing mail, further isolating residents from potential help. Special education programs have overwhelmingly focused on teaching compliance and done little to teach people with disabilities to be assertive or stand up for their rights. As a result of these and many other practices, people with disabilities have been systematically disempowered.[33]

Unfortunately, twenty years later these practices have not changed. Since abuse against disabled people is so widespread, many disabled people know other disabled people who have been abused and share their stories through informal disability communities, such as friendship circles. Often these are the only safe places to discuss abuse, and disability circles often develop strong support systems to support emotional healing and create strategic plans for reducing their risk of

---

31. Tairawhiti Community Voice. URL: http://tcvhub.co.nz/

32. *Abuse and neglect of adults with developmental disabilities: A public health priority for the State of California.* (2003). A report of Disability Rights California State Council on Developmental Disabilities USC University Affiliated Program The Tarjan Center for Developmental Disabilities, UCLA. URL: http://www.disabilityrightsca.org/pubs/701901.pdf

33. Sobsey, see notes 1 & 2.

repeated abuse. A useful indicator of the qualitative data collected is whether or not these grassroots resources are documented. Reports that show how disabled people survive the onslaught of abuse provide valuable insights into creating successful abuse prevention programs. Research that merely documents the problems without providing community-based insights on removing barriers is far less helpful.

Abuse in Medical Settings

Medical systems hold the deep-seated belief that disabled people are "broken" versions of nondisabled people. Even accomplished people who become disabled are told by medical professionals that their lives will now be tragedies. Alison Kafer (disabled), now a university professor, recalls the advice she was given after the accident that left her disabled:

> What my future did hold, according to my rehabilitation psychologist and my recreation therapist, was long-term psychological therapy. My friends were likely to abandon me, alcoholism and drug addiction loomed on my horizon, and I needed to prepare myself for the future of pain and isolation brought on by disability.[34]

The role of medical practitioners in abuse is rarely discussed except among survivors. Yet medical staff are often involved before, during, or after most forms of abuse. Medicine's role in silencing the voices of abuse survivors cannot be overstated. Most forms of abuse remain unreported, with the complicity of medical practitioners. Framing abuse as "medical" allows it to be explained and justified. In some situations medical professionals have directly supervised abuses, including Nazi exterminations, the Tuskeegee experiments, and the Ashley X "treatment."

During the Nazi era, disabled people were categorized as "useless eaters" and murdered in many different ways. From 1939-1941, people living in the community had their medical records secretly sent to clandestine medical panels for evaluation. During this T-4 program, 70,272 people were killed. After some protests, the T-4 program was officially stopped in 1941, but the murders continued in different ways. According to the Eugenics Archive, "Physicians assisted by nurses killed by starvation, injection, and administering deadly drugs. The groups

---

34. Kafer, A. (2013) *Feminist, Queer, Crip*. Indiana University Press. Bloomington, IN

killed included newborn babies, children, the mentally disturbed, and the infirm... The murder of thousands of disabled individuals through methods such as medication became known as 'wild euthanasia.' Approximately 250,000 people were killed."[35]

In the Tuskegee experiment, African-American men with syphilis were treated as human guinea pigs for over 40 years. This is part of a long history of withholding needed health care from disenfranchised groups so doctors could get the medical information needed to cure an enfranchised group, in this case white men. In 1932 the Public Health Service began a study of syphilis with 600 black men called the "Tuskegee Study of Untreated Syphilis in the Negro Male." The study ended in 1973 after a news report showed that the men never received treatment for their syphilis even after it became available in 1947, nor had they given informed consent. The medical researchers watched 399 men[36] with syphilis sicken and die from the disease.[37]

The 2004 Ashley X "treatment" is the latest, but not the last, way that medical professionals surgically alter the disabled bodymind, in this case for the convenience of caregivers. In Seattle "surgeons removed a girl's uterus and breast buds, while she was put on growth-stunting medications to keep her small, on the grounds that she would pose a 'hardship' to her family as she matured. That procedure has been used on multiple children in the subsequent years."[38] After both the parents and medical staff published positive reports about this procedure—and even after the hospital admitted that the procedure violated their own ethical guidelines and Washington state law—other parents have requested it for their own children, and medical professionals in other states have performed the "Ashley treatment."[39]

Sometimes medical abuse is a simple denial of needed medical treatment. Although rarely documented, this is the most common form of medical abuse. It's easier to see when you look at the rationing of expensive health care—specifically organ transplants. Disabled people

---

35. The Eugenics Archive. *Nazi Euthanasia.* URL:
http://eugenicsarchive.ca/discover/connections/535eed177095aa0000000242

36. In the study, 399 men had syphilis and 201 men were the control group (i.e. they did not have syphilis).

37. Brandt, A.M. (1978). "Racism and research: The case of theTuskegee syphilis study." *The Hastings Center Report.* URL: http://dash.harvard.edu/handle/1/3372911

38. Peace, W. (June 20, 2013). "Murder and hate crimes against people with a disability." *Bad Cripple (blog).* URL: http://badcripple.blogspot.com/2013/06/murder.html

39. See the 2008 interview with Ashley's parents. URL:
http://www.cnn.com/2008/HEALTH/conditions/03/12/pillow.QA/index.html; Also, Gunther, D.F. MD, MA; Diekema, D.S. MD, MPH. (2006). "Attenuating growth in children with profound developmental disability: A new approach to an old dilemma." *Arch Pediatric and Adolescent Medicine* 160(10). 1013-1017. doi:10.1001/archpedi.160.10.1013.

are routinely denied places on organ transplant lists. As Ari Ne'eman (disabled), Executive Director of the Autistic Self-Advocacy Network points out: "Doctors give faux medical reasons. On further scrutiny, they don't stand up." Ne'eman wrote a policy brief on the issue. "When someone with a disability is looking for a transplant, discrimination is the norm."[40]

Even though only a few examples of this denial are publicly known, disabled people and our families have received the message. As William Peace (disabled), a scholar and professor, notes: "I know with certainty that I will never receive an organ transplant. The reason for this bothers me: my existence is not valuable. Few people with a disability get an organ transplant and I no longer have any trust in the system that decides who lives and dies waiting for an organ."[41]

Even denial of medical care for minor health problems can cause disability. When disability rights leader Donald Galloway (disabled) was a child he had an injury to his eyes. His family tried repeatedly to get needed medical care, but they were repeatedly turned away, mostly for being black and poor. The extensive delay in medical treatment resulted in permanent blindness for Donald.[42]

Abuse in Institutions

Reviewing the reams of research on violence and disability shows that the lack of affordable and accessible housing creates the conditions that drive many people into institutions. Most people think of an institution as a large, locked building, frequently located in a rural area. In some places they are called "state schools" or "state hospitals." Most were formerly called "asylums." Over the past 30 years the institutionalization of disabled people has shifted from a few large institutions in each state to smaller, but equally disempowering, community facilities and nursing homes.

Self Advocates Becoming Empowered[43] defines institutions as "any facility or program where people do not have control over their lives. A

---

40. Ne'emann, A., Kapp, S., Narby, C. (2013). *Organ Transplantation and People with I/DD: A Review of Research, Policy and Next Steps.* Policy brief. Autism Self-Advocay Network. URL: autisticadvocacy.org/wp-content/uploads/2013/03/ASAN-Organ-Transplantation-Policy-Brief_3.18.13.pdf

41. Peace, see note 53.

42. Donald Galloway oral history in the *Disability Rights Independent Living Movement (DRILM) Historical Archives.* The Regional Oral History Office, The Bancroft Library, University of California, Berkeley. URL: http://bancroft.berkeley.edu/collections/drilm/index.html

43. Self Advocates Becoming Empowered (SABE) is an organization run by and for people with Intellectual Disabilities. URL: http://www.sabeusa.org

facility or program can mean a private or public institution, nursing home, group home, foster care home, day treatment program, or sheltered workshop."[44] These institutions look benign because they are often small and run by a small staff. However residents report having no access to food other than at meal times when it is portioned. No rights to privacy since all mail is opened, all phone calls monitored. No financial independence since all their monies are given directly to the institution. In short, their rights, well really their lack of rights, are the same at the community institutions as at the large rural institutions.

Even though many facilities are not called 'institutions,' restrictive community residential facilities such as group homes are also not desirable. People rarely voluntarily sign up to go into them. These facilities, according to numerous studies, operate by and for the convenience of the staff.[45] The lowest paid staff in these facilities do most of the direct services. They work long hours with a heavy job load for very little money.[46]

The lack of appropriate staffing levels and the lack of professional staff creates facilities where the disabled people (residents) rarely have any input about their daily schedule and are prohibited from leaving the facility. A friend of mine went to one of the "good" facilities, according to the hospital social worker, where she was crammed with two other residents into a room clearly designed only for two people. There was less than 24 inches between the beds. Her schedule was determined solely by the staff. She was bathed and dressed by 10am and put to bed at 7pm. Her mail was opened and read by staff, she was prohibited from leaving the facility, and she had no access to money, a telephone or a computer. When I suggested to someone I knew who had lived in a nursing home that I would be complaining, he urged me to wait until my friend had safely left the facility. "Otherwise," he told me, "they will punish her for the complaint."[47]

A bait-and-switch[48] approach often happens in senior Continuum

---

44. SABE position statement URL: http://www.sabeusa.org/wp-content/uploads/2014/02/POSITION-STATEMENT-Institutions.pdf

45. Bigby, C., Knox, M., Beadle-Brown, J., Clement, T., Mansell., J (2012). "Uncovering dimensions of informal culture in underperforming group homes for people with severe intellectual disabilities." *Intellectual and Developmental Disabilities* 50(6), 452–467.

46. Stone, R.I. (2001). "Who will care for us? Addressing the long-term care workforce crisis." *The Urban Institute*. U.S. Dept. of Health and Human Services. URL: http://aspe.hhs.gov/daltcp/reports/ltcwf.htm

47. Personal conversation with Lennis Jones (disabled), a mental health therapist who had lived in nursing homes for many years.

48. "Bait and switch" means that a person is promised one thing but then they are actually given something else. In this example, seniors are told that the decision to move into Assisted Living is their choice but, in fact, the decision is made by the staff.

of Care facilities.[49] During the public relations wooing, prospective new residents are shown the assisted living and nursing home on-site options, and assured that they, the new resident, will decide when it's necessary to move into them. It is only after they have given the facility a huge sum of money and moved into the facility that they realize that the decision of which level of care a person is placed in is a staff decision, not a resident's. Staff decides when a resident is moved from Independent Living to the more restrictive Assisted Living and then onto the completely restrictive Nursing Home. Community-based options, such as hiring a personal care attendant, are not discussed or encouraged. The minute someone needs personal care, they lose their place in the Independent Living section and therefore lose their rights and privileges as well. In 2010, there were 1,900 Continuing Care Retirement Communities in the U.S.[50]

Disability and the School To Prison Pipeline

In the U.S., disabled students, particularly male students of color, are disproportionately funneled into inferior educational settings. This means they often do not receive high school diplomas, an absolute necessity for adult employment. The numbers of disabled students completing school with a high school diploma is abysmally small, and barriers are disproportionally weighted against disabled students of color, particularly males. Sometimes termed the "school to prison pipeline," disabled students, particularly disabled males of color, are tracked towards incarceration from an early age.[51]

Public schools rarely provide role models or appropriate support for disabled male students of color, particularly if they are labeled with an emotional or learning disability. They do not "look" disabled, therefore they are often accused of being lazy or inattentive by teachers and administrative staff, who are usually neither disabled nor persons of color. If schools made even one small change, such as providing adult

---

49. These are facilities designed primarily for retirees, which offer a range of services from independent living in one's own apartment to full care settings, available as residents age and their care needs change.

50. Zarem, J.E., (ed.) (2010) "Today's Continuing Care Retirement Community." *Leading Age, Americas Senior Housing Association.* URL: http://www.leadingage.org

51. "The ACLU is committed to challenging the 'school to prison pipeline,' a disturbing national trend wherein children are funneled out of public schools and into the juvenile and criminal justice systems. Many of these children have learning disabilities or histories of poverty, abuse or neglect, and would benefit from additional educational and counseling services. Instead, they are isolated, punished and pushed out." from *School-to-Prison Pipeline.* American Civil Liberties Union. URL: https://www.aclu.org/school-prison-pipeline

disabled men of color as resources and models, these young men could develop some of the skills they need to navigate a disability-unfriendly world. Yet this almost never happens.

Having a disability creates multiple opportunities for getting put into jail.[52] Sometimes, a disabled person's stressful reaction does not match the police officer's expected response. This leads to the disabled person (usually a male) being brought to the police station, an environment that is hostile to all people and particularly stressful for disabled people.[53] This can be a best-case scenario because we know that all too often innocent black men with disabilities are shot and killed during their encounters with police officers.[54]

Once a young disabled person has a criminal record, it directly impacts all of his future possibilities. Emerging from juvenile facilities traumatized, abused, and without any marketable skills, his chances of ever being employed are minuscule.

Disabled men of color often get picked up and arrested on simple charges such as vagrancy and jaywalking.[55] As one study found, "People with epilepsy, with diabetes, who are deaf, who have other disabilities, have been mistaken as unruly [or] drunk."[56] Once inside the system, it can be extraordinarily hard to get out.[57]

Adult facilities, jails and prisons contain a large concentration of disabled men. Compared with non-institutionalized populations, the number of disabled men, particularly African-American and Latino

52. Ben-Moshe, L., Chapman, C., Carey, A., eds. (2014). *Disability incarcerated: Imprisonment and disability in the United States and Canada*. Palgrave MacMillan, New York NY

53. "Many mentally challenged people are abused and killed every year under the cover of law. Approximately half the victims of police violence are mentally dysfunctional." from Assistance to the Incarcerated Mentally Ill. URL: "http://www.care2.com/c2c/group/AIMI

54. *WE CHARGE GENOCIDE AGAIN! A Curriculum for Operation Ghetto Storm: Report on the 2012 Extrajudicial Killings of 313 Black People by Police, Security Guards and Vigilantes*. Prepared by Tongo Eisen-Martin. URL: https://mxgm.org/wp-content/uploads/2013/05/we-charge-genocide-FINAL.pdf

55. "Reginald 'Neli' Latson, a young man with Autism and Intellectual Disability, has been incarcerated since August 2013 as a result of behavior that results from his disability. He has been held in solitary confinement for most of that time and is presently at a Virginia state prison. Neli is not a criminal. He does not belong in a jail or a prison. His tragic situation is the result of events surrounding his initial detention which occurred, ironically, while waiting for the public library to open, and from subsequent mental health crises resulting from his confinement. In effect, Neli spends 24 hours a day locked in a segregation cell with minimal human contact for the 'crime' of being autistic; his lawyers wrote to Virginia Gov. Terry McAuliffe. 'Absent intervention, there is every reason to think he will remain there until the opportunity for effective treatment has been lost.'" URL: http://www.thearcofva.org/advocacy/current-advocacy-issues-and-activities/reginald-neli-latson/

56. Evans, S. (November 14, 2014). "The US prison system perpetuates "the criminalization of disability"." *Mint Press News*. URL: http://www.mintpressnews.com/us-prison-system-perpetuates-criminalization-disability/198878/

57. Neli Latson, see note 55.

men, is exceptionally high.[58.] The number of disabled men is so high that "the largest psychiatric facilities in the country are prisons."[59.] Note that the author did not say "in prisons." While a very high percentage of prison populations are men with mental disabilities, there are few psychiatric resources available to them.[60.]

A number of researchers and activists refer to this as the "criminalization of disability." Unfortunately these problems are not being discussed by anyone other than grassroots activists.[61.] In 2012, in New York, Rikers Island jailed as many people with mental illnesses as were in all 24 psychiatric hospitals in New York State combined. This amounted to, reportedly, 40% of the people jailed at Rikers.[62.] As counties across the country close down community mental health services, increasing numbers of people with mental disabilities are being funneled into the prisons.[63.]

Disability, Media, and Murder

When an actual crime is committed against disabled people and the perpetrator is white, there is often enormous support for not processing the violence as a crime. For example, in 1993, a Canadian man named Robert Latimer killed his 12-year-old daughter Tracy by putting her in the front seat of his truck and pumping in exhaust fumes until she died from carbon monoxide poisoning while he watched.

I was appalled and deeply upset when I heard about her murder. My feelings soon turned to anger when the local authorities decided not to prosecute Robert Latimer. In fact, they did not take legal action against him until disability grassroots groups took action. Even after national attention and activism, the government only charged him with second degree murder. He ultimately received a minimum sentence of 10 years at a minimum security prison.[64.] He was released in 2010 and lectures often to spread his support for the "mercy killing" of disabled

58. "Even when you're talking about the adult prison population, people with disabilities actually outnumber the percentage of people that are black or the percentage of people that are brown," Lewis said in Evans, S. See note 56.

59. Horowitz, A. (February 4, 2013). "Mental illness soars in prisons, jails while inmate suffer." *The Huffington Post*. URL: http://www.huffingtonpost.com/2013/02/04/mental-illness-prisons-jails-inmates_n_2610062.html

60. Ibid. (This means see previous note.)

61. Ibid.

62. Ibid.

63. Ben-Moshe, et al, see note 52.

64. 10 years is the minimum required for his life sentence. Source URL: http://www.raggededgemagazine.com/drn/latimer0402.html

people, with Latimer asserting that he killed Tracy to "end her suffering" from being disabled.

At the time, I thought her murder was an aberration, but decades of research by Dick Sobsey (nondisabled)[65] and others proved me wrong. Media coverage is hugely important in supporting the murderers of disabled people. Media coverage overwhelmingly connects the person's disability to their death, creating a link that basically states that disabled people are responsible for their own death. In this line of thinking, for example, the physical impairments of Tracy Latimer made her a burden to her parents, they made her "suffer" and this became her father's justification for murdering her.

In 2013 when off-duty police officers killed Ethan Saylor, a young adult with a Down Syndrome, they blamed his asthma and obesity for his death, not the fact that they were pinning him down with their bodies. His crime (in their eyes) was that he attempted to go to a second movie before his attendant had purchased the second movie ticket.

His attendant was trained by Ethan in how best to support him.[66] She went over and told the officers exactly how Ethan preferred to be approached in these stressful situations. Ethan knew that sometimes authority figures misinterpreted his fear for noncompliance, so he trained his staff to help him in those situations, but the officers ignored Ethan and his aide's expert advice. The aide called his mother as part of the safety plan that Ethan had devised. Unfortunately, the officers put

---

65. Biography: Dick Sobsey, Ph.D., is Professor of Educational Psychology and Director of the JP Das Developmental Disabilities Centre at the University of Alberta in Canada, where he also serves as an adjunct professor at the John Dossetor Health Ethics Centre. He has worked with children and adults with severe disabilities since 1968 as a nurse, a teacher, and a researcher. His current research explores the relationship between disability and violence. Dr. Sobsey is also the father of two children, including a teenager who has severe and multiple disabilities and is fully included in his neighborhood school. I mention Dick Sobsey because he is one of the only voices that has called attention to the ongoing violence against disabled people for the past three decades. He's done this difficult work year after year and provided 30 years of data for me to mine in writing this essay.

Source URL: http://products.brookespublishing.com/cw_contributorinfo.aspx?ContribID=3034&Name=Dick+Sobsey%2C+Ed.D.

66. Comment by Steamboatmom at
http://www.fredericknewspost.com/news/crime_and_justice/police/speaking-out-for-ethan-saylor/article_317b1a4e-4908-55a5-b938-e2dd96bc9444.html

"And another thing, he did not have an 'attendant.' Ethan hired his own support staff to assist him. His job coach assisted him to develop work skills or attend classes. His evening and weekend staff assisted him to pursue social activities. I do not know who you think you are talking about but clearly you did not know Ethan. His family did not need respite from him. He was pursuing the life of a young adult, going to a movie on a Saturday night with a friend/support staff is a normal thing to do as a 26 year old young man. He and his staff were friends, yes, friends. They enjoyed each other's company. They did things together for fun! He needed staff to assist him as he did not drive or handle his own money."

Ethan on the ground and pressed into his back until he died. Like nearly all of the murderers of disabled people, particularly if they are by law enforcement, the perpetrators were not charged with murder.

A major 2005 study reviewing the media coverage of 1,128 cases of developmentally disabled people who were murdered between 1980 and 2004 found these disturbing statistics: The United States had 700 murders in this period, followed by China (222), Canada (64), England (24), Japan (13) and other countries with 10 or fewer. In the vast majority (90%) of these cases the disabled people murdered were under the age of nine years old. Family members committed the most murders (308) followed by: Government employees or militia (268); Caregivers (212); Strangers (65); and Roommates (34).[67] Together, Government and Caregivers accounted for 63% of all murders of people with developmental disabilities.[68]

> The most common form of homicidal event [form of murder] was starvation. It accounted for 21.6 percent of cases. Other frequent events included beating or shaking (14.4 per cent), shooting (10.8 per cent), suffocation or gassing (9.6 per cent), burning or scalding (9.0 per cent), poisoning or drug overdose (7.2 per cent), and stabbing (6.0 per cent). Additional events included deliberate injury with a motor vehicle, deliberate infection, and dropping from a high place. In 7.7 per cent of cases the actual cause of death was undetermined or unknown to the researchers.[69]

Although these examples focus on the murder of people who had developmental disabilities, the data on people with other disabilities shows the same trends.[70] Of particular concern is the number of people with disabilities killed by law enforcement personnel. A 2014 New York Times article found "Although no agency or organization tracks the number of police shootings nationally that involve people with mental illnesses, a report by the Treatment Advocacy Center and the National Sheriff's Association, based on informal studies and accounts, estimated

---

67. The high number of murders in the government category include the disabled people killed in mass genocides.

68. Lucardie, R. & Sobsey, E. (2005) "Homicides of people with developmental disabilities: An analysis of news stories." *Developmental Disabilities Bulletin* 33(1 & 2).

69. Santos, F. & Goode, E. (April 2, 2014). "Police confront rising number of mentally ill suspects." *New York Times*. URL: http://www.nytimes.com/2014/04/02/us/police-shootings-of-mentally-ill-suspects-are-on-the-upswing.html

70. Sobsey is reviewing data that indicates that at least 25% of the deaths of people with cerebral palsy are murders. URL: http://www.researchgate.net/profile/Dick_Sobsey/topics

that half the number of people shot and killed by the police have mental health problems."[71.]

Encounters with law enforcement officers, both on duty and off, have an unusually high likelihood of resulting in the abuse and even murder of disabled people. On his blog, Bad Cripple, Bill Peace (disabled) expresses the outrage of many disabled people about the horrific problem.

> Exactly, how many people with a disability need to be murdered before people and the mass media get the idea: the murder of people with a disability is often a hate crime. How many people know the names Tracy Latimore [sic], Markea Blakely-Berry, George Hodgkins, Kyla Puhle, Tom Inglis, Daniel Kirby, Karandeep Arora, Leosha Barnett, Ajit Singh-Mahal, Gerren Isgrigg, and most recently Alex Spouralakalis [sic]. The violence is shocking. The murders are tortuous and premeditated.[72.]

The media has a direct role in increasing or decreasing the numbers of murders of disabled people. Between 1990 and 1994, the average number of Canadian murder cases in which parents killed their children was 34 each year,[73.] but after the widespread media support for Robert Latimer, who publicly presents his actions as "altruistic filicide," that is, he killed his daughter because that was in her best interest and that he did nothing wrong,[74.] the numbers of parents killing their children rose dramatically, with 62 cases in 1997 alone.[75.] The media often presented Latimer, as it has done with numerous murdering parents subsequently, as a loving father who just wanted to end his daughter's suffering.[76.]

Canadian researcher Dick Sobsey, also a parent of a severely disabled person, wrote as a parent about this type of "justification." I use his long quote because it shows many different aspects of family members killing disabled people:

---

71. Santos, see note 69.

72. Peace, see note 38.

73. Reynolds, D. (April 3, 2002). "Sympathy for Robert Latimer linked to increase in child murders." *Inclusion Daily Express*. URL:
http://www.inclusiondaily.com/news/crime/latimer.htm#100401

74. Cook, T. (2012) "Robert Latimer U.K.: Visa problems keep advocate from appearing at dying debate, say organizers." *The Huffington Post*. URL:
http://www.huffingtonpost.ca/2012/10/17/robert-latimer-uk-visa-problems_n_1975234.html

75. See note 25.

76. Sobsey, see notes 1 & 2.

I am also thankful that we do get some support as a family even if services are often inadequate or compromised by bureaucracy. Parents have been doing this for a lot of years with less supports. Here is something to think about. Paleoanthropologists tell us that spinal and cranial deformities have been found in older children and young adults among early humans and prehumans. These children could not have survived without parents or community caregivers. Since these skeletons date back as much as 990,000 years before the invention of the wheel, these families probably did not have very good wheelchairs. Those parents probably didn't get respite or other support services... I believe that our caregiving makes us a little more human today.

My real issue in the way society portrays parents who kill kids with disabilities is simple. I think it is tempting to portray these parents as tragic and maybe even heroic figures who care about their children, were treated badly by the system that should be supporting them, and who finally were driven to a desperate act. Sometimes these cases are used to point out how badly families are treated and to make the case for better family supports. I have attempted to ask one question, "does this portrayal increase or decrease the chance that another parent will murder their child?"

After studying well over 600 cases of parents who murdered their sons or daughters with developmental disabilities, I am convinced that this portrayal increases the chances that the next parent will kill their severely disabled child (and maybe themselves, too). Here's why...

To understand why parents (of children with or without disabilities) kill their children, we might ask "why does any parent kill a child?" The problem with this question is that all parents have instrumental motives to kill their children, raising any child makes demands on parents, costs a fortune, is stressful and complicated at times. These things may be more true with some children than others but they are basically true for all children.

So, we need to reframe the question to "why is it that most parents don't murder their children?" I think most parents would say it is because they love their children, that they could never hurt them or kill them. This is a good answer, but a slightly more technical answer says that most of us will never kill anyone because of inhibition. When people get depressed, angry, and frustrated, they may be tempted to do harm to their children or themselves. A lot of people get close to the edge, but only a few go over. Most of us control our antisocial impulses. This process is called inhibition and the breaking down of this process is called disinhibition. Some drugs, particularly alcohol and some stimulants, can be disinhibiting, but concepts and ideas can also be disinhibiting.

So parents who actually kill their kids are typically the ones who can convince themselves that their acts are in someway justified…When we portray these people as tragic heroes who were forced by others to take desperate action, we make it easier for the next person to commit an irrational act. So, I might have a little sympathy for the father if he threw the doctor out the window, but I have no sympathy for someone who displaces his anger to a vulnerable child.[77.]

Community Accountability

As Sobsey points out, there is enormous strength in local and immediate communities. In fact, that is how disabled people are surviving the abuse occurring daily, with the help of our friends. As more awareness comes to the prevalence of violence against disabled people, it is useful to look at what organizational strategies are having a positive impact on the problem.

Reporting abuse to a professional sometimes provides relief and safety for the disabled survivor. With these realities facing disabled people when it comes to reporting, how can communities support people who want to report?

In those cases where, for many disabled people, officially reporting the abuse is not a safe or available option, abuse prevention organizations suggest that the people who are not being abused provide direct support to the disabled survivor. Friends, family members and neighbors can help by:

    ✔ Breaking the silence and helping the survivor get

77. Sobsey, R. (2010). *Dr. Dick Sobsey Himself Replies.* URL:
http://severedisabilitykid.blogspot.com/2010/05/dr-dick-sobsey-himself-replies.html

support from violence prevention organizations.
- ✔ Becoming informed about violence in the home.
- ✔ Offering to go with them for help.

As a larger community, there are a number of structural issues that, if changed, would decrease opportunities for abusers to violate disabled people including:[78.]

- ✔ Start conversations about the daily presence of abuse.
- ✔ Examine the ways that the conversations about violence against disabled people are silenced.
- ✔ Investigate how local organizations address violence.
- ✔ Discuss reporting barriers with local service organizations and legal enforcement agencies.
- ✔ Provide specific disability-focused supports for a survivor during the reporting process.
- ✔ Assess the possibilities of legislative options.

At the local level, a critical resource is a commitment to address violence against disabled people by the organizations that provide services to them. Rarely do these organizations provide the needed resources for fighting abuse, yet they are uniquely positioned to do so. Most of these organizations are well aware of the access needs for the disabled people they serve. They know how to create support mechanisms because they are already doing it on other topic areas.

Organizations need to publicly name the prevalence of abuse in their local community. Our current system depends on individuals to carry out this job, and it is impossible to make change one isolated and not-believed survivor at a time. Systemic change comes when organizations make violence prevention a priority. A public discussion of violence provides a beginning. Organizations also need to commit to supporting disabled survivors who need emotional support services, who want to report the abuser, who need to learn how to tell their experiences so law enforcement can understand what happened. Most of all, organizations need to put a supportive and public face on the fact that abuse is occurring and that they support and believe the survivors.

A 2005 analysis of how news stories report the murders of disabled people reminds us of the need to take steps at both the individual and systemic levels:

---

78. "Few family members, friends, and providers are adequately trained to recognize signs of abuse in individuals with developmental disabilities and to assist victims to access the criminal justice and/or social service system." Disability Rights California, see note 32.

> [P]revention of abuse and discrimination of PWDD [People with Developmental Disabilities] needs to focus on empowering individuals to resist abuse, providing appropriate supports to and careful selection of caregivers and families, building safer environments, education and training, law and law enforcement, and changing attitudes. Deinstitutionalisation, normalisation, integration, and inclusion are positive steps towards normalising the environment of PWDD. With greater awareness of the risks for abuse and discrimination, more can be done to prevent PWDD from being victimized.[79]

It is important to note that while I discussed separately the social conditions that create opportunities for abuse, the specific types of abuse, the lack of consequences for abusers, and the community lack of awareness about abuse, they are interrelated and occur together.[80]

One of the best tools I have seen on developing community awareness and showing the nuances of violence are the short videos coming out of DeafHope, an agency working to prevent violence in the Deaf community.[81] The impact of these videos is strengthened by their quiet visual approach. Watching the videos, you feel like you are just hanging out with the couple at home. Although the scenes can be difficult to watch, they offer an important opportunity for us to notice the subtler forms of violence which can be damaging and are often unrecognized as abuse.

For too long we've been asking the wrong questions. Instead of asking the survivors, "Why didn't you leave? Why didn't you just get out?" the right questions are directed at the perpetrators by asking "Why are you hurting her? Why are you doing that?" Erin Esposito (disabled), a U.S. Deaf leader on domestic violence, stated during her keynote speech at DeafHope's Glimmer of Hope in 2011:

> Many agencies are working directly with communities to create "community accountability." In this model, communities become aware of the violence and take action, as a community,

---

79. The authors are professors in Canada, so the spelling is Canadian English and not USA English. Lucardie, R. & Sobsey, D. (2005). "Homicides of people with developmental disabilities: An analysis of news stories." *Developmental Disabilities Bulletin* 33(1 & 2), 71-98. URL: http://files.eric.ed.gov/fulltext/EJ844471.pdf

80. Sobsey, see notes 1 & 2.

81. The videos can be seen at DeafHope. URL: http://www.deaf-hope.org/videos/

to support survivors and confront abusers. Deaf[82] women have created agencies[83] to address violence in Deaf communities. In addition to fighting for access to non-Deaf violence prevention services, the Deaf women decided to target the specific conditions that both allow violence to occur and continue and to create Deaf-driven solutions to make Deaf communities safer. ... For so long we have done nothing or we have waited for something to happen then we do something. Now it is time do to something before anything else happens to make sure that we are all safe... It is time for us all to create the miracle of community accountability."[84]

As we have seen, there is a strong association between violence and disability. Both children and adults with disabilities experience higher rates of violence than other individuals. Four distinct but interrelated pathways connect violence and disability:

First, violence is a major cause of disability. One researcher asserts that nondisabled people can and do become disabled through abuse, "approximately 25% of all disabilities are directly caused by abuse."[85] Sobsey's 1994 book notes the confusion between disability, violence and causation:

> Violence often results in physical or mental harm that causes disability. For example, 10-15% of brain injuries and 15-20% of spinal cord injuries result from violence. In addition, abuse, neglect, and violence, even in the absence of gross physical injuries, contribute to cognitive and emotional disabilities. Since violence and abuse that take place in families or caregiving relationships is most frequently chronic, and it is difficult to identify an exact beginning of disabilities that may emerge or be identified over a period of years, it is often difficult to determine if maltreatment may have been a causal factor in an individual's disability... For example Elmer and Gregg (1967) in

---

82. In this paragraph I am capitalizing "Deaf" because throughout it I am referring to people connected through a cultural and linguistic community. If I were only referring to people with hearing disabilities, I would use lower case "deaf."

83. Deaf Hope. URL: http://www.deaf-hope.com

84. Erin Esposito, Keynote, Glimmer of Hope 2011. URL: http://www.deaf-hope.org/project/creating-the-miracle-of-accountability-erin-esposito-keynote-glimmer-of-hope-2011/

85. Balderian, N.J. (n.d.) *Abuse causes disability: A report from the Spectrum Institute.* Spectrum Institute, Culver City CA URL: https://archive.org/stream/ERIC_ED361929#page/n1/mode/2up

a follow-up study of physically abused children found that 50% had intellectual disabilities, but the study could not determine if the disability preceded or resulted from the abuse.[86]

Second, the presence of a disability increases the risk of victimization, partly due to impaired defenses and partly due to social responses to disability that increase risk. A 2003 California report showed that "people with disabilities are more likely to experience more severe abuse, experience abuse for a longer duration, be victims of multiple episodes, and be victims of a larger number of perpetrators."[87]

Restrictive settings and isolation also increase levels of abuse. The report also found that "While many feel that living in the community carries inherent risks, it is notable that some studies have found that crime rates are higher for victims with disabilities in institutions, group homes and other segregated facilities."[88]

Finally, most research over the past two decades has found that lack of the assurance of safety when reporting abuse, and lack of action by the people receiving the abuse reports, appears to increase risk for both violence and disability.[89]

I'm going to end by listing a few of the hundreds of disabled murder victims of the past few years. Some were murdered by their families and caregivers, others by police, and some by school districts.[90] In each case, the disabled person was unarmed. They were murdered "in cold blood" without any way to prevent the murder or protect themselves. As of this date, few of their abusers have been convicted of murder.

Tracy Latimer, 12 years old, gassed by her father, 1993. Wilkie, Saskatchewan. Robert Latimer served 7 years in prison for second-degree murder.

Idriss Stelley, 23 years old, killed 6-12-01 by police during a mental health intervention.

Isabella Herrera, 7 years of age, died after school bus driver failed to properly secure her wheelchair in January 2014.

86. Sobsey, see notes 1 & 2.

87. See note 25.

88. *Abuse and Neglect in California.* URL: http://www.disabilityrightsca.org/pubs/701901.pdf

89. Sobsey, see notes 1 & 2.

90. Brown, Lydia. (2 March, 2013). *Honoring the dead.* URL: http://www.autistichoya.com/2013/03/honoring-dead.html; Also at: http://www.Ollibean.org;

Jared Greenwood, 26, died of infected bed sores after being left in place and neglected by his mother. Bloomfield, NM. Sandra Greenwood was sentenced to serve two and a half years in prison for second-degree neglect. September 2007.

Richard Tims, 28 years old, March 15 2002, AIDS dementia, killed by police at a bus stop.

Anita Gay, 54 years old, schizophrenic, killed by police.

Christian Clay Jenkins, 14, given an overdose of oxycodone by his father. November 2008. Oak Hill, West Virginia. Henry Clay Jenkins was sentenced to life in prison with a possibility of parole for first-degree murder and child neglect resulting in death. However, the judge made a "mercy recommendation," meaning Jenkins will be eligible for parole after serving 18 years.

Damien Veraghen, 9 years old, poisoned and suffocated by his mother in a murder-suicide in January 2014.

Jennifer Caballero, 11 years of age, went missing from the middle school and was found dead six hours later in October 2013.

Angelica Auriemma, 20 years old, drowned by her mother, who first tried to electrocute her daughter to death. December 2013. Brooklyn, NY. Ioanna Auriemma served three years in prison for killing her daughter.

Keith Coty, 6 years old, died after school staff delayed in getting him help for a medical emergency, 2014.

Charles-Antoine Blais, 6 years old, drowned by his mother, November 1996. Montreal. Danielle Blais pled guilty to manslaughter and was sentenced to live in a halfway house for one year. She was then hired as a spokesperson for Montreal's autism society.

Peter Eitzen, 16, stabbed by his mother, July 2009. Blackiston, Australia. Beverley Ellen Eitzen was charged with murder but was acquitted because the judge found that she had been suffering a "major depressive episode" at the time of the murder.

Casey Albury, 17 years old, strangled by her mother, 1997. Feilding, NZ. Janine Albury-Thompson was convicted of manslaughter and sentenced to four years in prison, but her sentence was reduced to 18 months.

Pierre Pasquiou, 10 years old, pushed into the sea by his mother, 1998. Saint-Brieuc, France. Anne Pasquiou was given a three-year suspended sentence and served no jail time.

JUST THE FACTS MA'AM

70-85% of all parents who receive a prenatal diagnosis of Down Syndrome choose to abort.

Abuse is a daily part of life for disabled people.

96% of abusers are known to their disabled victim prior to the abuse.

In 2012 there were 1.3 million nonfatal violent crimes against disabled people.

RESOURCES

Curriculum on Abuse Prevention and Empowerment (CAPE). URL: http://wid.org/access-to-health-care/health-access-and-long-term-services/curriculum-on-abuse-prevention-and-empowerment-cape

Groce, N.E. (2005). *Summary report: Violence against disabled children.* UNICEF, United Nations, NY. URL: http://www.unicef.org/videoaudio/PDFs/UNICEF_Violence_Against_Disabled_Children_Report_Distributed_Version.pdf

Roguski, M. (2013). *The hidden abuse of disabled people residing in the community: An exploratory study.* Gisborne: Tairawhiti Community Voice. URL: http://www.communityresearch.org.nz/research/the-hidden-abuse-of-disabled-people-residing-in-the-community-an-exploratory-study/

Sobsey, Richard. (1994). *Violence and abuse in the lives of people with disabilities: The end of silent acceptance?* Paul H Brookes Publishing, Baltimore, MD

STAND! *How to Help Someone Who is Being Abused.* URL: http://www.standagainstdv.org/stayinformed/needtoknow_how.html

A full bibliography is available at my website: www.corbettotoole.com

9.

From Berkeley to Beijing

"Disabled women's issues are women's issues."
                    — Disabled Women: Visions and Voices (Video).[1]

Summary

In 1995 the United Nations held a worldwide conference on women in Beijing, China. Disabled women from around the world decided to go. I organized the North American disabled women and 50 of us went to Beijing.

In Beijing we held our own one-day conference, the International Disabled Women's Symposium. We attended the NGO Forum, which was for community organizations (the government people had a separate conference that I did not attend). The NGO Forum had over 30,000 women, 5,000 workshops and lasted for 10 days. There were a lot of access barriers at the NGO Forum and disabled women had to work hard to create access. Disabled women taught workshops to other women, disabled and nondisabled. Our time together in Beijing created networks that built an international movement of disabled women that continues today.

A tall Native American woman sits upright in her manual wheelchair at the foot of a long, steep stone staircase as I take her picture. The bright

---

1.   Levine, S. & Chadwick P. (1996). *Disabled women: Visions and voices from the 4th world conference on women.* [Online video]. Wide Vision Productions. San Francisco CA. URL: https://www.youtube.com/watch?v=adfHKfZdvzI&feature=youtu.be

sun illuminates her dark face and the basket hat she wears. Six Chinese men stand just out of the picture's frame, waiting to lift her up those stairs. She's leading a group of 40 disabled women up to the top of the Great Wall of China.

This image symbolizes disabled women's journey from our U.S. homes to the U.N. Forum on Women in Beijing,[2] China. Jene McCovey (disabled), a member of the Yurok Tribe from rural northern California, rarely travels outside the U.S. When she does, she always uses her power wheelchair. Yet she is far from home, at the base of dozens of stone steps, willingly allowing herself to be carried up to the top of the wall.

Jene came to Beijing to join over 200 other disabled women from around the world for the U.N. Non-Governmental Organization (NGO) Forum on Women. During the three weeks the disabled women were in China, we hosted an International Disabled Women's Symposium, attended the NGO Forum for Women, created the first Forum protest, recorded interviewed women from around the world and created a video commemorating it all.[3]

After decades of work by women, the United Nations finally decided to organize conferences on women's roles and rights. They held World Conferences on Women in Mexico City (1975), Copenhagen (1980), and Nairobi (1985). Disabled women had been excluded from them all by the total lack of access. When the U.N. announced there would be a fourth conference in Beijing in 1995, disabled women from around the world decided to attend.

The U.N. organized these conferences on two levels: the governmental conference, called The Fourth World Conference on Women, and the Non-Governmental (NGO) Forum on Women, which the disabled women would be attending. In what became the largest U.N. gathering in history, over 30,000 people, mostly women, held 5,000 official workshops during the 10 day Forum in Huairou,[4] a small town 35 miles outside Beijing.

For two years women's organizations around the world held local

---

2. The U.N. scheduled both the government conference and the NGO Forum in Beijing. In April, five months before the NGO Forum, the Chinese government announced that they were moving the NGO Forum to Huairou, a town 35 miles from Beijing. So while most reports of the NGO Forum talk about "Beijing," because that is where we slept, the actual Forum happened in Huairou.

3. See note 1.

4. When the Chinese government decided to move the NGO Forum, all the approved housing was in Beijing. They controlled what vehicles the NGO participants could travel in to get there, and closed the roads to prevent any deviations. They also severely restricted visas. A number of feminist filmmakers did not get visas to attend and document the NGO Forum.

and regional meetings to teach women's groups how to participate in the upcoming NGO Forum. Disabled women who attended these meetings reported a complete lack of accessibility to the meetings and a resistance by the meeting organizers to provide access, even in countries with strong disability access laws. The message was delivered even more clearly when, on behalf of disabled women in the U.S., I approached the U.S. planning committee and was told directly, "There are not enough resources for disabled women. We won't be providing any access or fighting with the Chinese government for access at the NGO Forum. Your people should not attend." Undeterred, over 200 disabled women from around the world attended the NGO Forum.

Although this discouraging response from national women's organizations was disappointing, it was not unexpected. Organized women's groups in the U.S. rarely provided access without significant pressure from disabled women. Twenty years of actively educating these groups and providing disability resources for them had done very little to change the perception by women's groups that disabled women were a burden and not an asset. Beijing was just more of the same.

Key organizers for disabled women planned for Beijing by providing our own access. We Brailled our own materials, brought our own sign language interpreters, had our own public speaking systems, paid for personal care attendants, and generally anticipated being on our own for access—which, in fact, proved to be the case. When Hillary Clinton, then First Lady, came to speak, she was required by American law to have American Sign Language interpreters at every public speaking event, but the nondisabled women organizers had made no commitment to accessibility, so Ms. Clinton's staff found out that we had ASL interpreters and asked to borrow ours. We graciously loaned them and requested that she acknowledge they were from our group, which she did.

Arriving in Beijing

I discovered quickly that the Chinese government, faced with an international gathering of feminists, made ridiculous assumptions that they enforced with a heavy hand.[5] I was the U.S. disabled women's organizer, and it was like being in a carnival house of mirrors. I felt overwhelmed and disoriented. I never knew when the next horrible-thing-that-I-had-to-deal-with would happen. Our first taste of being in

---

5. Some assumptions: feminists = lesbians = AIDS; spraying DDT would stop the spread of AIDS; feminists will strip naked anywhere. This meant that Chinese people who interacted with the feminists carried a sheet to cover the naked body quickly.

Beijing was at the airport. We arrived after 16 hours of travel from San Francisco to Tokyo, followed by a change of planes to Beijing. The plane was late, we were tired and desperately needed sleep. I anticipated that the biggest hassle would be getting a gaggle of disabled women, many of whom use wheelchairs, off the plane. I was wrong, oh so wrong. My epic Beijing nightmare was just about to begin.

The plane jetway led us to the second floor of the airport where there were two elevators side-by-side. They both went down one level and opened on the first floor. There was a painted line on the floor between the elevators. The distance between the two elevator doors was about a foot (12 inches, 3.48 cm). The left elevator was broken and had not worked for over two years. The right elevator worked fine.

Got the image? Side by side elevators—left one broken, right one working.

We assembled the 40 women, mostly disabled, at the elevator area. A United Airlines staff person, a very personable white man in his mid-30s, helped us to get oriented. He said we had to go downstairs to be processed in Customs. Those who could navigate three flights of stone steps began to head down. I led the rest of us towards the elevators. A Chinese security guard stepped in front of the elevators and pointed towards the stairs, clearly indicating that we should go that way.

I turned to the United Airlines guy and said that would not work for us. Some of our folks were pretty fragile, and even if they weren't, getting our people down three flights of stone steps was impossible. He explained that the left (broken) elevator was inside the painted line designating the Customs area on the first floor but the right (working) elevator was outside the Customs area. He started to sweat while he said that we had to go down the stairs. I conveyed his message to the other women, who now numbered about 20.

Many of these women ran organizations. They were not meek and compliant. They shook their heads showing their refusal to use the stairs. After all the elevators were side by side, the Chinese security staff could watch us move the two feet from one side of the line to the other once we exited downstairs. I turned back to the United Airlines guy and said "No way. That elevator is working (pointing to the one on the right), we are taking the elevator." He glanced over his shoulder at the guard and said, "There is absolutely no way they are allowing you to use that elevator. If you don't take the stairs they will arrest you or worse."

We were incredulous. We had traveled to attend an international conference with thousands of women. They wouldn't dare arrest us. We were wrong. Oh so wrong.

We spent the next 40 minutes fighting with them. It got so

contentious that the United Airlines guy started to cry because he feared what would happen to us. I was more afraid that a woman would be dropped and hurt, because the Chinese security officer had sent a group of men up the stairs to us, they surrounded one woman, reached down and began to lift her wheelchair. She attempted to show them where to hold so they could lift her safely.[6] They ignored her, as did their supervisor. She turned to us and asked for help. We surrounded the men and politely indicated that they should let go of her wheelchair. It was clear that not only did the men not have any training in how to do this safely but they were also being instructed to ignore our expert advice. This created a significant safety issue.

We talked among ourselves as each wheelchair rider made her own decision. Some of us got out of our manual wheelchairs and slid down the stairs on our butts while the men took our empty wheelchairs down the stairs. The women with enough strength and balance to carry a woman and her wheelchair volunteered to help. Disabled women gave explicit instructions and the volunteer women slowly carried them down the three flights of stairs. Getting us all downstairs took a long time, which also displeased the Customs and Security people who were forced to wait to process us. We did not win. We got a tiny taste of what it means when you have no disability rights. I wish I could say that was our last negative experience, but instead it was only the first hurdle on our trip.

Symposium

The disabled women who traveled to Beijing came with a fire for social justice and a desire to share knowledge. They'd spent a year raising the money to be there, and every minute together was precious. Everyone came a few days early to attend the First International Symposium on Issues of Women with Disabilities, with over 200 women representing 25 countries.

Everyone took the Symposium very seriously. Relying on email, with a supplemental fax or letter, we'd planned this Symposium across the globe. Each non-U.S. woman there was a designated leader in her region. Each came with stories and insights gathered from hundreds of women dealing with disabilities of their own or of a family member.

The depth of knowledge these women held about the international situation for disabled women was unsurpassed anywhere in the world.

6. Some parts of a wheelchair such as the armrests and footrests are designed to come off. If someone attempts to lift a wheelchair incorrectly using those parts, the part will disconnect from the wheelchair and the rest of the wheelchair, along with the person in it, will fall to the ground.

Here they were, all in one small, tin roofed room. We didn't mind that there were 200 women trying to communicate, or that only a few women spoke each of the 35 languages, or that the rains would pound the roof so hard we had to stop talking until the storm passed. We didn't care about the intense heat, the humidity, or the offensive sign outside the door that said "International deformity unite conference is here."[7] After a year of planning and fundraising, we were thrilled to be in the same room with each other.

As so often happened in international gatherings of the 1990s, the U.S. women dominated as organizers, speakers, and number of participants from one country. Susan Sygall (disabled)[8] from Mobility International USA (MIUSA),[9] Kathy Martinez (disabled)[10] from the World Institute on Disability,[11] and Kikki Nordstrom (disabled) from the World Blind Union[12] were the keynote speakers. Cindy Lewis (nondisabled) from MIUSA and I provided the facilitation. The goal of the day was to encourage women to share knowledge, to identify key issues, and to create talking points to focus on at the NGO Forum. We had not seen the town of Huairou yet so we had no idea of the enormous access barriers we would encounter at the Forum, but we already knew from our airport arrival that the Chinese government would not make our lives easier.

The day opened with introductions from each woman, which took a while and impressed all of us. So many women from so many places

---

7. Thanks to photographer Suzanne Levine (disabled) for finding a photograph of the sign.

8. "Susan has received numerous awards for her passionate advocacy for disability rights. In 2013, she became an Ashoka Senior Fellow and received recognition of her work in 2011 by being awarded the Kellogg Fellows Leadership Alliance Matusak Courageous Leadership Award and receiving an honorary doctorate from Chapman University. In 2000, she received the prestigious MacArthur Fellowship [nicknamed the 'genius grant']. In 1995, Sygall received the President's Award from President Bill Clinton for her dynamic leadership in international exchange programs for people with disabilities, for her mentorship of young people with disabilities, and for her active role throughout our country and the world in empowering people with disabilities. Sygall has also been honored with the Rotary Scholar Alumni Achievement Award, the Humanitarian Award from the Jewish Federation, and a Women to Watch Award from the *Jewish Woman Magazine*. She was also awarded a Graduate Rotary Scholarship and the Kellogg National Fellowship, which is awarded to approximately 40 outstanding leaders each year in the United States." Source URL: http://www.miusa.org/staff

9. Mobility International USA: Advancing disability rights and leadership globally. URL: http://www.miusa.org

10. Kathy Martinez is currently Assistant Secretary of Labor for Disability Employment Policy. URL: http://www.dol.gov/odep/AssistantSecretary.htm

11. "The mission of the World Institute on Disability (WID) in communities and nations worldwide is to eliminate barriers to full social integration and increase employment, economic security and health care for persons with disabilities." Source URL: http://wid.org/about-wid

12. "The World Blind Union (WBU) is the global organization representing the estimated 285 million people worldwide who are blind or partially sighted." Source URL: http://www.worldblindunion.org

had made it to Beijing, and into this room. Women came from all parts of the globe and all disability groups. Here we were sitting together in a stuffy room on a military facility in Beijing. Nearly all of us had been told we were not worthwhile human beings at one point in our lives. Yet here we sat, part of this historic international gathering poised to articulate and document the situation for disabled women throughout the world.

I had goosebumps as I sat in the front of the room looking out at the 200 women. My heart swelled and my words disappeared. I was witnessing history being made and I was part of it, and not because someone outside had funded us. We made it here, to this noisy room, on this day, because we had decided to be here. We had been discouraged from attending Mexico City and Copenhagen and Nairobi. We would not be discouraged from Beijing.

The U.S. Women provided the framework for the day. Susan Sygall (disabled), started the day celebrating that today was the anniversary of the day she became disabled. She talked about the opportunities she had been given, the places she went, the people who influenced her— all because she became disabled. We all nodded with deep understanding.

Whether we had been born with our disabilities or acquired them, we all agreed that being disabled opened doors that were not available to nondisabled people. Yes, we all knew the hardships that came with being in an oppressed group, but Susan offered a different story that we all also experienced—those moments when disability opened our lives, and did not close them. We had all had those moments and rarely could we share them, since they ran counter to the stereotypes that our lives as disabled women were tragic.

Laura Hershey (disabled), who'd attended the previous NGO meeting in Nairobi 10 years earlier, wrote a 1997 article where she stated that she would not take a magic pill to make herself nondisabled, because her disability experiences created and shaped her life—and she liked her life.[13] We all wished for less discrimination, fewer obstacles, but those happened because of how society treated us, not because of our bodymind differences. She wrote that article confident that she reflected a wider view because of how we all responded to Susan's story. It didn't matter how we came to disability, only that we accepted that our differences were ok, that problems came mostly from ableism, and that we wished more people knew and shared our viewpoint.

---

13. Laura Hershey. *From Poster Child to Protestor.* Originally published in the Spring/Summer 1997 issue of *Spectacle,* published by Pachanga Press, Burlington MA. URL: http://cripcommentary.com/frompost.html

Most of the U.S. women that came with my group had little international experience. They held typical beliefs that disabled women in the U.S. had the best resources in the world. They were shocked to learn from the international disabled women about the advantages of universal health care, paid maternity leave, and sophisticated regional and national disabled women's networks. We soon realized that other countries faced similar issues based more on their national support systems than on their geographic locations or economic status. Non-U.S. women whose only knowledge was through American media were shocked by the serious problems that American women faced, such as no universal health care, extensive poverty and restrictions on getting food and shelter. The Japanese gave everyone technology envy when they pulled out tiny wireless microphones and headsets and began translating the English speakers.

After a few more introductory keynotes, we broke up into small groups to discuss issues such as health care, education, employment, preventing violence, and parenting. Arranging the groups took a bit of time, since we needed enough women with shared languages to be able to communicate within each small group. Sometimes we had two or more groups discussing the same topic but in different languages. Most, if not all, of the non-U.S. women knew multiple languages and often served as interpreters between language groups. Dorothy Musakanya (disabled) was particularly valuable, since as a disability community organizer in southern Africa she worked in many countries and knew 10 spoken and 3 signed languages.

Around the world, many countries had national disability organizations. Although the disabled men usually dominated, many disabled women ran projects with and for other disabled women. Although the richest country in the world, in many areas the U.S. provided much less for disabled people—fewer safety nets for health care, housing, food, benefits—than many other countries. South Africa's recent Constitution guaranteed disabled people civil rights. Uganda had a Minister of Disability and Elderly Affairs and disability rights were named in the Constitution. Many northern hemisphere countries, particularly the Scandinavians, had long-term programs supporting southern hemisphere disability work. The U.S. women who'd believed that they would be sharing knowledge and be seen as the teachers, soon realized that in many situations they had the least to offer.

Disabled women from the U.S. were also the least sophisticated of the participants. All the other disabled women attending the Symposium had organized regional and national events and represented national organizations. The U.S. women led local groups and organized regional events. Few had any international experience, in contrast to the non-U.S. women who all had international experience.

Prior to Beijing, the opportunities for disabled women to come together with other disabled women rarely happened at the international level. Local and regional events occurred, but the ability to attend international events outside your region was a privilege that few disabled women had the financial or political clout to pull off. Nearly all international disability work was run by and for disabled men. The women who got to Beijing had worked with neighboring countries but rarely left their region, so coming to Beijing was a major event.

When the lunch break arrived, I gladly left the stifling building. Outside the meeting room a huge stone plaza slowly dried from the morning's rainstorm, leaving wide shallow puddles. I took off my shoes, picked up my daughter Joy (disabled), and rolled through the puddles dragging our feet in the cool water. Suzanne Levine took a photo of us that remains a treasured memory of that moment and hangs on my living room wall. In that photo, I wear the t-shirt that Pat Chadwick (nondisabled) designed to help us raise money for this trip. A large globe centers the shirt design with silhouettes of a blind woman walking with a guide dog, a woman riding a wheelchair with her arms above her head in a victorious "V", and a woman walking alone surrounded by the words "Disabled Women Change the World ... From Berkeley to Beijing."

Disabled Women's Tent

At the NGO Forum, women's groups who preregistered were assigned a "tent," which meant a flat concrete platform with pillars around the perimeter that held up a tin roof. There were no walls on the structures. The tents varied in size and were located throughout the town of Huairou.

Initially, the disabled women were assigned a tent in a remote area. Because the government only had a few months to build the tents, and these structures were designed to be temporary, the "walkways" to the tents consisted of flat stones, between one and two feet wide, placed near each other but not attached in any permanent way. Attempting to cross the rough stone surfaces with a wheelchair meant constantly having the front wheels fall into the spaces between the stones. It was a very slow and painful way to move. Rain fell daily during the Forum in Huairou, so very quickly the stones became tilted and unstable. The spaces between the stones filled with rainwater, washing away any dirt that might've provided a smoother surface.

The location of the Disabled Women's Tent was at the top of the hill, so the women who used wheelchairs and mobility devices had to roll across the uneven and widely spaced stones while going uphill. It became immediately apparent to us that most of the women with mobility devices were never going to be able to reach the Disabled Women's Tent. Some members of our group who could walk went and found the Forum's administrative offices, and after days of negotiating, got us moved to a different location. Of course, this meant displacing the women who were assigned to that tent, which did not endear us to them.

Our second tent was approximately 40 feet wide by 100 feet long and located on a main Forum route. The bricks there had more stability, and although it continued to be challenging it was flat enough that all of the disabled women could get to the new tent. For most disabled women, particularly those with mobility disabilities, the Disabled Women's Tent was the only place in the forum that was accessible to them.

The 5000 workshops spread over 10 days were all in inaccessible locations. Many of the disabled women faced a significant problem in figuring out how to participate with the nondisabled women. We held strategy meetings in the tent and decided that we would send representatives to all of the sessions marked for disabled women. Not only would we request that the session move itself to the Disabled Women's Tent, but we also offered signs that explained in English the new location of the workshop and why we had moved. Many workshop leaders accepted our generous offer and moved their session to the Disabled Women's Tent.[14]

Not all sessions had to be moved, because the sessions we planned after we arrived in China were held in the Disabled Women's Tent. When some of the major speakers became aware of the access barriers, they chose to hold their meetings or talks in the Disabled Women's Tent. In acknowledgement of disabled women's struggles, Madeleine Albright, United States Ambassador to the U.N., gave her internationally broadcast speech in the Disabled Tent.[15]

---

14. We had no ability to plan the moves in advance. Workshop leader names were provided, but no one had a working cell phone, nor were the leaders' contact information listed in the program. So moves had to occur at the beginning of each session. In a few cases, particularly on the later days of the Forum, workshop leaders were aware of the problem, came by the Disabled Women's Tent to schedule space for their workshop and took our signs to notify workshop participants of the change in location.

15. Madeleine Albright was the first woman to represent the U.S. in regards to foreign affairs as the Secretary of State.

Bella Abzug, one of the first women in the U.S. Congress, was a distinguished elder in the women's movement.[16] She had co-founded the National Women's Political Caucus and led many of the women's efforts to encourage the U.N. to take a stronger stand in support of women's rights. By 1995 her body no longer supported her easily and she used a manual wheelchair, but she never spoke to women's groups from her wheelchair. She would be pushed to the door and then stand and walk in to give her presentation. I met her at one of the Preparation Committee meetings and discussed disability politics with her. I honestly didn't think it was making any difference.

When she arrived at the Forum, her staff approached us to ask if she could give her keynote presentation from the Disabled Women's Tent. We were thrilled. She had many responsibilities and gave many well-attended talks at the Forum. When she gave her presentation in the Disabled Women's Tent, she spoke while she sat in her wheelchair. She talked about the struggles of women, the need for change, and about being a woman with a disability. It was a moment I did not expect to see and I was really grateful to be there to witness it.

The Forum provided a rare opportunity for disabled women to get professional skills trainings. Jan Sing (nondisabled) from Whirlwind Wheelchairs[17] taught a build-your-own-manual-wheelchair class.[18] Women cut steel pipes, bent steel for frames, welded pieces together, made spokes for the large drive wheels, and sewed fabric for the seat. Many disabled women had never touched a screwdriver much less welding and power tools, but Jan guided them through the safety procedures and soon the women, working together, built a wheelchair together. People walking by often stared at the women as they worked. Few had seen disabled women employed, much less using tools

---

16. Bella Abzug, one of the most colorful American activists to emerge from the 1960s, often claimed to have been born yelling. She ran for the United States Congress in 1970 on a peace and feminism platform, and represented her Manhattan district from 1971 to 1976. She died in 1998. Her biography can be found on the Jewish Women's Archive. URL: http://jwa.org/womenofvalor/abzug

17. URL: http://www.whirlwindwheelchair.org/

18. Ralf Hotchkiss taught this class at SFSU for many years and invited community people to take it. In his class each person built their own wheelchair. I'd taken his class years ago. Bending and welding steel requires concentration and skill. I learned the skills during the class, although cutting the steel at the correct angles for attaching the caster wheel always eluded me, and I depended on others to mark the steel for me. I loved welding even though the safety table was at the height of my chest and sparks often flew in the direction of my face. I felt protected in the welder's helmet, gloves and apron, and I never got hurt. For sheer Superman-posing, nothing beats bending steel. A central metal spool was bolted to the workshop floor with the top forming a flat surface. We'd add the dies needed for the bends required—different ones for bending the side frame and hand rims. Sitting down did not provide the needed leverage so Ralf rigged up a car jack and I used that to bend the steel around the dies. I never felt stronger or more butch than I did in that class.

typically associated with men. For these women, building this wheelchair was the highlight of the Forum, and many requested the photographers to document their work so they could show the people back home.

Judi Rogers (disabled), a woman with walking cerebral palsy and one of very few U.S. health professionals with a disability, had shaped her Occupational Therapy skills into an expertise on disabled women taking care of young babies. She'd developed numerous pieces of equipment to make diapering, feeding and carrying a baby much easier for disabled women. She even used my then 2-year old daughter, Joy (disabled), as her "model" to show various baby care techniques such as diapering, feeding and bathing. Her expertise made her a highly sought resource.

While there were many formal classes and speeches, the majority of the time disabled women were networking and sharing resources informally. Every day of the Forum women worked, teaching and taking classes from each other.

The tent provided unexpected opportunities for connection. Sarah (disabled) arrived one day with her mother. Sarah lived in England and had left school twice because of bullies. She felt isolated from other teens and disabled adults. We rapidly embraced her, since other than my daughter, Joy, there were no disabled children at the Forum. After a few minutes of conversation, it was clear that Sarah was competent and resourceful. She was immediately drafted to be Joy's babysitter. I was very busy at the Forum and although the group shared care of Joy, I also wanted to attend workshops, make videos, and network with other participants. Sarah showing up was an advantage to us both—she got paid work (a first in her life), she did not have to follow her mom to boring (to her) workshops, and I got a break from childcare.

To me this was the most significant achievement of the forum— women sitting together sharing their experience and knowledge, building an international community, valuing each other's skills, and negotiating through their similarities and differences.

This networking could happen because we planned for accessibility. At the Symposium, disabled women identified their language skills and we kept a list of who could communicate in which languages. Our interpreters from the U.S. not only spoke American Sign Language but also the International Sign Language,[19] Gestuno.[20] We also brought people who could fix wheelchairs, provide personal attendant services,

---

19. Rights of sign language. URL: http://wfdeaf.org/human-rights/crpd/sign-language

20. Gestuno is a sign language designed for the same purpose as the spoken language Esperanto—to allow people to have one language that is spoken by everyone.

read and write Braille, and communicate with plain language. Each disabled woman was encouraged to ask for the access she needed, and collectively we did our best to provide it. So while everyone did not get the full access that they might have had at home, everyone got enough access to participate fully at the forum.

As our visibility increased, nondisabled women soon learned about the access challenges we were facing. Many of them came by the Disabled Women's Tent for conversation and networking. In one memorable conversation we brought together an international funder, who was funding a women's economic development program in Zimbabwe through a women's organization, and a disabled woman, who was leading disabled women's economic work, but who was not on the radar of the local women's organization. That one conversation built a bridge that dramatically increased economic development options for disabled women in Zimbabwe.

Sometimes I think that bad weather is a great ally for creating and encouraging communication and networking. Huairou and Beijing were blisteringly hot the entire time we were there. Complaining about the weather and helping each other in preventing heat-related illnesses created fundamental human bonds that quickly smoothed over political and regional differences.

Forum Protest

Since the government seemed very cautious of the NGO folks, as evidenced by the sudden move of the NGO Forum from Beijing to Huairou, there was a requirement that all taxis that went to the Forum had a large sheet stored within easy reach of the driver so that when, as they feared, we took off our clothes on the streets of Beijing, they could easily and quickly cover us. The drivers received training to identify specific English words such as 'protest.' The extensive tent area was sprayed nightly with DDT to, as they told us, "stop the spread of AIDS that the women carried, especially the lesbians." We didn't know whether to laugh or cry at the poisoning of the land and our bodyminds or the massive disinformation about AIDS.

DDT was also used around the military hotel to 'manage' the plants. The smokestack, where all garbage was burned daily, was shorter than the surrounding hotel buildings, so the smoke went into our rooms as well as into the sky. At that time, Beijing was already on the 'top ten most polluted cities in the world' list. Just before the cameras arrived for the opening of the governmental U.N. Conference on Women, the

Chinese government ordered the thousands of incinerators to stop running so that the sky over Beijing would not look so polluted on international television.

Hotel staff and police went through our luggage daily. Even the normally exempt international television personnel had their rooms searched every single day. There was no attempt to hide the searching. We all learned to bring anything important with us each time we left the hotel.

As was typical of the way the Chinese government handled the Forum, there was a designated "Protest Area" far from the main Forum areas. Frustrated with all the access and other problems of the conference, we decided to stage a protest. Since the Protest Area had no accessible pathways, we held our protest in the central part of the Forum, which gave us a lot of media coverage. We handed out flyers stating the access problems and asking women's groups to commit to make access a priority.

To say that we were frustrated with the pervasive lack of accessibility did not even begin to scratch the surface of our displeasure.[21] The lack of access to the elevator at the airport set the stage for our time in China. Since no conference transit had any wheelchair accessibility, we paid the Chinese government for a bus to transport us to and from Huairou. The bus had only a few seats and no way to secure our wheelchairs. On the bus, we rattled along the bumpy crowded roads an hour each way from Beijing to Huairou, jamming our wheelchairs against each other and hoping that we were not hurled across the bus. There were twenty of us crammed into each one, accompanied by the omnipresent government monitors who brought college students studying special education as our "helpers."

One memorable day, the rains came early and very hard, so we decided to leave Huairou at noon. We took our soaking wet bodies to the bus where we discovered that today's bus had no windows, so the rain came inside. Tired and more than a bit cranky, we expected to go back to the hotel, but the handlers decided to punish us for protesting outside the official and remote protest area. So we sat wet with the rain coming in, while the Chinese students went into a local cafeteria and had their lunch hour. When we asked to leave, we were told to be grateful that we had a ride back and that the bus would leave when the handler decided. After sitting in the rain for hours a number of us got

---

21. By the end of the trip I had absorbed so many traumas that when I came back to the U.S. I was unable to enter a Chinese restaurant or to be around Chinese businesses for nearly a year. While I am thrilled with the work of the disabled women, my personal survival of the trip was precarious.

sick with colds. Some of our immune systems began to deteriorate and we developed air pollution sickness.

As we expected, we were punished for protesting outside the designated Protest Area. Our buses were cut off for a day. Only repeated complaints and the support of the hotel manager got them returned.

Forum Video

Disabled women documented the Symposium and Forum with video, photos, interviews, research, and audio recordings. I decided that I wanted to videotape short interviews with some of the international disabled women. I built a three person video crew. I found the folks I wanted to interview and asked them the questions. My 2 1/2 year old daughter, Joy, played quietly by my side throughout the filming.

This was my first big video project.[22.] In the early 1990s a few disabled folks had died in my Berkeley disabled community without leaving an oral history, most notably Ed Roberts in April 1995. I realized the importance of capturing disabled women's oral histories. I didn't have much money to do this, but then I never do, so I planned on doing thirty-minute interviews with whoever appealed to me. That really was my criteria—to find disabled women whose stories interested me and then get them on videotape. I would later record other interviews at other sites, but this was my first. I'd raised money to buy a decent VHS recorder and Pat (nondisabled), the sound person, brought her own radio-production quality sound system.

I deeply believe in the power of women telling their own stories, unfiltered through a reporter or a video editor. I wanted women to just look into the camera and talk about what was important to them, in their country, at this time. Since so many disabled folks do not work, my question was never "What are you working on?" but instead more generally "What is interesting you these days? What is important to you as a disabled woman?"

The women talked with open hearts. Most had never been videotaped before, so I worked hard to make them comfortable. We used small lapel microphones that clipped onto their shirt so they could soon forget about the microphone. I sat next to the video camera so they could talk directly to me and not have to stare at the camera. If the woman didn't speak English or American Sign Language, then we asked

---

22. These videos are being uploaded and will be available as a supplement to the book. See www.CorbettOToole.com for additional information.

a disabled woman who spoke her language to be the interviewer. We'd fuss over the set up, but once we turned on the camera we all did our best to be unobtrusive.

Poignant stories fell out of their mouths and souls. Women talked about how the incorrect use of anesthesia caused nondisabled women to become disabled during their labor and delivery of their babies; how when they became disabled their husband and children permanently left them as per the local custom; of disabled women raped while the community took no action, even when it was reported; of the lack of opportunities to participate in either the projects of nondisabled women or disabled men. These women were on the front lines of fighting for disabled women's rights and services, although they were unpaid and often unrecognized for their incredibly hard work.

While other filmmakers interviewed people for the purpose of fitting them into the filmmakers' pre-written script, I deeply believe in the necessity of disabled women telling the stories that are important to them. Having unfiltered interviews provides invaluable insights into the lives and communities of disabled women from around the world. I continued videotaping disabled women at the 1997 International Leadership Forum for Women with Disabilities in Washington, the 1998 Changing Borders: Women with Disabilities Learning from Each Other, and the 2000 Employment of American Indian Women with Disabilities Meeting.[23]

Post-Beijing

Although some of the issues important to disabled women got included in The Beijing Declaration and Platform for Action,[24] by and large disabled women and our issues continued to be ignored by women's organizations both in the U.S. and internationally.[25] We met with

23. See note 22.

24. The Beijing Declaration and the Platform for Action, adopted unanimously by 189 countries, is an agenda for women's empowerment, and it is considered the key global policy document on gender equality. It sets strategic objectives and actions for the advancement of women and the achievement of gender equality in 12 critical areas of concern: Women and poverty; Education and training of women; Women and health; Violence against women; Women and armed conflict; Women and the economy; Women in power and decision-making; Institutional mechanism for the advancement of women; Human rights of women; Women and the media; Women and the environment; and The girl-child. Source URL: http://www.unwomen.org/en/how-we-work/intergovernmental-support/world-conferences-on-women#sthash.JEvemjjF.dpuf

25. Follow-up to Beijing:

2000: The General Assembly decided to hold a 23rd special session to conduct a five-year review and appraisal of the implementation of the Beijing Platform for Action, and to consider future

funders who supported women's projects but did not include any women with disabilities—even after we connected them to disabled women in their funding area.

The International Leadership Forum for Women with Disabilities in Washington, D.C., in 1997 brought together 612 women from 80 countries.[26] This work built directly on the Disabled Women's Symposium. The D.C. Forum followed a more traditional international conference format of panels and plenaries rather than the Beijing Forum two years earlier. The Beijing Forum seeded the international disabled women's work that continues today.

Nancy Ward (disabled), who founded Self Advocates Becoming Empowered (SABE), saw me videotaping in D.C. and told me that I structured the video work like a sheltered workshop, paying my employees next to nothing but expecting fully employed skills and workload. I loved the irony of that statement, since Nancy had previously "worked" in a sheltered workshop for the typical payment of 12 cents an hour. She quit the day that they refused to hire her as the supervisor at the nondisabled pay (and status) and then hired an inexperienced nondisabled person and told Nancy to train her. I love that story. I love that Nancy knew when to kick their asses with their own oppression. I wish I had known her before Beijing so that she could have gone with us.

In 2002, Venus Ilagan (disabled) became the first woman Chairman

---

actions and initiatives. Women 2000: Gender Equality, Development, and Peace for the Twenty-First Century took place in New York, and resulted in a political declaration and further actions and initiatives to implement the Beijing commitments.

2005: A 10-year review and appraisal of the Beijing Platform for Action was conducted as part of the 49th session of the Commission on the Status of Women. Delegates adopted a declaration emphasizing that the full and effective implementation of the Beijing Declaration and Platform for Action is essential to achieving the internationally agreed development goals, including those contained in the Millennium Declaration.

2010: The 15-year review of the Beijing Platform for Action took place during the Commission's 54th session in 2010. Member States adopted a declaration that welcomed the progress made towards achieving gender equality, and pledged to undertake further action to ensure the full and accelerated implementation of the Beijing Declaration and Platform for Action.

2015: In mid-2013, the U.N. Economic and Social Council requested the Commission on the Status of Women to review and appraise implementation of the Platform for Action in 2015, in a session known as Beijing+20. To inform deliberations, the Council also called on U.N. Member States to perform comprehensive national reviews, and encouraged regional commissions to undertake regional reviews. Source URL: http://www.unwomen.org/en/how-we-work/intergovernmental-support/world-conferences-on-women#sthash.JEvemjjF.dpuf

26. "The International Leadership Forum for Women with Disabilities was one of the most heralded, far reaching and successful events of 1997. Held June 15-20 in Washington, D.C., the Forum attracted legislators, artists, advocates, organizational executives, trainers, international assistance experts and grassroots development specialists from around the globe. All the world's cultures and regions were well represented in the group of 612 participants from 80 countries and territories" Source URL: http://wid.org/publications/downloads/INternational%20Leadership %20Forum%20June%201997%20Final%20Report.pdf

of Disabled Peoples' International, a U.N. recognized consultant group on disability. In 2002 the U.N. Convention on the Rights of Persons With Disabilities started working on an international document that included rights for disabled women, and after many years, in 2006 it was adopted by the U.N. and sent to individual countries for signatures. As of 2015 the U.S. still has not signed the convention, but over 150 other countries have done so.

In many ways disabled women's work continues to be the undervalued and neglected work of both the disability rights movement and the women's movement. At Beijing+5, a gathering five years after Beijing to assess progress, disabled women and our issues continued to be ignored and marginalized, as stated in the report.[27] At Beijing+15 in 2010, this trend continued. The number of individual disabled women and individual disabled women's organizations increased, but support from male dominated disability groups and women's groups continues to be minimal. Without these ongoing bases of support, projects to help disabled women continue to be short-term and underfunded around the world, and it falls to disabled women to continue the needed supports and services unpaid and unrecognized.

JUST THE FACTS MA'AM

1995 — U.N. Conference on Women in Beijing, China, and U.N. Non-Governmental Organization (NGO) Forum on Women in Huairou, China. Over 200 disabled women from around the world attend the Disabled Women's Symposium at the NGO Forum.

1997 — The International Leadership Forum for Women with Disabilities in Washington, D.C., brought together 612 women from 80 countries.

2006 — The U.N. Convention on the Rights of People With Disabilities is formulated. To date over 150 countries have signed it. The United States has not.

---

27. We made it to what I call the comma list ... refugees, disabled, seniors... but no commitment or action was ever taken The report may be viewed at this source URL: http://www.un.org/womenwatch/daw/followup/beijing+5.htm

RESOURCES

Freeman, J. (1996). *Beijing Report: The Fourth World Conference on Women*. Published as "The real story of Beijing." In *Off Our Backs* 26(3), 1, 8-11, 22-27.

Levine, S. & Chadwick P. (1996). *Disabled women: Visions and Voices From the 4th World Conference on Women*. [Online video]. Wide Vision Productions. San Francisco CA. URL: https://www.youtube.com/watch?v=adfHKfZdvzI&feature=youtu.be

A full bibliography is available at my website: www.corbettotoole.com

10.

Disability Queered

"If you must err, do so on the side of audacity." — Sue Monk Kidd[1]

Summary

In the 1970s as people in Berkeley, California built a disability rights movement, they asked queer people (lesbian, gay, transgendered, asexual, bisexual, and others) to help them. Many queers volunteered to help. Some queer people were disabled, some were not. But in 1982, when HIV/AIDS emerged, the queer communities asked the disabled rights movement for help. The disability rights movement did a little bit to help, but mostly ignored the people with HIV/AIDS.

I was a disabled queer working in the disability rights movement starting in 1974. I became very upset by the lack of support for queers in disability communities so I began to dream about a conference for disabled queers. In the year 2000 I worked with other disabled queers to create the first international Queer Disability Conference in San Francisco. Over 200 people attended the conference. In this essay, I write about the ways that being in that queer disabled space made me feel happy and fully welcomed. We ended the conference with a wild and fun dance.

I had no idea. I expected that I would be happy, intrigued, challenged. I never imagined that my whole body would vibrate, that my hips would swagger, that my nipples would stand at attention so often. I anticipated

1.   Kidd, S.M. (unknown). (2014) *The Invention of Wings*. Viking, New York, NY.

the intellectual challenge but not the liberation. Hyperbole you say. Nonsense, I reply. You were not there. You do not know what I mean. You think you can imagine but you cannot. What happened is too ephemeral.

I've been a disabled queer since 1974. I was part of the 1970s Berkeley disabled community—a very queer friendly space in those days. I had queer disabled friends, went to queer disabled parties. I thought I knew how freedom and wholeness felt. Then the Queer Disability (QD) Conference happened in San Francisco in 2002 and I realized how wrong I was. Well, I did not intellectually realize it—my body did.

At the QD Conference, sex permeated the entire space—the ways people glided into meeting rooms, the intimacy of queer space, the outrageously public flirting. Even though my conference experience primarily consisted of dealing with problems that inevitably arise at conferences, rarely attending a session or having time to just hang out and relax, I soon found myself flirting with participants as we passed each other on the walkways, exchanging approving looks, sharing smiles across the distances. We seemed to have agreed to queer norms where sexual energy was expected and appreciated.

I always thought I felt fully able to be queer in disability spaces, but the QD Conference showed me how much I had inhibited myself. The week after the Conference I went to the movies with Linda (nondisabled), an old friend. I started to comment on her cute ass, out loud, in a flirty voice but as soon as I began to speak my thoughts I realized that was not allowed. That freedom had disappeared with end of the QD conference.

I don't think of myself as inhibited, nor do most people who meet me. Many would say that I am the poster child for living out loud—being fully able to be queer and disabled and proud. But QD belied that belief. I had always been the queer in disabled spaces and the crip in queer spaces.

I keenly felt the isolation and restrictions on being disabled in nondisabled spaces. The ways that what I needed would be evaluated on measurements of inconvenience and expense. I would be allowed to participate only at the level of their willingness. I rarely noticed the ways I controlled my queer impulses in disabled spaces. The tightness in my body, the restraint in my speech. There was no "Hey girl," shouted across a room in disabled spaces. No "Oh baby you look good." I thought those, but did not speak them. To do so violated the unspoken rule of tolerating queers without creating queer spaces. This was often reinforced when disabled leaders would have same-sex relationships that they did not discuss or name publicly.

In the 1970s disability rights movement, the queers were expected to keep their silence. This was framed as, "being public would expose our leaders to the distraction of homophobia, and we needed them to be effective fighting ableism." So we kept silent. In one situation famous to us but hidden from the world, a major disability organization created a new branch office across the country because two women lovers broke up and neither would leave the new agency. The official word was that it was time for expansion. Thirty years later, no one has publicly stated otherwise.

My body embraced queer disability space with joy. My hips led the way.[2] They twitched when an interesting queer came near. With over 200 participants, by the middle of the first day my hips felt like they were hula dancing. My hands soon followed. They would move in wider arcs providing emphasis. My chest puffed out. My voice pitch rose. My eyes showed appreciation for the beauty before me.

Like shaking off a sleepy body, I moved fully into my own desire, reveling in the strong, proud community I shared. Later at the QD Dance, a hot butch would put her pendulous, leather-encased breasts against my face in a dance of sheer momentary desire. This was not "fall in love with me forever" desire—this was "we are here and you are beautiful" desire. It might last the length of a passing in the hallway or a long club version of a dance song. But even as we expressed appreciation and desire, we simultaneously enacted a "just here, right now" attitude.

Hour by hour, my body relaxed into its natural expression. I never realized how tightly I held myself, never noticed that even at my loosest when I was in disability spaces, my safest places, I was only half-loose, not only in how I held my body but also how I controlled my speech.

In this queer disabled space my teasing became both more nuanced and more complex, as if I had gone from singing children's nursery songs to singing opera. I offered compliments to people that honored their individual beauty and style. These included and acknowledged their queerness and disability. So while I might feel safe to say, "You look really good" in a disability space, here I could speak my fuller truth by saying approvingly "Honey, those pants, your ass—so hot!"

Other participants relaxed too. In large part that was possible because we had planned for the fullest access we could make. The folks with environmental illnesses participated at a level rarely accessible to them, since we had a strict no-scent policy. Instead of being the person

---

2. Some people think that because I sit in a wheelchair, that my hips are not active. That is a mistaken belief.

who had to leave the conference because the scents made them sick, here they could just be a regular participant.

The genderqueer folks did not have to go to their dorm room every time they needed to pee, since we created non-gendered bathrooms throughout the conference and in the food and sleeping spaces. We had a strict policy of not making medical decisions for participants, so when people had epileptic seizures we did not call an ambulance but, as they requested, we provided people to monitor them and keep their environment safe.[3]

Safety is an often ignored part of being able to freely express ourselves. Safety does not mean freedom from conflict, but it does mean acknowledgement of differences, the need for access accommodations, and an environment that allows for respectful discussion of privileges.

It's now 12 years since the QD conference. And what I miss most of all is that freedom to express myself, to honor the wondrousness of people with sexy sassy remarks, to be queer and disabled, accepted wholly as beautiful selves. Oh, I get short tastes of it, but nothing like an entire environment of free expression for three days. We were our unfiltered, unmitigated selves and we thrived.

QD Background

Beginning in the late 1950s, I spent every year from age 7 to 14 at Camp Caravan for disabled kids. I loved the disabled kids at camp. I loved how I felt surrounded by disabled people living 24/7 for a month at a time with no families allowed, no outsiders coming and judging us. Those years of spending a month or two at summer camp were the only times in my life that I did not experience any microaggressions because of my disability. In 1974, I had only recently found the disability community, the grown up versions of kids from summer camp, as we all came together in Berkeley, California.

I was newly immersed in the heterosexually-focused disability

---

3.   A recent conversation on Facebook highlighted the different treatment that epileptics receive based on race. The white epileptics reported that when they had a seizure in public people often called emergency services and an ambulance and police arrived. They reported being taken to the hospital (which none of them wanted). The black epileptics reported that they were arrested because, they were later told, the police presumed their epileptic behaviors to be induced by street drugs. All epileptics stated that they hate the default of being removed from their surroundings and being separated from their families, friends and sometimes important items such as wheelchairs, school books and computers. The cost of being taken by ambulance and admitted to the Emergency Room for what they consider to be a typical and nonfatal medical situation creates enormous financial hardship. See footnote 21 on the cost of ambulance transportation.

rights movement when I met two disabled lesbians at the disabled women's rap group that I started.[4] I was a little scared, but mostly I was thrilled to have a name for what I'd always felt. When I realized that I was queer, deeply thoroughly queer, when I realized that for me being in a romantic connection with a woman was so profoundly different for me than being in a romantic connection with a man, I knew I was unassailably queer.

Through the 1970s and early 1980s I worked diligently in the disability rights movement and found myself a niche in education and women's issues. I did my damnedest to be useful. I thought that because there were other queers in the organization, that somehow being queer and disabled would be okay. I did not realize that the disability rights movement was by and large crafted, right from its origins, to be a single issue movement. It's only about disability access and not about intersections.

The disability rights movement's issues focused on access for white disabled men, particularly wheelchair users, by the way in which the needs of disabled women, disabled people of color, and disabled queers, even now 40 years later, are not a priority. It does not matter how many reports or conferences or studies were done in the past two decades showing the need, the American disability rights movement never has (and I would argue never will) prioritize disabled people who are not white, are not male, are not straight, and don't have a physical disability.

The Berkeley area disability rights movement spent the 1970s working with other social justice groups to say "Disabled people are important, disabled people are being disenfranchised, we need our civil rights. We want to be in the struggle with you, we want your support, we want to be part of all parts of society, and we have the right to do so." We had spent over a decade working with, and sometimes working in, various queer communities, bringing our message to them.

In 1974 I was just beginning to have an inkling of the single issue focus of the disability rights movement. When AIDS hit, the marginalization of queers became impossible to ignore. By 1982, the AIDS epidemic hit hard in the San Francisco Bay Area. Hundreds of men had been diagnosed, or if they didn't have an official diagnosis they had the symptoms, and by 1982 some of them were going blind and needed disability services.

When AIDS caused disabilities, specifically vision loss, the gay men came to the independent living centers to seek services. Now, I do not know the history of what happened in San Francisco, but I noticed the

---

4. See more on this in "Center for Independent Living, Berkeley" in this book.

men from San Francisco came to the Center for Independent Living in Berkeley, where there was a blind lesbian on staff in Blind Services who made sure that the men were welcomed and that they received the services they needed. As the AIDS epidemic grew, the need for the services started to grow, and CIL needed to make a decision whether to expand and serve this population or not. They, like the rest of the independent living centers in the U.S., decided not to.

Since many of my lesbian friends provided care for the newly diagnosed gay men, I became more aware that there were increasing numbers of gay men with AIDS. It seemed to me a natural alliance, that we should be networking with these newly disabled people, but the disability rights movement did not see it that way. By and large they ignored the AIDS crisis, and in many cases they rejected gay men outright.

In 1992, the National Council on Independent Living (NCIL) based in Washington, D.C. held its national meeting in Oakland, California, next door to Berkeley. It was the first time that NCIL held its meeting on the west coast, and we were all very excited. I had noticed that my disabled friends were not thinking about or discussing safe sex, so I approached Kathy Simpson (disabled), a health educator at Planned Parenthood, and we proposed a workshop on safe sex for disabled people. Kathy was thrilled because there was very little material available on disease transmission among disabled people, so getting people information by word of mouth was the primary method available to us.

Over 100 people, all of them directors or top staff of independent living centers from across the United States, attended our workshop. We started by giving an overview of safe sex practices and ways they could be adapted for people with various disabilities. But as we looked over the audience we saw the people's eyes were glazing over. So we paused and asked them, "What are you using for safe sex?" And they told us, "We don't use anything."

Kathy and I were pretty shocked by this attitude in 1992. It was pretty clear that AIDS was an epidemic that was not going to stop anytime soon, and at that point in history it was a debilitating and often terminal diagnosis. We pushed a little further and asked "Okay, Why aren't you using any safe sex practices?" They looked around the room at each other, nodded knowingly, and told us "Well, we're not gay men so we don't need to do anything about AIDS."

Since 1982, the Centers for Disease Control (CDC) had documented that HIV/AIDS was transmitted through certain sexual behaviors, through blood transfusions, and through IV drug use. Sexual identity, while sometimes useful for identifying specific populations at risk, was not helpful in identifying individuals or other kinds of populations at risk for HIV transmission. It was a little scary to Kathy and me that this group of highly educated national disability rights leaders did not think that HIV was something they or their agencies needed to think about.

We then asked them "What safe sex information are you providing in your AIDS training in local disability communities?" Again they looked around the room at each other and said, "We don't do any training about AIDS, because that's really not a problem in our community." Kathy and I were getting increasingly concerned about this line of thinking and the risks to our communities from HIV/AIDS, so we asked how they handled requests for services from people with HIV/AIDS. These leaders answered, "We just tell them we don't serve them." Our level of disbelief grew at their answers, and more importantly at the flippancy with which they thought their answers were totally acceptable.

We confirmed by saying "When people call your independent living agency for services, if they say their disability is HIV or AIDS, you don't serve them?" They replied, "Yes." Someone in the audience volunteered, "They don't have to say they have HIV/AIDS. If we think they are gay, we don't serve them either. Like if they were referred to us by a gay or AIDS agency." At this point Kathy looked at me and saw my face getting red, a sign of my blood pressure rising. I was ready to throttle the entire gaggle of the "leadership of the disability rights movement" across the United States. In 1992, they were stating publicly, and without any hesitation, that they would not serve clients who have legitimate disabilities, which they were required by law to serve.

At that moment, I realized how deeply embedded and how completely acceptable homophobia was in the disability rights community. The pat on the head attitude of, "Yes, gay issues are important to us," and "We'll get to your issues in a few minutes because you're really one of us" that I received in the 1970s in the disability rights community was, I now realized in hindsight, really "We're never going to get queer issues because we're not queer, our movement's not queer and we're not going to have anything to do with queer people."

Pondering this, I reflected back to the early 1980s, when the disability community did nothing about AIDS, even when it impacted presumably heterosexual disabled men—hemophiliacs. Hemophiliacs rely on plasma, blood products that are distilled from hundreds if not thousands of blood donors.[5]   Very early in the AIDS epidemic, as early as 1982, the Centers for Disease Control met with all of the major hemophiliac organizations, including their medical specialists, and discussed the risk of AIDS transmission in blood products.[6]   The hemophilia community rejected the CDC's suggestions to stop using potentially infected blood plasma, which is the concentrated blood product with hundreds or thousands of contributors, and to go back to using single blood resources and having the treatments occur as needed in a medical facility, as opposed to at home.[7]   The resulting deaths of thousands of hemophiliacs was largely preventable.[8]   In the early 1970s the blood processing companies had learned that Dr. Edward Shanbrom had developed a technique for purifying blood plasma.[9]   The purifying was necessary because industry standards placed the plasma donation centers in poor areas, including prisons, where a high percentage of donors had communicable diseases.[10]   Prioritizing costs over lives, the blood processing industry skipped the purification and released plasma

---

5.   "The concentrated clotting factors came onto the market in the mid-1970s. Because they were so effective in stopping bleeding, they changed hemophilia from a disease that caused enormous pain and disability and that often led to an early death into one that allowed people to live normal lives. People with hemophilia infused the clotting factors into their own veins, treating themselves whenever they feared bleeding was coming on…. Concentrated factors gave birth to a new catch phrase for people with hemophilia. "Infuse early and often," they say their doctors told them." Kolata, G. (December 25, 1991). "Hit hard by the AIDS virus, hemophiliacs angrily speak out." *The New York Times*. URL: http://partners.nytimes.com/library/national/science/aids/122591sci-aids.html

6.   Evatt, B.L. (2006). "The tragic history of AIDS in the hemophilia population 1982-1984." *The Journal of Thrombosis and Hemeostatis* (4), 2295-301. URL: http://www1.wfh.org/publication/files/pdf-1269.pdf

7.   Ibid. (This means see previous note.)

8.   Ibid.

9.   "Soon after they began producing the substance, [Dr. Shanbrom] noticed that the lab workers developed jaundice after breathing the plasma mist in the cold rooms. Suspecting hepatitis, he conducted tests on the liver enzymes of experimental patients, which showed pathological changes. 'It was obvious there was some kind of virus there', he said later. He did not consider withdrawing the product; like everyone who had seen its miraculous effects on hemophiliacs, he had no doubt that the benefits exceeded the risk. Yet he felt that, given the product could spread a chronic disease, the company should try to minimize the risk. He notified his superiors to take preventive measures, such as closing its collection centers in hepatitis hot spots. They ignored his suggestion, and he eventually left Hyland."

"Dr. Shanbrom approached the [CDC] hoping to interest them in using and studying his detergent process of viral inactivation. The response was a letter from the CDC that he has saved to this day. The CDC expressed interest in Dr. Shanbrom's process but regretted that it did not have enough chimpanzees to enable researchers to conduct experiments with it. For want of adequate funding to the CDC for chimpanzees, clotting factor remained infectious. . . .He also later apologized for not doing more to reprevent the epidemic." COTT, see note 30

Coleman, N. and Friedman, M.. (2002). *Red gold: The Epic Story of Blood: Blood Collection*. Educational Broadcasting Company. New York. URL: http://www.pbs.org/wnet/redgold/printable/p_bloodcollection.html

10.   Ibid.

with HIV to patients first in the United States and then overseas.[11.] Hemophiliac activism confronted the industry, but in the end it was stymied by legal maneuverings.[12.]

I was at the heart of what it is often called the "mothership of the disability rights movement," and not once did I see any serious discussions occur about the fact that these were our disabled brothers who were dying. We could have taken all the powerful political capital that we had generated in the 1970s, and used even the tiniest bit of it to help hemophiliacs and gay men who were infected to fight their battles. Instead, we pretended like neither group of men was part of "us," and we ignored them. I mourn the needless deaths and my/our part in ignoring the crisis.

The QD Conference

This painful history spurred in me a burning desire to have a conference —a gathering of some sort for disabled queers. I'm a very slow learner and it took me 20 years to realize that the disability movement was never going to care for queer disabled people. Beginning in 1997, everywhere I went for the next few years, I talked about the need for a queer disability gathering. Different people would nod their heads and say, "What a good idea," but nobody was ever willing to put the energy in until around the year 2000, when a small group of us decided to take on this project.

At that time everyone in the planning group was poor, and many were full time students. We were unfunded. Yet each one of us, in a profoundly transformative way, wanted and needed queer disability community. We had no money, we were spread across the country, we had never worked together before—yet with a lot of help we pulled off the first international conference by and for queers with disabilities.

Eli Clare (disabled) was working a full-time job. I think at that time he was the only one of us that worked at a regular job. Samuel Lurie (nondisabled) was doing contract work on health. Ellen Samuels (disabled) and Allison Kafer (disabled) were full-time graduate students. Jay Williams (disabled) was a full-time undergraduate student. And by then I was living on government benefits. We were all white, all poor,

---

11. Wellington, D.L. (May 28, 2014). "The twisted business of donating plasma." *The Atlantic*. URL: http://www.theatlantic.com/health/archive/2014/05/the-twisted-business-of-donating-plasma/362012/

12. See: MacNeill, T. & Murphy, M.L. *Hemophilia Historical Record*. URL: http://www.cott1.org/blog. Also, Rosenberg, M.P. (May 1992) "Causes and effects of the hemophilia/AIDS epidemic." *Action Now*.

and except for Samuel, all disabled.

Jay, Ellen, and I all lived in the San Francisco Bay Area. Allison was in Los Angeles, Eli in Michigan and Samuel in Vermont. We divided the tasks based on our interests and availability. Eli and Samuel looked for ways to make the conference more trans friendly. Eli and Allison took the lead on the conference program, sent out the call for presentations, reviewed the incoming suggestions and created the final program. Ellen and Jay took the lead on ensuring that the conference space was as environmentally safe as possible. We provided scent free products, had a scent free cleaning provision put into our contract for both the meeting rooms and the dorm room cleaning, and provided as many food options as possible to accommodate food allergies.

In many ways I functioned, as I often do, as the camp director. I would suggest big picture directions, try to find networks that would assist us, and generally just try to provide support to keep us happy and productive. As we went along, other people joined us. The Denver-based group of Laura Hershey (disabled), Robin Stephens (disabled), and Carrie Ann Lucas (disabled) brought the resources from the street activist world of ADAPT,[13] such as where to get good political T-shirts made. Patricia Chadwick (nondisabled) created a beautiful T-shirt and conference design for us. Paul Longmore (disabled), a major figure in disability studies and a history professor at San Francisco State University, worked together with Eugene Chelberg (disabled), who was a newly arrived top administrator at San Francisco State, to create a welcoming home for the Queer Disability Conference. The Society for Disability Studies loaned us both credibility and resources that allowed us to get a little bit of federal funding to pay for some of our access needs.

We knew from the start that we were a group of white people and that was going to create some problems for us. It meant that only some of the voices in the community were going to be heard loudly and clearly throughout the planning process. It also meant that we were going to miss important connections and important issues because of our whiteness. Knowing this contradiction, we plowed ahead with planning the conference.

We did all this in the early 2000s, when the only tools we had available for communication were email and landline telephones. We had no cell phones, no social network sites, no live chat rooms, no video chats. During our 18 months of organizing we met in person only once.

---

13. ADAPT is a national grass-roots community that organizes disability rights activists to engage in nonviolent direct action, including civil disobedience, to assure the civil and human rights of people with disabilities to live in freedom. URL: http://www.adapt.org/

While the conference attendees were largely queer disabled people, we had intentionally scheduled the conference to be a few days before the Society for Disability Studies (SDS) conference on campus. Most of the organizers regularly attended SDS, so having both conferences the same week was useful. The Society for Disability Studies advertised the Queer Disability Conference on the SDS promotional materials, including allowing people to register for both conferences at the same time. I had organized previous pre-SDS events (mostly one day events on disabled women) that SDS had enthusiastically supported, with shared interpreter and meeting room costs. So when we discussed planning QD2002, we decided that having the two events in the same week benefited us all.

Eugene Chelberg helped us select conference dates so that we were the only group on campus at that time. This was an enormous help to us, because we needed to control the physical environment to create some degree of safety for people with environmental illness. It was much easier to do that when we were the only group in the cafeteria and the dormitories.

We also needed to make the space work for trans people. To do that, we needed to control the bathrooms, shower rooms, and dormitory rooms. We marked the bathrooms, particularly in the dorms, which had shared bathrooms, with phrases such as "gender nonspecific" or "everybody welcome," but the signs were soon queered and cripped. People added their own preferred language such as boi, dyke, gay, butch, grrl, queer, transman, crip, and many other terms of endearment.

With over 200 people, the Queer Disability Conference amplified the message that queer disabled people exist and have unique needs and issues.[14] Let me give you a little more understanding of why that's so significant. We brought over 200 people together. You could put 20 queers in a room and there would 40 different opinions, and we brought in over 200 queers and put them in one room, and people worked together. That does not mean they agreed. There were lots of people, like me, for whom the trans stuff was really new. They were lots of old lesbians who clung tightly to specific identities like "lesbian" and were cranky and pissed about the shifting language because they felt that losing specific terms like "lesbian" ignored the sacrifices of women who had died because of their sexual identities. There were lots of gay men who had issues with how lesbians ran things. The environment was ripe for conflict, and the fact that we had so very little conflict speaks

---

14. Queer Disability Conference program URL: http://www.disabilityhistory.org/dwa/queer/program_grid.htm. For general QD2002 info and some online papers: http://www.disabilityhistory.org/dwa/queer/index.htm

volumes to the absolute thirst we all had for community.

There are many things about the Queer Disability Conference of which I am extraordinarily proud. We provided a gathering space for over 200 queer disabled people—an accomplishment that has never been duplicated. We created a space where variations of queer were prominently displayed. In our feedback from the conference, people often said that they wished there was more of the queer perspective that they were personally representing or identifying with, yet almost no one said that the conference was an unsafe space in which to be queer. Considering that we were bringing 200 strangers together under a very broad umbrella called queer, the fact that there were not more feelings of exclusion is a major accomplishment.

That's not to say that this was not without a significant learning curve. Let me give you one small example of my own. Samuel and Eli recruited heavily in the trans community, both for speakers and volunteers. One of their trans friends named Francisco (disabled) came early to volunteer. Francisco's disability, epilepsy, is not easily visible, so when I asked him to stand in the driveway and direct conference participants to the parking area to the designated parking areas, I wanted him to be easily identifiable with the conference. Now, Francisco is a small man and I am a large woman. This was the first time Francisco and I had met. While we were standing talking in the parking lot, I realized that I wanted him to be more visibly identified as being part of the conference. I was wearing one of the new conference shirts that clearly said queer disability, and he was wearing a regular T-shirt. I asked him it was okay for him to wear my conference shirt while he was directing traffic. He said fine, so I took off the shirt I had and gave it to him. Then I walked away and thought nothing about it, went about my business for about an hour, and came back and checked on him.

When I came back around, he seemed a little apprehensive, and I could not figure out why. I felt like I had approached him in an okay manner before, that our communication was good, yet he seemed kind of anxious. So after I checked in about the parking issues, I said to him, "You know it seems like something's not right." He said, "Well..." and he kind of looked down at his shoes and said, "You know, I don't want to be rude, but you know, this shirt is really big on me." I looked at him and noticed that he had taken the hem of the shirt and tied it in a knot, so that it hung closer to his hips and not his knees. And he said, "You know, I don't want to be rude, but this kind of feels like a dress on me, and I'm really not okay with wearing a dress." We both looked at my very large shirt on his very small body and laughed together. I looked him in the eye and said, "I'm sorry, it never occurred to me. I will go and get you a shirt that fits you. Thank you for telling me. Please tell me what size you need."

I didn't know what I didn't know. Francisco was gracious enough to work the shift directing traffic in clothing that made him feel very uncomfortable because he was committed to doing the service. He also knew that I had not given him the shirt to in any way dishonor his trans body, even though it did, but because I was fat and he was not. Other things happened during the conference that drew him and me closer together, but I think that was really the basis for our trust in each other —that moment in the parking lot.

Queer Disabled Keynotes

As conference organizers, we were very careful and very intentional about our keynotes. It was really important for us to reflect a range of disability, a range of queer, and as much as possible, to highlight disabled people of color. We knew from the beginning that all of our keynotes would be disabled people. We were absolutely clear that every single keynote was going to be a queer disabled person. We needed to find people who lived in multiple communities of disabled, queer and something else, but who, while they were leaders in their own intersectional communities might not be known outside their circle.

Eli Clare later wrote about this. I will have him set the stage for you:

> In the last three decades disabled people and lesbian, gay, bisexual, and transgender peoples have taken to the streets and entered the academy. We've built movements for social change, created culture and community, and shaped our own theory and analysis. But the issues, concerns, and experiences of queer disabled people have rarely been placed front and center.
>
> With these thoughts about marginalization, identity politics, and community building, a small group of organizers—myself included—created the first-ever Queerness and Disability Conference, which happened in 2002 at San Francisco State University. We envisioned bringing together artists, activists, and scholars to explore a whole host of issues, ranging from the medicalization of bodies to queer crip relationships, from using personal attendant care to queer performance, crip style. And

what came to be was an incredible, high energy, two day gathering of three hundred people where the sparks of connection and challenge, community and conflict, flew.[15.]

The keynotes were given by three speakers, two of whom were Deaf.[16.] It is extraordinarily rare (even at an event related to disability) that a Deaf person is a keynote. I have never seen another disability conference that highlighted two Deaf speakers on the same plenary. We asked Raymond Luczak[17.] to speak because he is a leader on queer Deaf issues. The second speaker, Vicky D'aoust (Tanis Doe),[18.] was a biracial (Métis)[19.] woman who talked about living and researching in the borderlands of multiple communities. We closed with our third speaker, Emi Koyama,[20.] a leader on intersex issues, who explored cultural assumptions of gender.

---

15. Eli Clare. URL: http://eliclare.com/what-eli-offers/lectures/queer-disability

16. "Deaf" refers to people who are affiliated with the cultural and linguistic community of people with hearing impairments who communicate primarily through American Sign Language. Small "d" "deaf" means people who have hearing impairments. So all Deaf people are deaf, not all deaf people are Deaf.

17. From the QD Conference program:

     RAYMOND LUCZAK edited the Lambda Literary Award-nominated anthology *Eyes Of Desire: A Deaf Gay and Lesbian Reader* (Alyson); he also wrote *St. Michael's Fall: Poems* (Deaf Life Press). The Tactile Mind Press is publishing his next two books—*Silence Is a Four-Letter Word: On Art and Deafness* and *This Way to the Acorns: Poems*—at the same time this July. Excerpts from his deaf gay novel, *Men With Their Hands*, have appeared in various periodicals. Seven of his plays have been workshopped and produced around the country; his next show, *A Pair of Hands: Deaf Gay Monologues* will premiere on Friday, June 28th as part of the Queer@HERE Theater Festival at the HERE Theater in New York City. A screenwriter and filmmaker, he lives in New York City where he is completing his debut feature film *Ghosted*, which he produced and directed. He has just completed his first DVD project called *Manny ASL: Stories in American Sign Language*, which he also directed; it is coming out at Deaf Way II this July. His web site is www.raymondluczak.com.

18. When she wrote about disability issues, or any topic other than queer issues, she used the name Tanis Doe. When she wrote about queer issues, she used the name Vicky D'aoust. The Queer Disability Conference was the first time that she publicly stated in any media that Tanis Doe and Vicky D'aoust were in fact the same person. From the QD conference program:

     VICKY D'AOUST began writing for *Lesbian Contradiction* shortly after adopting her daughter over 15 years ago. Since then, she has been published in legal journals, three book-length anthologies about lesbian identity and disability parenting, and many other collections of stories. She watches *X-Files*, doesn't usually attend conferences, and prefers the virtual life to the corporeal one. This will be her first major appearance since Outrights Conference in Vancouver in 1991. She is a bi-cultural, bi-polar, borderline academic with multiple disabilities.

19. Métis means heritage from an indigenous parent and a european-heritage parent.

20. From the QD program:

     EMI KOYAMA is a multi-issue social justice slut, synthesizing feminist, Asian, survivor, dyke, queer, sex worker, intersex, genderqueer, and crip politics. These factors, while not a complete descriptor of who she is, have all impacted her life. Emi is currently the Program Assistant for Intersex Society of North America, and the Community Board Chair for Survivor Project. Emi lives in Portland, Oregon, and has been putting the emi back in feminism since 1975.

Like most conference organizers, I saw very little of the actual program other than the opening and closing keynotes because there are always a million things to do to keep the conference moving. Our conference, for some reason, seemed to be a hotbed for grand mal seizures so, for me, those are some of my most vivid memories.

We had four multiple-hour-long grand mal seizures during the conference, most of which began in meeting rooms during sessions. Michael, a volunteer, traveled with a seizure dog and had a higher level of expertise and knowledge about epileptics than anyone else. When the first person had a grand mal seizure, I was immediately called over and I requested assistance from Michael. Unfortunately, because of the many extremely long seizures, Michael also saw very little of the conference. Luckily, we had taped the conference and were able to provide him with audio tapes.

All of the epileptics except for Michael had previously been sent to the hospital any time they had a seizure around other people. In the U.S. healthcare system, that meant a $4,000 dollar or more hospital bill, plus another $300 for the ambulance.[21] People had asked us very clearly to let them manage their own disabilities unless they were a danger to themselves or others. Michael had enough expertise to help us assess each situation.

More significantly, none of the people other than Michael had ever had feedback from the people witnessing their seizures. This meant they did not know what was happening as they were coming out of the seizure, or what, if anything, was really triggering them and continuing the length of the seizure. Or even what kind of help might be useful. One participant, who had two grand mal seizures a day apart, received important information about her seizure management. We realized that as she came out of her seizure and started to move, her seizure would return. What she needed immediately after her seizure was an extended period of immobility in order to stop the seizure cycle. Although she had decades of seizures (many undoubtedly in the presence of medical "professionals"), this was the first time she had been given this valuable information.

For some people the Queer Disability Conference happened in the meeting rooms, for some at The Dance and for others in these quiet moments of disability intimacy. We shared community in all these ways. We lived our principle that disabled people should always be in charge

---

21. In San Francisco an ambulance change can range from $300-1,500 depending on which ambulance company responds to the call. Source URL: http://sanfrancisco.cbslocal.com/2011/05/18/consumerwatch-ambulance-calls-can-hurt-your-wallet/

of the decisions in their lives and that our job as organizers was to create a structure that valued this as much as we valued having an interesting keynote speaker. Along the way, we all learned a lot about ourselves and each other.

Eli Clare describes the feeling of being in a plenary room:

> The room is jammed, full of people using wheelchairs, crutches, ventilators, canes, service dogs, full of queer crips and our friends, allies, and partners. There's a team of people doing real time captioning and another team sign language interpreting. Whatever our differences, most of us bring a shared sense of queerness as familiar and good; a shared understanding of disability as neither tragic nor pitiful, but rather as an integral part of who we are, the social conditions of ableism as big a concern as the bodily, cognitive, sensory, and/or emotional impairments we face.[22]

The Conference created openings for discussions that rarely happen in disability spaces. One of the most important was the closing keynote. Originally envisioned to be a conversation between Eli Clare and Diana Courvant (disabled), by lunchtime on the final day we realized that caucuses needed that time. So Eli facilitated the presentations of the caucus statements and the discussions.

The people with psychiatric disabilities presented first.[23] They discussed the need for safe places to be at the conference, including a quiet room, the availability of voluntary peer counseling, a conference statement clearly committing to non-institutionalization of attendees and a commitment to allowing the disabled person to make all decisions regarding their own bodyminds.[24]

The People of Color caucus presented next. They raised the issues of the whiteness of the organizers and programming, the need to prioritize issues facing disabled people of color, and the need to openly discuss race and class issues. The presentation ended with: "In conclusion, we must recognize issues of race, class, gender, sexuality, disability, religion, age, and so forth as many rivers that have separate qualities, but are also part of the larger water system. In essence, the confluence of the waters is representative of a larger and more desirable

---

22. Eli Clare. URL: http://eliclare.com/what-eli-offers/lectures/queer-disability

23. I am using the term preferred by the person presenting the caucus information.

24. A full transcript of the caucus presentation is here:
    http://www.disabilityhistory.org/dwa/queer/panel_closing.html

act of decolonization."[25.]

These two thoughtful caucus reports provided both a closing and an opening. They marked the end of the conference while pointing at directions for growth. I, unfortunately, was not ready to hear their wisdom. I was angry that my perfectly imagined (and white-led) conference was ending with dissension. Mostly I was angry because they were right.[26.]

For many years I could not re-read these statements, but writing this essay required me to do so. I am struck by the incredible kindness contained in them. The gentle prodding that asked people to examine their own work and make commitments to include people not like ourselves. Over a decade later, I am still struggling to learn the lessons that they asked us to learn.

The first international Queer Disability Conference created many new networks, provided important learning opportunities, and solidified a bridge between queer and disability work in academic and community circles. For most of us, the conference provided a rare validation of our own work exploring the borderlands of queer, disabled and other worlds. We no longer felt quite so alone. We found some travelers to accompany us. We took the germ of an idea and with a lot of work and almost no money, we blew it up to a major conference that, in many ways, created the networks and developed the ideas for new Queer Disability theories and writings.[27.] And, as always in the best disability circles, we ended with a dance.

Queer Disability Dance

We ended the conference with a crip dance. Simi (disabled) and David (nondisabled) Linton had started the tradition of a dance at the Society for Disability Studies (SDS). They offered to host a dance for the Queer Disability Conference. They arranged for the booze, paid for it even, and we commandeered the large recreation room. This was the great part of being the only group on campus—we could pretty much arrange things how we needed them, and we *really* needed to dance.

---

25. See previous note.

26. For more on race and disability, see the essay in this book. I look at this statement, and the reasons it was needed and I shake my head at myself. Yes, I knew that we were all white and yet I chose to ignore that. I never again participated in an all-white organizing effort. I apologize for having created this space that was so unwelcoming for many people of color.

27. Before QD there were queer studies and disability studies but after QD there was Queer Disability Studies. Before QD 2002, the field was starting to grow, but after the networking, the sharing of resources, and the presenting of new ideas, the Queer Disability Studies grew exponentially.

We all needed a space to blow off our tension and our conflicts—to move and shake and just celebrate our freaky bodies. Cathy Kudlick (disabled) and Jim Ferris (disabled) are both usually quiet, but they jumped up and started a cane dance. Some folks balanced their canes in their hands, others twirled them like batons. Cathy's blind white cane extended far beyond her body while Jim's shorter walking cane's handle provided perfect ballast for balancing it in his hand. As leaders, their tame reputations fell away and they became the wild ones.

The QD dance came at the end of two full days of erotically charged engagement with ideas and each other. Sexuality flowed through our movements. I'd brought my manual wheelchair, which I much prefer for dancing. A disabled butch dressed in black leather pants and a black leather bra which did not contain her 44DDD breasts came over to me. We started dancing face to face but soon she went behind me, placed her legs between my wheels, leaned over and said "May I put my tits on you?" I stammered assent and she rose up and slowly placed her right breast on my right shoulder. It promptly slid forward, the mass too great for my shoulders, the weight pushing it forward, her nipples reaching for mine. Her left breast soon followed. I reached my arms up encasing her tits. She reached her hands down holding my arms in place. My head leaned back pushing deeper into her, her tits muffling the loud dance music. We rocked until the song ended. A blissful few minutes etched forever into me.

Sexuality flowed in all directions. David Linton and I always tried to find time to have one dance together. A superb dancer, David is particularly comfortable with dancing with wheelchair folks, a rare skill. With sexy moves he is captivating to watch. Simi loves to watch us dance and encourages others to sit with her while she comments "OH NO, what is happening?" with an inquiring falsetto and fake inquisitive eyes.

David is my favorite sexy dancer, in large part because he offers me opportunities to touch him while he dances erotically. He drops his hips, pushes his legs wide and straddles my legs while thrusting his crotch forward. He treats me as a sexually desirable dance partner, something that never happens in non-crip dance spaces. I reciprocate by showing my appreciation of his excellent dance moves.

Later that night David encouraged me to find a way to dance with him in my power wheelchair, which I dislike using for dance because it inhibits my movement. The ever prescient David realized that I would be using it more as time went on, though, and he encouraged me to explore the possibilities more.

We started our dance in the usual way then as he came closer he put his left thigh on my right armrest. I looked up and smiled. I slid the left joystick outwards. Encouraged, he put his right thigh on my left armrest. Now his entire body balanced on my armrests as we faced each other. He looked back at the floor and then smiled at me. I nodded my agreement.

I leaned back into my wheelchair gaining additional balance. I reached and held his belt firmly in my right hand. He slowly dropped his head down towards my feet. Looking around to ensure that we had clearance, I slowly began to spin my wheelchair. He raised his arms above his head to maximize his extension.

People pulled back farther so he would not hit anything and I cranked up my speed and we spun—increasing our speed, not really seeing anything but feeling the tenuous connection of my hand on his belt, his legs hugging my torso. His always wild hair floating across the floor until I began our descent. Slowing my speed, allowing him to regain orientation. As he pulled himself up onto my lap, other dancers applauded in celebration.

They recognized the difficulty of the moves we did, honored our courage in the attempt and our skill at execution. Like any dancer on any dance floor.

We, along with everyone in the room dancing and observing, spent a few hours honoring our authentic movements, showing off our gnarly bodies, and allowing others a rare glimpse of our unrestrained joy. The Queer Disability Conference ended too soon and even now, 12 years later, I miss that amazing space of acceptance.

JUST THE FACTS MA'AM

1970-2002 — Queers with and without disabilities work in disability rights organizations and fight for disability rights, but disability rights organizations do not equally support gay rights, even disabled gay rights.

1992 — At the National Council on Independent Living (NCIL) the directors of independent living centers state in an AIDS prevention workshop that their agencies do not serve people with HIV/AIDS.

2002 — International Queer Disability Conference held at San Francisco State University in San Francisco, California.

RESOURCES

Kafer, A. (2013) *Feminist, Queer, Crip.* Indiana University Press,
    Bloomington, IN.
Queer Disability Conference website. URL:
    http://www.disabilityhistory.org/dwa/queer/
Wood, Caitlin, Editor, *Criptiques.* Publisher: May Day. Criptiques blog
    URL: http://criptiques.com/

A full bibliography is available at my website: www.corbettotoole.com

II.

Welcome to India: Parenting Disabled Children

"We do this with no capital except our valuable time. We do this because the world we live in is a house on fire and the people we love are burning."
— Sandra Cisneros (unknown)[1]

Summary

I am a mother, and my daughter is disabled. I wanted her to feel comfortable in both the disabled and nondisabled worlds. She grew up going to school with nondisabled students and teachers. After school and on weekends she spent time with disabled adults and other disabled kids.

I talk about how disabled children, who are usually raised by nondisabled people, really need to be around disabled adults who can give them and their families many resources. Nearly all the professionals that work with disabled children are nondisabled people who do not know any disabled adults, so the professionals do not know the many useful things that disabled adults have discovered to make their lives better. Professionals think a lot about what is "wrong" with disabled children, but parents and disabled adults think a lot about what is "right" with disabled children.

It is important for disabled children to have disabled adults in their lives, so that they can know successful and happy people who have bodyminds like them.

---

1. Sisneros, S. (1991). *The House on Mango Street.* Vintage Books, New York, NY

❖ ❖ ❖

In 1994, when I adopted my daughter, she lived in Japan, so I had to go through Japanese customs in order to fly home with her. The customs agent seemed very befuddled that a middle-aged white woman using a manual wheelchair wanted to take an 11 month old Japanese baby to the United States. My total lack of Japanese created language obstacles. We attempted many words and phrases in hopes of finding a common English vocabulary, because unlike me the customs agent knew Japanese and English (and I suspect other languages as well). Our conversation continued so long I feared missing my plane when unexpectedly this gatekeeper's face broke into a large smile. He tilted his head expectantly and said "New mother?" My affirmative reply broke through the linguistic logjam. He checked the appropriate box on his form and sent us to our plane.

I thought of that moment often while raising my daughter— moments of struggling to find the right words, to find a shared vocabulary—not with her, but with the many and ever changing 'professionals' in her/our life. Throughout her childhood, I sat with my daughter nearby while various professionals, who I thought of more as 'gatekeepers' than helpful people, tried to fit our lives onto their predetermined, normed-for-anyone-but-not-us forms.

Like many parents of a disabled child, I was given the short piece by Emily Kingsley called *Welcome to Holland*,[2] in which she offers the metaphor that a family planned a trip to Italy (having a nondisabled baby) and instead ended up in Holland (having a disabled child). In this story from the 1980s, the family prepared for an Italian holiday and suddenly found themselves in Holland with a different language and different customs than they expected. Yet as some commentators observed, Kingsley's family is still going from one white European environment to another, and European countries, in a global perspective, are much more similar than they are different. My experience was more complex.

I know many prospective parents who planned for a nondisabled child (a trip to Italy), but instead ended up with a disabled child. Suddenly being thrust into the world of disability is not like being in a similar place like Holland, but more like India, an entirely different country on a different continent, and it disorients them. I use India as an example because it shares many features for the parents of disabled children. The disabled child may look like their parents, may speak the

---

2. Kingsley, E.P. (1987). *Welcome to Holland.*

same language but the experience of being suddenly brought into the land of disability can be as disconcerting as an American arriving unprepared in India.

They are not only thrust into an environment that is different from what they expected, but in fact they are in a community and culture that bears almost no resemblance to their home country. Some families, to continue the metaphor, go out into this new world and begin to learn the local language and customs. Others function like expatriates: they create little enclaves of their former (nondisabled) world, closed off and attempting to pretend that there's not very much difference from before their child came, and after. But as parents of disabled children know very well, having a disabled family member changes everything.

Can we imagine a world where disabled people are different but equal, a variation on humanness? That is the world I wish to see, because quite frankly that is the world that I live in. In my world disabled adults are a full spectrum of human: some are kind, some evil; some skilled, some not; some successful, some unsuccessful; some are parents, some are not; some are working, some are not. In my world disabled children are encouraged to meet disabled adults and to develop a variety of skills and interests.

Indulge me for a minute while I imagine a world where disabled children are seen in their wholeness. The playgrounds that they go to provide a variety of ways of interacting with the equipment, and many opportunities for engaging other children, so that it is a pleasant and physically challenging environment. It might include a slalom course for kids with wheels, whether they ride skateboards, tricycles or wheelchairs. There would be quiet spaces that can be darkened so that children can interact in a low stimulation environment. There would be maps that include Braille information so that all parents would know about the equipment and the layout. There would be running water in a bathroom that is fully accessible. There would be a variety of seating options on the grass, at tables, in sun and shade so that people could rest and eat.

In this imaginary world, accessibility is built into the environment. In school, everyone learns sign language as well as spoken language so that everyone has the opportunity to be multilingual. Education is designed around the student not the student around the tests. Learning happens in lots of different environments. Some students learn through music, others through reading and still others through math and the sciences. At every level students work in groups based on affinity for the subject and not based on age or perceived gender. In this world all children's learning styles are welcomed. What started out as an attempt to create access for disabled children ends up creating options for all students.

Deficits and Isolation

Back in the real world of the U.S. in the early 21st century, nearly all disabled children are labeled as deficient. Rarely does anyone outside their family talk about the child's strengths. This approach imagines a mythical nondisabled child who meets mythical milestones of development and learning, against whom the disabled child is compared and found wanting. Viewing disabled children in this way creates problems not only for the disabled child but for the parents as well.

Right from the beginning, the cultural presumption is that a disabled baby is deficient. Professionals talk about what they cannot do and measure them against very strict nondisabled standards. Early intervention programs are geared to "help the child catch up," and never focus on the child's strengths, except to assess how they can help the child support "deficits." So a three-year-old who gets around the house by crawling is considered a failure. Parents are pushed to enroll the child in physical therapy, agree to surgeries that might put the child at risk, and use equipment and even medications to support the goal of standing and walking. The fact that the child is completely mobile and extremely successful at crawling is completely ignored. Simply adding a mobility device such as a wheelchair would give the child mobility outside the house. In the medical model the child's creativity, flexibility, and success in mobility are completely obliterated in favor of the often unattainable nondisabled goal of getting the child upright, with the final goal always focused on walking. As occupational therapist Judi Rogers (disabled) says, mobility is necessary and there are many options, but "walking is overrated."

One only has to look at a small sample of physically disabled adults to see myriad ways of navigating the world. Gregor Wolbring (disabled), a world famous bioethicist, has created an entirely floor-based home environment. Crawling is his preferred modality, and he's moved everything of importance in his house down to floor level so that he can access it easily. He uses a wheelchair only for going outside and for more traditional nondisabled environments. His creativity and adaptability means that his everyday life works very well for him, and what he's learned would be invaluable for disabled children and their families. Yet nondisabled families are either unaware of or unwilling to make use of resources like these.[3] Nondisabled professionals do not see Gregor as a brilliant adaptor but see his life as a failure of physical therapy.

When their son was born with disabilities, Megan and Hal Kirshbaum (both disabled) started an organization, Through the Looking Glass.[4] They were already connected to disabled adults like Hal who led wonderful busy lives, so they were shocked when they encountered negative attitudes about their lovely and lively son. As Megan says, "Well, I just felt a lot of the approaches to family and to disabled babies were very pathological in focus. I think that it was because it was based in the medical model and a way of thinking that was pathology focused. A lot of things people would experience with their babies—and that I was experiencing with my baby—were assessments where they would look for what was wrong with your baby. They didn't look at who your baby was as a little person, or what was wonderful about your relationship with your baby or something, they looked at what part of his body wasn't functioning right, or what kind of deficits did he have, or how his body might become more abnormal in time."[5]

In the medical model of disability, where disabled people are viewed as incomplete versions of nondisabled people, there are always reminders to disabled people that they are an inferior position.[6] If you think I'm exaggerating, just notice what happens when a person becomes permanently disabled, particularly if their disability is visible. How has their life changed? Did their employment stay the same? Where they lived? For most people, in fact for pretty much all nondisabled people, having a significant visible disability would completely change their current lives.

---

3. Gregor Wolbring, and other disabled adults, can be seen in the film *Fixed: The science fiction of human enhancement*. New Day Films. URL: http://www.fixedthemovie.com/

4. Through the Looking Glass (TLG) is a nationally recognized center that has pioneered research, training, and services for families in which a child, parent or grandparent has a disability or medical issue. TLG is a disability community-based nonprofit organization, which emerged from the independent living movement, and was founded in 1982 in Berkeley, California.

  Our mission is "To create, demonstrate and encourage non-pathological and empowering resources and model early intervention services for families with disability issues in parent or child which integrate expertise derived from personal disability experience and disability culture." URL: http://www.lookingglass.org/who-we-are/mission

5. Megan Kirshbaum, oral history in the *Disability Rights Independent Living Movement (DRILM) Historical Archives*. The Regional Oral History Office, The Bancroft Library, University of California, Berkeley. URL: http://bancroft.berkeley.edu/collections/drilm/index.html

6. "Most educational programmes for autistic toddlers aim to suppress autistic behaviors, and to make children follow a typical developmental trajectory. None is grounded in the unique way autistics learn." from Mottron, L. (2011). "Changing perceptions: The power of autism." *Nature* 479, 33-35.

Parents of disabled children know that their children will face challenges, not because of who they are, but because of how they are perceived and treated as disabled people. It always troubles me that nondisabled professionals who work with disabled children choose not to know disabled adults, because those adults hold the keys to many resources and creative ideas for living with a disability. Unfortunately the nondisabled professionals pass this prejudice against creating links to disabled adults and disability communities on to parents of disabled children.

In my research for this essay, I looked at lots of children who were different from their parents in significant ways. Some are disabled while their parents are not. Some appear very different from their parents in how their races are perceived. So? A biracial child might look more like one parent than the other at different ages. It was only when I looked at the writings of adults who had been adopted as young children by people of a different race that I began to find another way to explore my thinking about children who do not share the same experiences as their parents, even when they all live together lovingly.

After World War II, American families that were unable to get pregnant turned to adoption. Most families wanted children who looked like themselves and could pass in public as being their birth children, so children were often matched by skin color, hair color, eye color, and sometimes even religion to their adoptive families. As the demand for adoptable children grew, the availability of babies that matched Caucasian middle-class families shrank. White families now had a dilemma: they could continue to adopt domestically within the U.S., or that they could start to look for children outside the country. A number of families worked with international adoption agencies and adopted children from Korea. That generation of the Korean adoptees are now adults and they are telling us about their experiences.[7]

International adoptees talk about feeling greatly loved by their white parents but also about the isolation of being the only person of color in an all-white family, at their school, on the recreational sports teams. They write about the love of their adoptive parents, the care and concern and, frequently, middle-class privileges that came to them. They report that love was not enough; they longed for people who looked like them to be a part of their life and their families' lives. They

---

7.   Much of the writing in the section on transracial adoption is based in conversations I had with adult transracial adoptees and their white adoptive families at conferences for transracial families. See also: *Korean Adoptees: Dilemmas of Racism in Transracial Adoption* by Elizabeth Dawes Kim. PACER, Apr 5, 2014. URL: http://pacer-adoption.org/2014/04/05/korean-adoptees-dilemmas-of-racism-in-transracial-adoption/

tell us that while the world might have overlooked their nonwhite status when they were young children accompanied by white parents, as their activities separated them from their parents—during the teenage years, moving to work environments, going away to college—the world increasingly separated them, as a person of color, from their families. For many children this was an excruciating and painful process of losing class and temporarily borrowed racial privilege. As adults, the world sees them as people of color, yet they have no skills as people of color because their families did not include adults of color who have important survival knowledge in their lives.

For many of these transracial adoptees, an adult life which includes many people of color is completely separate from their childhood life, which included almost exclusively white people. They tell us of yearning for adults who could inform them and guide them in being people of color in predominately white environments. In the past two decades, books and conferences have focused on helping white adoptive parents understand this, encouraging them to bring adults of color into their children's lives and into their own lives.

Although it is rarely framed this way, I have observed that disabled children have a similar journey. They are isolated and kept away from disabled adults, and their families do not know any disabled people who are like them. They grow up in nondisabled homes where their families have nondisabled friends. They go to nondisabled schools, practice their religion in nondisabled environments, and are asked to participate in a nondisabled world that pretends they are welcome and no different. Their struggles as disabled children to survive in these environments, their need for disabled adults to give them strategies and resources, goes unnoticed by the nondisabled adults in their world. Without role models or connections to disability communities, young disabled people are forced to make their way on their own.

The impact of isolation versus being raised in community can be seen very dramatically when you look at children who grow up inside disability communities. Two disability groups, although very different in many ways, have created strong and supportive environments for disabled children. The dwarf community not only births children who are dwarfs, but also, through Little People of America,[8] has created an organizational structure to identify dwarf babies throughout the world and assist them in finding homes with dwarf parents. Similarly, in the Deaf community all children are taught sign language, whether they are hearing or deaf, so that they can fully participate in the culturally Deaf

---

8. Little People of America. URL: http://www.lpaonline.org/

community.[9]

Rebecca Cokely grew up disabled, had parents who were also dwarfs and knew other dwarf adults her whole life. As President of Little People of America she observed close-up how nondisabled parents dealt with having dwarf children, as she says here:

> The struggle is that the awesome parents, the ones who get it, get it because they care what their child thinks. They want to understand how adults with the same disabilities feel about things, so they can see what they may need to anticipate in their own kid. What gets me is when they totally dismiss or marginalize the opinion of the adult with a disability and think they have the right, or the privilege to tell us what our narrative should be.[10]

The research on students who attend schools for the deaf shows dramatic differences between children raised in homes where American Sign Language is spoken, particularly by native speakers, and children who grow up in all hearing environments without any access to sign language until they get to school. The children who grow up signing at an early age develop language as infants and acquire English as a second language much more readily, since they're already building on the strong language base of American Sign Language. Their school success is dramatically higher than children who come from all hearing environments. Yet the ongoing presumption that the nondisabled hearing environment is superior to a deaf or disabled environment permeates the perspectives and approaches used by hearing professionals working with deaf children.

It is striking and extremely disheartening to me that nondisabled families sincerely believe that raising children in completely nondisabled environments is acceptable. Imagine for a minute if our culture decided that all boy babies should be raised exclusively in the world of girls and women; that adult men would be completely absent from their lives even though adult men existed in the society. The society would be structured such that boy children would never meet or know an adult male until they themselves were adult males. People find this example ludicrous, and yet that is exactly the environment that we are providing for disabled children.

By raising our disabled children away from their communities of

---

9.   Capital "D" Deaf means people who are tied to the culture and language of American Sign Language. Lower case "d" deaf means people who have hearing disabilities.

10. Cokely, R. "The struggle is that awesome parents…." *Facebook*, December 10, 2014.

disabled adults, we are telling them that their difference is undesirable, because what societies value are the things we put into the community. If society valued disabled people, we would see them at all levels of society. They might be delivering our mail, be the pediatrician, teach at our children's schools, and be our neighbors. Disabled people would appear as one of many characters throughout all the children's books, would be present in all of our media, magazines, television, and internet. Familiarity with and knowledge about disabled people would be commonplace. The absence of disabled people from disabled children's lives tells them that disabled people are unwelcome in their world.

Before my daughter was born I read a research study about disabled children in public schools. The study found that by and large disabled children succeeded well prior to middle school. Regardless of their school environment, whether it was an all disabled classroom, a mixed disabled/non-disabled classroom, or an entirely nondisabled environment, the disabled kids were learning, socializing and fairly happy.

Beginning in middle school, as the social structure of the schools striated, disabled children were increasingly at a disadvantage. Many academic options became closed to them, such the science laboratory or advanced placement classes. In fact, a number of disabled students were told that they were not allowed in advanced placement classes because they also were enrolled in special education services and required accommodations such as Braille, sign language interpreters or a class note taker.

By middle school, nondisabled students begin to enact adult norms, and their childlike acceptance of diversity disappears. For the first time, many disabled children get a taste of the discrimination that is ableism.[11] The absence of disabled adults from their parents' lives and from their own means they are forced to navigate these difficult and often unfriendly environments without supports or resources that are available within their own community. Disabled students realize that their parents are not able to understand or assist them when they are being bullied at school for being different, so frequently they learn not to give their parents that information. By and large disabled students struggle alone until they reach adulthood when, if they are lucky, they encounter their first disabled adults.

Being aware of this problem I consciously decided to build disability support into my daughter's life from a very early age. While

11. "Ableism—a set of practices and beliefs that assign inferior value (worth) to people who have developmental, emotional, physical or psychiatric disabilities." URL: http://www.stopableism.org/what.asp

her school environment was entirely staffed by nondisabled adults, her afterschool programs, weekend and summer activities were in environments that were led by disabled adults.

I found my whole family benefitted when I brought disabled adults into my daughter's life—people who move like her, who share her disability experience, who have strategies for succeeding. We all need to know that there are people who look like us, move like us, have brains like ours. Disabled children rarely have that in their home, family or neighborhood, so parents need to seek out folks and make them visible to their child. Some families enroll their children in classes led by disabled adults. Other parents seek out disabled adults in their communities, create informal mentoring and attend disabled-run events. Whether the community is large or small there are disabled adults living there who can be beneficial to both disabled children and their families.

Nondisabled Professionals

Nondisabled staff in many educational, medical and therapeutic contexts that disabled children and their families must interact with rarely know any confident disabled adults who are directing their own lives. By and large they are working from a medical model of disability that views the disabled children as deficient.

They rarely see or honor the strengths that the children bring, nor can they even envision a disabled person's life that is happy and sexy and interesting and engaging. In other words, the nondisabled people working with disabled children do not envision those children as having lives as rich and fulfilling as their own or their own nondisabled children's.

That means that disabled children are constantly surrounded by people who neither see their potential nor believe in their full capabilities. Unfortunately for many disabled children, these attitudes are mirrored in their homes. Very few disabled children have an opportunity to learn skills from disabled adults and be seen in their wholeness. This is a huge loss to both disabled children and the nondisabled community.

I do not have a shared vocabulary with nondisabled people who are hired by other nondisabled people to decide what, if any, services my daughter can have. Note that I did not say "that my daughter is entitled to" because that is rarely, if ever, the determinant. She is *entitled* to be treated with full citizenship in all areas of civic life—to go to school, ride the bus, visit the library, play on the playgrounds, go to an amusement park, be in a carpool, join clubs, swim at the Y, take a plane.... Yet these activities are too often deemed by nondisabled people to be for other nondisabled people only.

Disabled people, as we are so often reminded, are the exception, the unexpected, the unwanted intrusion. In this view, to include us would cause expense, adjustments and inconvenience. In order to receive access to medical, educational and other public services, our families must interact with nondisabled professionals who accept such assumptions uncritically. To me, they are not 'service providers' or 'teachers,' they are gatekeepers. Their job is to keep the status quo, which means keeping disabled people out as much as possible, or, if they allow us in, they make sure that we know we are an exception and will only be allowed to stay if we are not too much of an inconvenience (meaning we accept their limited, and usually illegal, accommodations without complaint).

Every encounter with nondisabled gatekeepers requires strategic planning. Before I meet with them I must arm myself with knowledge about how their system works, what they are usually willing to do for kids like mine, what they will do if pressured, what kinds of pressure works and what approach they respond to best. My best source for this information is parents who have navigated this system before me. We, as parents, know that our children are entitled to these public services, but we also know that few of our kids ever get to use them. Always foremost in my mind are the consequences for my child if I do not navigate the gatekeeper's world properly, if I fail to get her through that gate.

With each gatekeeper, I struggled to learn their vocabulary and perspective. Do they call disabled children "handicapped" or "special needs" or something else? I learned from other parents that using the gatekeepers' preferred labels made them more likely to hear my points. Since each gatekeeper had different labels, I had to keep note of which words to use with which gatekeeper. They seldom bothered to find out and use my own preferred identities. Sometimes, if I slipped and used 'disabled person,' they would inform me that the correct term was 'a person with a disability.' Since my daughter and I were both 'persons with disabilities,' you would think we might know how we would like to be described, but to keep my daughter's options open, I would bite my tongue and try to get back to the point of the meeting.

In most situations the gatekeepers have names and titles, and when more than one of them was in the room, they would call each other by those. But I was always "Mom" as in, "I reviewed the request and called Mom who said...." I never had a name, even though I introduced myself at the beginning of each meeting, even though they always had both our names on their paperwork that was usually in front of them, even though I had 25 years of disability advocacy experience, a lifetime of living with a visible disability, peer-reviewed journal articles and my standing as a national expert on women and disability. None of that buffered me from being called "Mom." I was not a person, I was a placeholder, an interchangeable human who did not deserve the dignity of a name and certainly did not merit respect.

Raising a disabled child is a full-time, unpaid, 24/7 job. Yet I was expected to accommodate fully-salaried, 9-to-5 gatekeepers who expected me to meet at their convenience, always during their working hours, and to get to their preferred locations, however inconvenient for me and my daughter (who was usually required to be there so that the gatekeepers could see the object of their comments). Not only is there no financial compensation for attending these meetings, the paid gatekeepers would repeatedly question my previous decisions and remind me of the importance of following theirs. I had to comply if I wanted any hope of getting past them and getting the needed program for my child.

Disabled children interact with numerous systems, medical and educational. Each one generates reports that have significant impacts on the child's life as they determine what services the child can receive. Agencies often do not work together, so parents are required to fill out the same forms multiple times. A speech therapy evaluation might be needed for a child's Individualized Education Plan. A doctor's report might be necessary to get a disabled transit pass, but most agencies will not accept the doctor's note that's already been generated for a different agency, putting families and medical professionals in a constant revolving door of needing a statement to prove the child's disability over and over again.

These barriers to services, this gatekeeping of eligibility, means that families that have more money and are closer the white middle-class heterosexual norm are more likely to get services than families without those privileges. Even with those class privileges, services are so limited that many disabled children never receive them.

A child who becomes disabled early in life generates thousands of pages of documents. In theory, some systems provide paid Case Managers to handle this. But in reality, the parent is the actual Case Manager. Unpaid and outnumbered, the parent Case Manager is forced to not only document the child's needs in order to be eligible for services, but also to fight bureaucratic systems.

As Henry Frost, a middle school student in Tampa, Florida,

discovered, having a middle school across the street from your house does not make you eligible to attend if you have a disability and the 'assigned' program for your disability type is across town.[12] It mattered little if he could do just fine at the school across the street, because his disability label restricted him, in the school district's practices, to only attending the one special program at a middle school across town. It took Henry and his parents over a year of fighting and hosting a national campaign, I Stand With Henry, before the school district allowed him to go to school across the street. Of course, as often happens, the district refused to provide him the little bit of support that he needed, support that was written in his IEP, so that he would eventually fail.

In my home state of California a state ballot initiative designated funds for children from birth to age five. Each child born in the state now receives three nurse visits to provide support and early intervention. If the child has a disability or seems at risk of needing additional supports, then the state will provide more nurse visits and a paid Case Manager.

At a state forum for community input, I testified that my daughter, who was then twelve years old, had had eleven different Case Managers from three different systems—her early intervention program, the state's developmental disabilities agency and her school. None of them talked to each other. The only way a subsequent Case Manager got any materials was through getting copies from me. They were all paid Case Managers (in my state those jobs start at $35,000), but all the parents were untrained and unpaid.

I argued that in our system, parents should always be our children's primary Case Managers, and we should be trained and paid. The decision makers smiled at me and dismissed me. None of them were parents of disabled children or disabled themselves. They had no knowledge of how their systems even worked. So parents continue to teach other parents how to become Case Managers and advocate for their children.[13]

Children with some disabilities become eligible for school-based services at age 3.[14] Schools are some of the most rigid entities that

---

12. Zurcher, A. (October 15, 2012). "Henry's fight for inclusion." *The Huffington Post*. URL: http://www.huffingtonpost.com/ariane-zurcher/henry-frost-school_b_1962091.html

13. Under IDEA, every state has at least one Parent Training Information Center (PTI), usually staffed by parents of disabled children, which offers disability information and helps parents find resources and navigate Early Intervention and Special Education systems. A PTI locator can be found at http://www.parentcenterhub.org/find-your-center/

14. "The Individuals with Disabilities Education Act (IDEA) is a law ensuring services to children with disabilities throughout the nation. IDEA governs how states and public agencies provide early intervention, special education and related services to more than 6.5 million eligible infants,

parents will encounter. Typically, schools have predefined classrooms for disabled preschoolers, and they attempt to shoehorn all of the disabled children in their school district into their pre-existing programs. Although state and federal laws require schools to provide disabled children with a "free, appropriate education," by and large they do not.

Individualized education plans (IEP's) were designed to be contracts between school districts and parents to ensure an appropriate education for their child, however most parents are seen as little more than a nuisance by most school districts. Although my daughter was extremely bright, her multiple disabilities required accommodations in school settings. At every single IEP meeting at least one staff person said to me, "It's not really realistic for your child to be in the normal classroom." These comments occurred even years after she had proved her ability to succeed.

IEP meetings typically consisted of me, sometimes my daughter, and a multitude of school employees. Often IEP goals were pre-written (which is against the law) and presented to me as a fait accompli. I soon learned to bring friends with me to the IEP meeting. Their entire job was to fill the room and provide support for us in contrast to the numbers of school employees.

Each year of my daughter's life, we would pick a few battles to wage. Keeping what we already fought for was the first priority. In our case, that meant keeping her in the regular curriculum at her public school with a notetaker and computer technology support. Keeping the existing gatekeepers happy in her other services became the second priority. Each year, she and I would discuss what she wanted to do— summer camp, afterschool activities, learning to use the library, etc. Then I would contact other parents about their experiences, and I would report back to my daughter. She evaluated the options and barriers and would identify those she wanted us to take on. Thus, not only did we navigate systems together, but my daughter also gained self-advocacy skills.

I was always struck by how the nondisabled professionals in these meetings wanted to show that they understood the need to teach disabled youth to 'speak for themselves,' so they required my daughter to attend meetings where they always talked about her in ableist and derogatory ways. She hated attending those meetings and begged me to get her out of them.

Each time I tried, though, the professionals would state that I was being 'overprotective' and 'limiting her independence.' I didn't really care what they called me, but they refused to take action about her needed services unless she was in the room. They also refused to let her bring her iPad, which comforted her, into the meetings. The entire situation was abusive and completely disregarded her needs. Since we were both required to be in those horrible rooms to get her services, we would discuss the ways in which she was being required to perform their idea of a disabled student, how she felt, and how we were going to provide healing from the trauma of being bullied by larger, more powerful people.

We used the preparations for these meetings as opportunities on how to navigate disability-related bureaucracies where nondisabled people were always in charge. We developed tools for surviving in those rooms as well as creating comfort and support after those meetings. For me, that meant crying on the phone with another disabled mom. For her, it meant getting an iTunes gift card and downloading comforting entertainment.

The preschool years are a good training ground for parents of disabled children to learn how to navigate their school district. Sometimes the best lesson you learn from those years is to change school districts. An adversarial atmosphere between parents and school districts is so pervasive that one group of parents formed an organization called Mothers from Hell.[15] On their website, stories of actual encounters between parents and school personnel are documented, with heavy emphasis on the absurd humor that occurs in those encounters. The premise is if we didn't laugh at how horrible they are, we would become violent.

In short, I, like so many parents, was an unpaid, full time advocate, awareness educator, medical and educational expert (I had to explain to them what the other gatekeepers' reports meant), and case manager (who else had all the reports on my child?).

The actions and decisions of parents are judged, criticized and evaluated as part of the gatekeeper's process. If the parent seems in any way suspect, the gatekeeper may not only deny services to the child but may also report the family to Child Protective Services. One disabled parent with four disabled children told me that she gets reported annually by someone in her small town—a school aide, a bus driver, a

---

15. "Mothers From Hell... is a national group of parents, relatives, friends, and anyone who just plain 'gets it' fighting chipped tooth and broken press-on nail for the appropriate education, community acceptance, desperately needed services, rights of and entitlements for people with disabilities.... Our name is not about our advocacy philosophy, but a name bestowed on us for daring to stand up for our kids." URL: http://www.mothersfromhell2.org/

medical person—because the idea that a disabled woman can be a single parent to disabled children is incomprehensible to the person reporting her and therefore must be dangerous to the children.[16.]

Gatekeepers all see their systems as beneficial and nondiscriminatory, so navigating their resistances meant framing my approach in a way that was completely upside down to me. For example, my daughter wanted to participate in a school-run afterschool program. The gatekeeper saw her need to be in the program as 'extra' and 'inconvenient' and 'costly.' My daughter just wanted to play with her friends in a supervised but social environment. If I wanted my daughter to get past the gatekeeper, I had to push for her right to be in the program without pressing the point about how they were violating the law.

Parent advocates often say, and I agree, that the parent is the only person who sees and loves and believes in their child—their wholeness just the way they are right now. The gatekeepers see difference and difficulty. Parents will spend their life fighting for their child's rights, and it is exhausting and discouraging and oftentimes very upsetting.

The system is rigged so that parents of disabled kids have to work harder with fewer resources in order to achieve even a modicum of access to nondisabled environments for their children. The process is exhausting and isolating. I've even heard parents of preschoolers say "I've spent enough time on this child, now I'm giving my attention to the rest of my children."

Closing

Disabled people, regardless of impairment, have figured out how to live happy and fulfilling lives. A study by Through the Looking Glass shows that disabled parents excel at problem-solving and creativity. These are gifts that every family could use, but keeping disabled and nondisabled people separated in our society means that this valuable knowledge is not shared.

Parenting a disabled child provides an opportunity to expand and include more cultures in the family, and to participate in both the nondisabled and disabled worlds. It is deeply sad that so few families choose this option. Instead, nearly all families put their energy into trying to get the disabled child to fit into the predetermined mold of inadequate and broken disabled person, one who will never quite succeed. Until we begin to imagine a world where disability is a

---

16. See the essay on disabled parents in this book for more about the topic.

difference, not an inferior status, we are trapped. And disabled children pay the price.

JUST THE FACTS MA'AM

- Over 6 million disabled children receive special education school services in the United States.
- Almost no schools have disabled teachers.

RESOURCES

Mothers from Hell 2. URL: http://www.MothersFromHell2.org
Ollibean. URL: http://www.Ollibean.com
Parent Training and Information Centers. URL:
    http://www.parentcenterhub.org/find-your-center/

A full bibliography is available at my website: www.corbettotoole.com

12.

Disabled Parents

"Disability is an ingenious way to live." — Neil Marcus (disabled)[1]

Summary

Disabled people are told repeatedly that they should not be parents, that they are not safe with children and that they should not pass on their disability to the next generation. Disabled people are sterilized to stop them from ever getting pregnant. If they do have children, many disabled parents lose them because someone complains to Child Protective Services, and the people evaluating them as parents do not believe that disabled people should have children.

Many disabled adults are great parents. Their children are happy and safe. Like all parents, when they have support and resources they can manage any parenting challenges. Often the best support comes from other disabled parents. When the evaluators believe that disabled parents are capable of being good parents, then they see the many wonderful ways that disabled parents take care of their children.

Four children, three all girls, in five years. That's the birth clump in my Irish-American Catholic family. Three teenage girls, all at the same time. My dad did not have an easy time with us. He often yelled with exasperation, "I can't wait until you have kids of your own. You'll see what it's like." One day he started his well-practiced rant as he looked up to see which daughter he was yelling at this time. When he realized

---

1. Marcus, N. *Storm Reading.* URL: http://vimeo.com/26988933

it was me, he stopped his rant mid-sentence and stammered "Oh forget it." In that moment I realized, with that simple interruption of his rant, that he believed that I would never have children, never raise children. I would never be a mother.

Luckily I never believed him.

There were no adult disabled women in my childhood. I worked my way through high school as a babysitter, the only job available for the girls of my era. It was widely viewed as the training ground for girls to learn childcare skills that they would use when they became mothers. Yet no one ever talked to me about becoming a mother, although that message was embedded in everything the adults told my sisters.

Even at the disabled children's summer camp[2] that I attended for many years, we would discuss the boys we liked, but we never discussed the possibility of having children. Most of us were unclear about whether the definition of 'mother' included disabled women at all. If we imagined ourselves as sexual beings we were only allowed the option of being heterosexual, and it was always implied if not directly stated that our future husbands would be nondisabled.

After college and for the next two decades, I longed to become a mother. In the disability community, I was everyone's favorite babysitter, and I welcomed to the opportunity to play with their kids. During my early 20s, I had made a few somewhat passive attempts by "accidentally" forgetting my birth control pill. During my 30s I tried to get pregnant by artificial insemination, but that did not work. By the age of 42, I had given up any hope of parenting.

It was in this context that, in 1993, I had the unexpected opportunity to adopt a disabled child. It was a complete surprise when, at a meeting at the Women's Foundation in San Francisco, my friend Atsuko Kuwana (disabled) said "Corbett, would you like a baby?"

"Yes!" I replied, without hesitation, "Tell me more."

Atsuko and her husband Michael Winter (disabled), both wheelchair users, had adopted their son, who had clubfeet, from a foundling home in Japan. The Director of the home had written to them about the difficulty of finding a home for a baby girl with cerebral palsy. Atsuko thought immediately of me. Their relationship with the Director was strong enough that their recommendation would ensure a placement. We agreed that I would think about it overnight and give her an answer in the morning. My joy carried me not only to the next

---

2. Camp Caravan, Royalston, Massachusetts. Camp Caravan still exists, but it is no longer a summer camp for disabled kids. It is run by the Millers River Educational Cooperative. URL: http://www.campcaravan.org/

day, when I told them yes, but for the 20 years since.

Disabled Parents

Until the early 1990s there was very little research on disabled parents. The prejudice against disabled people becoming parents was so strong that no one bothered to actually evaluate them fairly. In the past twenty years, two organizations, Through the Looking Glass in the United States and the Disabled Parents Network in the United Kingdom, have provided nearly all of the available data on disabled parents that presumes they are capable of being safe parents for their children. This essay relies heavily on these two sources, both of which have published dozens of articles and reports on disabled parents. Through the Looking Glass also provided significant assistance and input to the U.S. National Council on Disability for their 2012 report on disabled parents, *Rocking the Cradle: Ensuring the Rights of Parents with Disabilities and Their Children*. As a disabled parent, I have conducted some research with Canadian disabled parent and researcher Tanis Doe, Ph.D. in the 1990s, and in 2013 I interviewed five disabled mothers, and one nondisabled mother married to a disabled man, who collectively have 11 children. This essay uses these four data sources extensively.

Even with forty years of disability rights activism in the U.S. and U.K., disabled women rarely receive any encouragement to become mothers. The barriers might take different forms for different types of disabilities, but the underlying message is the same—motherhood is an important job, and disabled women can never meet the standard reserved for nondisabled women. As is stated in *Rocking the Cradle*:

> Although the right to be a parent is generally regarded as fundamental, this right is not always assumed for people with disabilities. According to Megan Kirshbaum and Rhoda Olkin of Through the Looking Glass (TLG), "Parenting has been the last frontier for people with disabilities and an arena in which parents are likely to encounter prejudice."[3]

The archetype for motherhood embeds the nondisabled body so deeply that any deviation from that illusionary body is deemed unacceptable. Our society allows disabled people to have different ways and levels to participate in sports and to be useful to our local

---

3.   National Council on Disabilities. *Rocking the Cradle: Ensuring the Rights of Parents with Disabilities and Their Children*. URL: http://www.ncd.gov/publications/2012/Sep272012/

communities, but the job of parenting is held to an impossible standard. We celebrate the glowing pregnant woman, the beautiful young woman holding her new baby, and the self-sacrificing mother who creates the successful child. Into these images we infuse race (the mothering standard is white), class (mothers stay at home and raise their children), and lack of disability (mothers must have unlimited physical and mental prowess). So when it comes to parenthood, disabled women join women of color and poor women as a category that society attempts to restrict and control, especially in terms of reproduction. Since many of us are in more than one category, the restrictions come in many layers.

How do you keep disabled women from becoming mothers? The gatekeepers such as social workers and medical professionals control their bodies as much as they can. Disabled women, especially women with cognitive or psychiatric disabilities, are frequently sterilized or put on contraceptives.[4] When that doesn't work and the woman has children, the children may be forcibly removed. But always, disabled women are told they are not fit to be parents. As the National Council on Disability parenting report states:

> The power of the eugenics ideology persists. Women with disabilities still contend with coercive tactics designed to encourage sterilization or abortion because they are not deemed fit for motherhood. Equally alarming, a growing trend is emerging toward sterilizing people with intellectual or psychiatric disabilities.[5]

Even if we are white, middle class, disabled women, our disability makes us unfit for motherhood.[6] We are seen primarily as a danger to our children. We have learned to navigate a hostile world, we have resourcefulness, wonderful problem solving skills and tenacity, yet these skills are rarely appreciated by the nondisabled world. In fact, none of our gifts are even seen by the nondisabled world. We are just broken people, and we are not allowed to be parents.

In 2012 the National Council on Disability undertook the first major research on parents with disabilities in the United States.

---

4.   *Rocking the Cradle.* See previous note.

5.   Ibid. (This means see previous note.)

6.   For those of us who are not white and/or not middle class and/or not straight and/or not partnered with someone of the opposite gender, we are much more likely to be viewed as unfit for parenting. Discrimination in child removals shows heavy race, gender, income and sexual orientation bias in addition to disability bias.

Analyzing data from the 2010 American Community Survey, TLG[7] estimates that at least 4.1 million parents with reported disabilities in the United States have children under age 18; meaning that at least 6.2 percent of American parents who have children under age 18 have at least one reported disability."[8]

Although the report does not specifically report on grandparents, Through the Looking Glass works with all the child's primary caregivers and provides specific resources to grandparents and other older family members who are increasingly being relied on to provide a parenting role. Aging also increases the probability of some types of disability, although grandparents are rarely included in data on parenting.

Because of the scarcity of substantive data at the local and national levels, parents with disabilities in the U.S. remain mostly invisible.[9] According to Paul Preston, co-director of the National Center for Parents with Disabilities at Through the Looking Glass, "Erroneous assumptions about the low prevalence of parents with disabilities affect the availability of resources or the motivation to create new resources specifically for parents with disabilities and their families."[10]

The presence of disabled parents is nearly invisible in American society. In part this is because we consider the role of parents and the role of disabled people as so separate that we cannot imagine disabled people as parents. When a disabled parent is shown in the media, it is typically a disabled father with a strong and healthy nondisabled wife. The implicit assumption is that she is the caregiver. When the disabled parent is the primary caregiver, challenges to their parenting come in many forms and sometimes even result in losing custody of the children.

Disabled people, especially disabled women, are widely discouraged from even considering parenting. Medical professionals offer

---

7.   Through the Looking Glass (TLG) is a nationally recognized center that has pioneered research, training, and services for families in which a child, parent or grandparent has a disability or medical issue. TLG is a disability community-based nonprofit organization, which emerged from the independent living movement, and was founded in 1982 in Berkeley, California.

      Their mission is "To create, demonstrate and encourage non-pathological and empowering resources and model early intervention services for families with disability issues in parent or child which integrate expertise derived from personal disability experience and disability culture." URL: http://www.lookingglass.org

8.   *Rocking the Cradle*, see note 3.

9.   In the U.K. the Disabled Parents Network has substantially increased the visibility of disabled parents, has changed government policies and has developed governmental supports specifically for disabled parents.

10. *National Center for Parents with Disabilities*. Through the Looking Glass. URL: https://lookingglass.org/services/national-services/71-ncpd. Also, see note 7.

sterilization,[11] geneticists offer abortion, and social services are set up to find problems, not solutions, for disabled parents. Through the Looking Glass researchers Megan Kirshbaum (disabled) and Rhoda Olkin (disabled) point out that:

> [M]uch of the research on parents with disabilities has been driven by a search for problems in these families.... As a result of pervasive pernicious practices, disabled parents face the artificial obstacle of presumed incompetence. As this stereotype becomes enacted through custody and policy practices, disabled parents experience extraordinarily high rates of family disruption through actual or threatened loss of custody. Despite this harrowing history, many people with disabilities still choose to become parents. The desire to become a parent traverses all cultural, physical, and political boundaries.[12]

Far too often, the entire emphasis of stories about disabled parents focuses on perceived problems, and almost never the joy of parenting, which is usually the focus of stories about nondisabled parents. While I will spend some time discussing the long-standing problems facing disabled people who want to be parents, I will spend an equal amount of time documenting the ways in which being a disabled parent offers both children and society new resources and ideas. As performance artist Neil Marcus (disabled) says, "disability is an ingenious way to live."[13] In my research with disabled parents, I found similar results to research conducted by the Disabled Parents Network in the UK[14] and Through the Looking Glass in the United States. Their research found that the resourcefulness required for being disabled in a world geared for nondisabled people translates beautifully to handling the everyday challenges of parenting.

Barriers For Disabled Parents

Most people hold attitudes similar to my dad's; they just can't imagine disabled people as parents. When my dad stumbled over the idea that I might have children, I was walking with crutches, which does not seem

---

11. "The first half of the 20th century was plagued by the eugenics movement. As a result, by 1970 more than 65,000 Americans had been involuntarily sterilized." *Rocking the Cradle*, see note 3.

12. Ibid.

13. See note 1.

14. URL: http://disabledparentsnetwork.org.uk/

to me to be a huge barrier to being a mom. Yet even that level of disability excluded me from society's idea of motherhood. Another disabled woman put it this way, "Before I got pregnant, I was told by my father that it would be irresponsible of me to have a baby because I would be an unfit mother. This is the view of most of society."[15]

Yet study after study shows that the main problems disabled people face are the presumptions that they are unable to be parents. Because this assumption is so deeply embedded in America, there are very few services or resources designed to support disabled people as parents. While the social services stereotype is that having a disability automatically makes a person an unfit parent, disabled parents argue that the problem is the negative attitudes of the people evaluating disabled parents.

Disabled people often do not lack skills, but instead often lack the resources we need to parent successfully. All parents, including disabled parents, need supports, unbiased services, food, and shelter. As one study for the Disabled Parents Network in the UK showed:

> For some years, disabled parents themselves had been arguing that inaccessible and inadequate services, and a lack of support, create problems for them and their children. It is not impairment, learning difficulties or mental health needs that are primarily responsible for the difficulties they face. Instead, it is negative attitudes towards disabled parents and unequal access to support that too often undermine family life.[16]

Even children's books about disabled people almost never portray them as parents.[17] Materials on parenting almost never include disabled people. Strong negative societal attitudes that presume that disabled people will automatically be unfit parents provide daily roadblocks. Two disability groups, the dwarf[18] and the Deaf[19] communities,

---

15. *Rocking the Cradle*, see note 3.

16. "The Task Force received evidence that disabled parents commonly face the assumption that their impairment or illness in itself, and inevitably, leads to child deprivation, potential harm or abuse. In contrast, Task Force members argued for an approach which recognises that these risks are created and/or exacerbated by the lack of appropriate support, unequal access to mainstream services, negative attitudes, and the poverty and poor housing which can be associated with physical/sensory impairments, learning disability and mental health difficulties." Disabled Parents' Network. see note 14.

17. *Mama Zooms* by Jane Cowen-Fletcher is a rare exception to this.

18. The preferred language is "dwarf" or "little person."

19. Capital "D" Deaf means that people are tied to each other through the culture and language of American Sign Language. Small "d" deaf means that people have a hearing impairment. So all Deaf people are deaf, but not all deaf people are Deaf.

intentionally challenge these stereotypes.

Little People of America (LPA)[20.] hosts regional and national conferences where disabled parents are the leaders. Young people attending these conferences see disabled parents in a variety of roles: they organize the conference, coach the sports teams, and work in a variety of jobs. In addition, Little People of America maintains a database of dwarf children worldwide who are available for adoption. LPA provides support systems, both formal and informal, to help dwarf parents adopt dwarf children. The Deaf community has a similar support structure.

Outside of these two uniquely supportive communities, disabled people encounter hostility and significant barriers to becoming parents. Although disabled parents have been taking care of children for generations, the challenges to their parenting has meant that they are largely invisible, in many cases for fear of losing their children. For example, we don't know how the frontier's blind women navigated parenting. There must have been women who did, we just don't know who they were or how they did it.[21.]

Most of our contemporary beliefs about whether or not something can be accomplished are based on our knowledge that someone has already done it. So when a woman with Down Syndrome announces her desire to become pregnant, the massive resistance she encounters is largely because neither she nor the people around her have any knowledge of how people with Down Syndrome manage parenting tasks. Instead of encouraging her and finding creative solutions, society is structured to prevent her from getting pregnant.

Women with Down Syndrome are currently parenting, many of them successfully.[22.] Yet finding information about their strategies is incredibly difficult. In part, social service professionals do not want to document the successes of Down Syndrome parents for fear that more

---

20. Little People of America (LPA) is a nonprofit organization that provides support and information to people of short stature and their families. URL: http://www.lpaonline.org/

21. I use this example to make a point. Blind people have always been able to live in nondisabled society so there must have been some blind women parenting on the frontier—whether they started out blind before they became parents or they became blind.

22. "Most of these studies have focused only on identifying parents with intellectual disabilities who provide inadequate childcare, rather than identifying predictors of adequate childcare such as coping and skill acquisition—despite the fact that a substantial number of parents with intellectual disabilities have provided adequate care." from Working Together with Parents Network. (In the UK people with intellectual disabilities are called 'people with learning difficulties' or 'people with learning disabilities.'). Source URL: http://www.bristol.ac.uk/sps/media/WTWPN_documents/intro-to-parents-with-learning-diffs-july-2014.pdf p. 232

people with Down Syndrome will want to become parents. Eugenics[23] has moved out of sterilizing women in the operating theater and into restricting their reproductive choices and child custody.

In a study that I conducted with Tanis Doe we found that:

> In general, with rare exceptions, people with disabilities do not get asked if they want to have children. They don't get asked if they want to be sexual. The silence around sexuality includes their parents, their counselors, their teachers, and most health professionals. Yet these same people sometimes counsel in favor of involuntary sterilization.[24]

Research in the past decade by Through the Looking Glass and the Disabled Parents Network has repeatedly shown that, with appropriate supports, nearly all disabled people are capable of being safe and effective parents. The problem is that our society holds tightly to the belief that disabled people are incapable of being safe and effective parents, so all efforts are geared to preventing parenting rather than supporting it.

> In addition to the myth of asexuality and skepticism regarding their ability to attract partners, women with disabilities have been discouraged from having children for a variety of other reasons. Concerns that they will give birth to 'defective' babies and prejudicial assumptions about their capacity to care for children often underpin the resistance that they may encounter.[25]

Often it is only the disabled person and their immediate support system that believes in them as successful disabled parents. Preparing their "arguments" for their ability to be a safe parent is exhausting. "The most difficult preparations were those to mentally ready ourselves for the likely probability that there would be—and will always be—people who doubted our abilities and worth as parents."[26]

While parents with disabilities may face big challenges, with

---

23. Eugenics: The study or practice of attempting to improve the human gene pool by encouraging the reproduction of people considered to have desirable traits and discouraging or preventing the reproduction of people considered to have undesirable traits. URL: http://www.thefreedictionary.com/eugenics

24. *Rocking the Cradle*, see note 3.

25. Ibid.

26. Ibid.

appropriate supports many can be great parents. Just like other parents, they do not have to be responsible for every part of childrearing all by themselves. All parents rely on supports to help raise their children, such as day care, carpools, schools, babysitting co-ops, or advice from other parents. Those with disabilities might need other supports, such as an adaptive crib or the use of a mobile device to help remember tasks, or personal supports designed to assist them, such as in-home parenting training, respite care, budgeting assistance, or homework assistance. It can be a relief for parents with disabilities to realize that, just like other parents, they do not have to be responsible for every part of childrearing all by themselves.[27]

There are very few in-person disabled parent support groups, so disabled parents have created online communities. Often these online groups are the only place that disabled people considering parenting can get accurate information and support. Parents share the specifics of how they manage different situations, but most importantly, they share the attitude that safe and effective parenting is not only possible but within their reach.

> The ability to be a good mother does not reside in the ability to chase around after a toddler, nor in the ability to teach your child how to ride a bike. Neither does it include protecting your child from being teased about her parent's disability; all children find something to tease each other about and a sturdy, self-confident child will emerge unscathed.[28]

Pathologizing Disabled Families

When disabled people do become parents, they often experience extreme prejudice. If the disabled parent has a nondisabled partner, it is usually presumed by nondisabled people that the nondisabled partner is "the real parent." If both parents are disabled, nondisabled people frequently ask who is taking care of the children. In a study that I conducted with Canadian researcher Tanis Doe (disabled), which was cited in the NCD report, disabled parents who were out in public with their children reported being asked "If it is ours; who is the parent?; where is the parent?; or 'why are you holding it?'"[29]

27. Brillhart, L., Lightfoot, E., & Yuan, S. (2012). "A chance to parent." *Exceptional Parent* 42(2), 39-41. ERIC #: EJ968423 IN PARENTING RESOURCES. URL: http://eric.ed.gov/?id=EJ968423

28. Carrie Killoran NCD, *Rocking the Cradle*, see note 3.

29. Ibid.

Pervasive prejudice exists even among those closest to pregnant disabled women. In the *Rocking the Cradle* report, one disabled woman reported that she was persistently advised to adopt, since both she and her male partner have a genetically based disability. They chose to get pregnant, but "many people did not express happiness regarding Kathryn's pregnancy until tests revealed that the baby did not have their disability."[30] Even announcing the news of a pregnancy can be a disappointing experience for disabled parents. When another disabled woman announced that she was having twins, her mother's reply was "Now your husband has three babies."[31] This lack of support is unfortunately very common.

In addition to the common misconception that a non-disabled partner is "the real parent" and caregiver to the children, children of disabled parents are typically perceived to have a more burdensome life. One disabled couple found that people assumed they had adopted their apparently nondisabled son so that they could acquire a caregiver.

> They didn't say it directly, but I knew what they were thinking. But I did not ask my son to help me, because I don't want people to see him as my little helper. Now he's 21, and I think when he was young I did more for him than nondisabled parents do. It was always in the back of my head, both in Japan and the U.S. I don't want people to see my son as my little helper.[32]

As long as people presume disabled people are not qualified to be parents, the barriers and prejudices will continue unabated.

Embedded in all of this is the presumption that only nondisabled people should be parents. This assumption is so strong that children of disabled parents are removed from the home at very high rates. Yet every single research study shows that nearly always the basis for removal is prejudice against disabled people, not inadequate parenting by disabled people.

> Perhaps the biggest hurdle faced by disabled parents is the deep-seated assumption that their children would be better off with non-disabled parents. Social workers – and society generally – need more examples of the positive outcomes when disabled

---

30. *Rocking the Cradle*, see note 3.

31. Ibid.

32. From my interviews with disabled mothers.

parents are supported to look after their children.[33]

Breaking Up Families

The rate of removal of children from families with parental disability—particularly psychiatric, intellectual, or developmental disability—is ominously higher than rates for children whose parents are not disabled. This removal is carried out with far less cause, owing to specific, preventable problems in the child welfare system. Further, parents with disabilities are more likely to lose custody of their children after divorce, have more difficulty in accessing reproductive health care, and they face significant barriers to adopting children.[34]

Perhaps most disturbing are state laws that consider parental disability as a risk factor for child abuse. According to the 2012 *Rocking the Cradle* report, every single state allows the fact that a parent has a disability to be a determining factor in terminating parental rights.[35] In theory, evaluation for removing a child from a home should be based on whether or not the child is in danger or being caused any harm. Since the people doing the evaluations have no knowledge about how disabled people can successfully parent, evaluations are typically based on negative, ableist stereotypes that disabled people are unfit to be parents.

Let me give you one example. In the late 1980s in California a disabled mother who uses a power wheelchair was undergoing a Child Protective Services parental fitness evaluation. The social worker required her to show how she changed the baby's diaper. The mother carried the baby into the bedroom and laid him on a changing pad on top of the bed. She knew from experience that the bed was the safest place to do the diapering. She used appropriate sanitary procedures such as using a washable diaper pad. The mother liked the bed because the baby sank in a little bit, which prevented him from rolling around. This made diapering more stable for both the baby and the mother. But the social worker had never seen a disabled person change a diaper, nor did she ask the mother what the advantages were of changing a baby on the bed.

Instead, she required the mother to change the baby on the kitchen table. The mother objected, saying that she knew it was not safe. The social worker said, "If you cannot change your baby safely on the table,

---

33. *Rocking the Cradle*, see note 3.

34. Ibid.

35. Ibid.

you cannot keep your child." The interaction was videotaped, and it indeed showed a mother who could not safely change her baby on the kitchen table. This was later used in court to demonstrate that she was not a safe mother.

The woman's lawyer brought in an expert on disabled parenting who reviewed the videotape but also videotaped the mother changing the baby's diaper on the bed. The expert told the court that this mother had in fact figured out a safe and sanitary way to change her baby's diaper by doing it on the bed. The courts followed the prejudicial recommendations of the social worker, and the mother lost custody of her son. And since she was pregnant at the time, she also lost custody of her second child as soon as he was born. This is a very common occurrence.[36]

Disabled parents do everything they can to stay off the radar of social service systems. Research by Through the Looking Glass and the Disabled Parents Network over the past decade shows that once social service systems get ahold of disabled parents, they are likely to lose their children. Although there are different rates of removal of children depending on the type of disability, all disabled parents risk losing their children. The rate of removal averages between 40 and 80%. That means that out of 100 disabled parents, between 40 and 80 of them will lose custody of their children before the child turns 18 years old.[37]

If you think that losing their children only happens to poor women or to disabled parents who have no friends and resources, you would be completely wrong. Even successful disabled people with lots of resources are threatened with losing their children. No one is immune to the threat of breaking up the family. Megan Kirschbaum, a leading researcher on disabled parents, found in her 2001 research that that even highly skilled and networked parents are presumed incompetent by nondisabled social service systems.

> Parents with disabilities were being pathologized by professionals, or underestimated. There were a lot of attitudinal problems they experienced with professionals who were assuming that they wouldn't be able to take care of their babies, or wouldn't be able to take good care of their babies. Most of these parents who were interviewed were extremely competent people. They were mostly prominent, competent people in the

---

36. Megan Kirschbaum, oral history in the *Disability Rights Independent Living Movement (DRILM) Historical Archives.* The Regional Oral History Office, The Bancroft Library, University of California, Berkeley. URL: http://bancroft.berkeley.edu/collections/drilm/index.html

37. *Rocking the Cradle*, see note 3.

disability community. It was rather startling that they would be questioned in that way. They were people with quite a lot of resources, as far as support systems and finances and things.[38.]

One person who has experienced a lot of challenges to her parenting is Carrie Ann Lucas (disabled), the Director, Founder and staff attorney at the Center for the Rights of Disabled Parents. She is also a disabled single parent with four adopted disabled children. Even though she runs one of the only legal centers for disabled parents, owns her own home, and is a successful practicing lawyer, at least once a year someone reports her family to child protective services. These reports have been filed by people as different as a school aide, a neighbor, and even someone driving by their house.

One of Carrie's daughters is very stubborn and does not like doing things for herself. Carrie deeply believes that her daughter needs to have independent living skills in order to survive as an adult. So whenever her daughter refuses to drive her own wheelchair up the 10 foot ramp into the house, Carrie just sits at the top of the ramp waits for her to do it. A stranger driving by observed her daughter sitting at the bottom of the ramp on a warm sunny day for 10 minutes while Carrie sat the top of the ramp waiting for her. This stranger decided that two disabled people in electric wheelchairs sitting by themselves outside for 10 minutes must mean that they are stranded and in need of nondisabled assistance, and he called Child Protective Services. Because of Carrie's extensive expertise, and the fact that her home is a safe and loving place for all of her children, these complaints are easily dealt with, but it's extremely troubling to me that we've created a system where disabled parents are presumed so incompetent that sitting outside on a sunny day with their child is cause for filing a Child Protective Services report.

Sometimes there doesn't even have to be a formal report filed, because just the threat of involving social services is used against the disabled parent. A common tactic in divorce proceedings is for the nondisabled parent to threaten to inform the social services systems of how the disabled parent accomplishes child care tasks. Most often disabled parents are pressured to sign away all rights to child support and alimony and agree to whatever custody arrangements are proposed, in order to maintain some visitation and custody of their child.[39.]

---

38. Kirshbaum, see note 36.

39. *Rocking the Cradle*, see note 3.

Positives

Some disabled people become parents through pregnancy, some through adoption. However they become parents, disabled people have to fight hard to make their family and to keep their family intact, but the joy of being a parent overcomes all the barriers. As one of the disabled women I interviewed in 2013 stated:

> Being someone's mother is not something special, because I am a woman, a human being. Although I am a disabled person, I want to have an education, a job. I want to marry. I want to have a kid. To me it is nothing special, but the society doesn't think so. I always tell myself I am doing what other women do. I hope that for young disabled women, I want them to be whatever they want to be. I hope we become good role models for young women with disabilities.[40.]

Some disabled people who are already choosing adoption choose to adopt children with disabilities. One woman who grew up attending Little People of America conferences says: "I grew up in dwarf culture knowing I'd likely adopt a dwarf kid." Other disabled parents who found disability community, support, and culture as adults also choose to adopt disabled children. For them it is a gift to be able to raise disabled children within a disability community. Nearly all disabled children grow up in entirely nondisabled environments. While this teaches them how to survive in those environments, they are rarely connected to adult disability communities. They are cut off from finding resources and strategies that could make life easier living in the nondisabled world. Since the vast majority of nondisabled people raising disabled children prefer to be disconnected from disabled adults, there's very little overlap between communities of disabled parents and parents of disabled children.[41.]

I really wanted to adopt a kid with a disability. I wanted to share my joy at being part of a disability movement, and I wanted to spare one disabled kid the isolation of growing up with only a nondisabled world perspective. Another disabled parent I spoke to sees it this way:

---

40. From my interviews with disabled mothers.

41. See "Welcome to India" in this book.

> I think what makes us different than nondisabled parents is that we don't have to 'make sense' of our kids' disabilities. They just are. I see other parents trying to make sense of their kids' disabilities through cliché, sentimentality, etc. My kids aren't like everyone else. I'm not like everyone else.

In *Rocking the Cradle* Megan Kirshbaum, co-founder of Through the Looking Glass, reported that disability culture holds certain values that assist parents with disabilities to be effective and successful parents: awareness of social stigma and obstacles, familiarity with different strategies used by disabled people, ability to differentiate which strategy will be effective in each situation, respect for expertise and adaptations derived from personal disability experience, non-pathological focus, empowerment, disability culture as a support, interdependence, respectful orientation (i.e. presumption of competence).[42]

Perhaps the clearest way to see the positives about disabled parents is to look at a few who intentionally chose to adopt disabled children. I conducted research with five disabled mothers and a nondisabled mother who was married to a disabled man. Among them there were 11 disabled children. Being disabled before they became parents gave one mother a distinct advantage. One couple who was white applied to adopt children of color.

> We had to go through "training" to adopt transracially. I remember a discussion about how when people adopt across race, they become a "conspicuous" family and that some white people really have a difficult time dealing with being so conspicuous. I see my disability as an asset in this regard. My family gets stared at constantly, but when I'm not with them I'm always stared at because of my visible disability. Now we're just a little more interesting to be stared at. But I know that I can manage the staring and conspicuousness a lot better than people who've never had that experience. I have a lot of tools in my toolbox for dealing with that.[43]

For disabled children, having in-home adult disabled role models is extremely rare, although the absence of disabled adults in the lives of disabled children is rarely mentioned as a concern in the literature. Yet,

---

42. Kirshbaum, see note 36.

43. Transracial adoption means adoption of a child by parents of a different race. Also, this quote is from my interviews with disabled mothers.

it is well documented in the transracial adoption literature of the past decade that the presence of adults who look like the adopted child provides important role modeling.[44] According to accounts by many of these now-adult children, lack of adult role models profoundly shaped their childhood. For disabled children, the absence of disabled role models in their lives is the norm, not the exception. The absence is so severe that some children maintain a fantasy of cure based on the lack of role models, while others presume death upon adulthood.[45]

Some disabled parents see great value in sharing their connections to the disability community, such as in one family where the husband is disabled and the wife is not:

> Our overall disability perspective is a social/civil rights model; that disability is a difference that should be acknowledged, but that it's not a negative thing in itself. I think that has affected our daughters in that we didn't expect anything different from them than if they had not been disabled. Plus we connected them with other disabled adults who are role models (my husband is disabled but I'm not). I think we 'normalized' it.[46]

Disabled parents find that passing on disability culture, sharing knowledge of how social service systems work, networking and teaching problem solving skills to their children are important aspects of disabled parenting. But above all else, maintaining a sense of humor is critically important. One parent I interviewed notes that, "having a sense of (dark) humor about disability stuff, especially the things people say to you or your kids," is important for their kids to learn to deal with negative stereotypes about disabled people. Another parent found that her disabled son was so used to using his disability as an excuse with his nondisabled foster parents that he was brought up short when it didn't work with his adoptive disabled mother.

> One day, right after placement (we did 9 months of preplacement visits, so kid is very attached here), my youngest, when arguing about having to make his bed said: 'You know I'm

---

44. Much of the writing in the section on transracial adoption is based in conversations I had with adult transracial adoptees and their white adoptive families at conferences for transracial families. See also: *Korean Adoptees: Dilemmas of Racism in Transracial Adoption* by Elizabeth Dawes Kim. PACER, Apr 5, 2014. URL: http://pacer-adoption.org/2014/04/05/korean-adoptees-dilemmas-of-racism-in-transracial-adoption/

45. *Fixed: The science fiction of human enhancement.* New Day Films. URL: http://www.fixedthemovie.com/

46. From my interviews with disabled mothers.

handicapped, I can't make my bed.' I just laughed and said, 'Look around dude, we all have disabilities. That excuse doesn't fly here.'[47]

Some disabled parents find that being the only disabled adult during social services and school meetings can be an unexpected advantage. Often, the disabled adult is the only person in the room who actually knows successful disabled adults, so they can advocate for the resources that will enable their disabled child to have the most options and skills for learning and growing. As one parent with a visible disability that I interviewed, who also has a Ph.D., found:

> Medical professionals get the message pretty quickly that I'm an informed and strong advocate, and when they find out I'm a professor in disability studies (they think it's something medical, they don't really get that I'm an artist!), they tend to give me more respect.[48]

Perhaps the best gift that disabled parents give their children, disabled and nondisabled, is seeing the value in different ways of being. Disability is not a rigid continuum. It's a sphere of many different possibilities. All children benefit from having parents who offer and support multiple ways of being in the world. Research shows that disabled parents' expectations of their children are welcoming of more diverse learning styles.[49] Disabled parents have already learned that there is never just one way to accomplish a task. Sometimes this knowledge is mundane, such as showing a child a different way of opening a jar. Other times this supportive and welcoming attitude makes a huge difference, as this disabled parent reported when I interviewed her about her son:

> When we first figured out my son had severe mental illness, I could explain to him "You have a disability. It's not in your legs like mine; it's in your head and it makes it hard for you to control your emotions." At age 5, he looked at me with the biggest look of relief on his face and said, "Oh, Mommie, I'm glad I'm disabled; I thought I was a bad person." For him, he had

---

47. From my interviews with disabled mothers.

48. Ibid.

49. Grace, E.J. (2014). "Your mama wears drover boots." In Wood, C. (ed.). *Criptiques*. May Day Publishing. URL: http://www.criptiques.com

a context, a positive context related to disability.[50]

A little bit of humor helps too. Disabled parents often get asked a lot of questions by strangers. Our children grow tired of the questions, of the negative presumptions about our families. When my daughter was 8 years old she decided she wanted to do something in response to the questions, but she wasn't sure what to do until she talked with other kids who had disabled parents. One of the kids told her that he charges one dollar for each answer he provides. My daughter loved this approach. The typical questions were: "What's wrong with your mom?" and "Who is she?" (They asked while pointing to me, her mom). Strangers were taken aback by the small child requesting money for an answer. But my daughter was happy whether they paid her for an answer or they just walked away. Since she came up with the strategy, I let her keep the money.

Conclusion

Disabled people have always been parenting, sometimes more publicly and sometimes with less visibility. Other than inside specific disability communities,[51] it's never been safe to be both disabled and a parent. In 2012 the National Council on Disability created a comprehensive report on disabled parents called *Rocking the Cradle: Ensuring the Rights of Parents with Disabilities and Their Children.* I leave you with their findings:

> **Finding 1:** There are few accurate and comprehensive sources of information on the prevalence of parents with disabilities.
>
> **Finding 2:** The child welfare system is ill-equipped to support parents with disabilities and their families, resulting in disproportionately high rates of involvement with child welfare services and devastatingly high rates of parents with disabilities losing their parental rights.
>
> **Finding 3:** Parents with disabilities who are engaged in custody or visitation disputes in the family law system regularly

---

50. From my 2013 interviews with disabled mothers.

51. Nora Groce's book documents her research on the isolated island of Martha's Vineyard where until the early 1900s the hereditary deafness there meant everyone learned sign language whether they were deaf or not. *Everyone Here Spoke Sign Language: Hereditary Deafness on Martha's Vineyard* by Nora Ellen Groce. 1988: Harvard University Press.

encounter discriminatory practices.

Finding 4: Parents with disabilities who are involved in dependency or family proceedings regularly face evidence regarding their parental fitness that is developed using inappropriate and unadapted parenting assessments. Resources are lacking to provide adapted services and adaptive parenting equipment, and to teach adapted parenting techniques.

Finding 5: Prospective adoptive parents with disabilities face significant barriers to adopting children, both domestically and internationally.

Finding 6: People with disabilities face significant barriers to receiving assisted reproductive technologies (ART), despite its importance for many people with disabilities who want to procreate.

Finding 7: Personal assistance services (PAS) are a crucial support for many people with disabilities but usually may not be used to assist them with their parenting activities.

Finding 8: Parents with disabilities face significant barriers to obtaining accessible, affordable, and appropriate housing for their families.

Finding 9: Many parents with disabilities face barriers to traveling with their families using paratransit services.

Finding 10: Parents with disabilities have significantly less income and more frequently receive public benefits.

Finding 11: People with disabilities, especially women, face significant barriers to receiving proper reproductive health care.

Finding 12: Parents and prospective parents with disabilities face a significant lack of peer supports.

Finding 13: Social service providers often do not know, or overlook the parenting roles of consumers.

Finding 14: Formal Individuals with Disabilities Education Act

(IDEA) Part C Early Intervention (EI) programs and other non-Part C early intervention and prevention model programs are an appropriate service option for many children of parents with disabilities.

Finding 15: Parents with disabilities involved in dependency or family law proceedings face significant barriers to retaining effective and affordable legal representation.

Finding 16: Centers for Independent Living (CILs), with appropriate training, can provide services to parents with disabilities.

Finding 17: Despite limited funding and little national attention given to parents with disabilities and their families, a number of programs and support services have begun to emerge across the nation; they must be replicated nationally to provide consistent capacity to support parents with disabilities and their children.

Finding 18: The impact of disability on the integrity of American Indian/Alaskan Native (AI/AN) families has been utterly neglected by professionals in the fields of law, policy, and research.

Finding 19: Federal legislation, similar to the Indian Child Welfare Act, must be enacted to address the systemically disparate treatment faced by parents with disabilities throughout the country.

Finding 20: The United Nations Convention on the Rights of Persons with Disabilities (CRPD) reinforces the rights of people with disabilities to create and maintain families.[52]

JUST THE FACTS MA'AM

- Over **4 million** disabled parents have children under age 18.
- **65,000** disabled people were sterilized prior to 1970.
- **40-80%** of disabled parents have their children removed from the home.

---

52. *Rocking the Cradle,* see note 3

RESOURCES

Disability, Pregnancy & Parenthood. URL: http://www.dppi.org.uk/
Disabled Parents Network, UK. URL:
   http://disabledparentsnetwork.org.uk/
National Council on Disabilities. *Rocking the Cradle: Ensuring the Rights of Parents with Disabilities and Their Children.* URL:
   http://www.ncd.gov/publications/2012/Sep272012/

A full bibliography is available at my website: www.corbettotoole.com

13.

Dancing Forward

*"In imagining more accessible futures, I am yearning for an elsewhere—
and, perhaps, an "elsewhen"—in which disability is understood otherwise:
as political, as valuable, as integral."*   — Alison Kafer (disabled)[1]

Summary

The stories and histories of disabled people are important and must be
preserved in permanent archives (libraries for people's stories and
work). To date, disability rights organizations have saved the stories of
mostly white disabled people, especially people who have physical
disabilities. It's important to save more stories. We also need to save and
celebrate the wonderful ways that disabled people move and think.

Disability history is complicated, messy, and mostly invisible. This book
attempts to tell you just one perspective on that vast history. If you
take away nothing else from this book, take this: write, sing, video,
audio your history. Every day we lose entire libraries as disabled people
die and leave no record behind. We need to capture those histories.[2]
No matter when you became disabled, you have been in situations
where you are the first. You might be the first person with that
disability to hold a job or become a parent or write a blog. The

---

1.   Kafer, A. (2013). *Feminist, Queer, Crip*. Indiana University Press, Bloomington, IN.

2.   As I write this there are a number of efforts to do this work: The University of Toledo;
     University of Texas, Arlington; the University of Massachusetts, Amherst; and the University of
     California, Berkeley. More information can be found on my website: www.corbettotoole.com

nondisabled people that love us do not share our experience of being disabled in the world. They have their own stories, and they need to be recorded too.

Whatever you have done, whether it seems newsworthy to you or not, it's critically important for the history of disabled people that your history is preserved. Right now, the primary stereotypes being captured and saved are reflected in the media stories of the inspiring Christopher Reeve (disabled),[3] and the brilliant but locked-in Stephen Hawking (disabled).[4] Just for a minute think about what little history you grew up knowing about disabled people. If you grew up in the United States, your disability history was pretty much limited to President Franklin Delano Roosevelt (disabled)[5] and Helen Keller (disabled), but only as the child with the miracle worker.[6]

Throughout history, disabled people have been present, doing interesting and ordinary things. Bones of young adults with significant physical disabilities from 990,000 years ago have been found preserved in ancient human dwelling sites. In reporting this, Dick Sobsey (nondisabled) jokes that since the wheel was not yet invented, "these families probably did not have very good wheelchairs."[7]

Even when our bodies are present, our disabled selves are often erased. In 2010 I visited the Boston Museum of Fine Arts's new exhibit on Pre-Columbian artifacts.[8] There were two small statues that clearly showed disabled bodies—one of an adult with achondroplasia, a form of dwarfism, and another adult with osteogenesis imperfecta (brittle bones). Yet one was labelled as a nondisabled child and the other as an imaginary figure.[9]

---

3. Christopher Reeve was the handsome actor who played Superman. He became quadriplegic in 1995, after a horseback riding accident.

4. Stephen Hawking is a brilliant physicist, professor, and writer who is paralyzed from Lou Gehrig's disease and uses a wheelchair and a voice synthesizer.

5. Franklin Roosevelt was the 32nd President of the United States, during the Great Depression and World War II. He had polio and used a wheelchair.

6. Helen Keller was the first deafblind person to receive a Bachelor's degree. Her success is often attributed to the work of her teacher and companion, Anne Sullivan, the "miracle worker," who taught her language by spelling words into her hand.

7. "Parents have been doing this for a lot of years with less supports. Here is something to think about. Paleoanthropologists tell us that spinal and cranial deformities have been found in older children and young adults among early humans and prehumans. These children could not have survived without parents or community caregivers. Since these skeletons date back as much as 990,000 years before the invention of the wheel, these families probably did not have very very [sic] good wheelchairs" [caps in the original] from Sobsey, R. (2010). *Dr. Dick Sobsey himself replies*. URLs: http://severedisabilitykid.blogspot.com/2010/05/dr-dick-sobsey-himself-replies.html

8. Pre-Columbian refers to life in North and South America before the arrival of Europeans.

9. Museum of Fine Arts Boston Art of the Americas collection. URL:

The disability rights organizations had created access to get disabled people into the museum, but disability history had not yet reached the museum curators to correct this error. Luckily an artist had preserved their images, documenting that disabled people were there.

As is so often the case, disabled people are hidden in plain sight. For the most part, our history never got recorded or documented, and that needs to change. If we don't leave our histories in permanent archives, all that will be left is the same old mythologies, written by and for nondisabled people.

Who Do We Want To Be?

In this book I have made a lot of statements that will ruffle feathers. I want to spend a few minutes addressing some of them. The first topic I want to take on is disability rights organizations. Throughout the book, I have shown both the amazing work they have accomplished and also their failures. I have deep respect for the powerful work that disability rights organizations have accomplished over the past 40 years. A group of ragtag activists built an international movement that has changed societal attitudes, created civil rights laws and brought disabled people into the awareness of society. That's an amazing accomplishment.

The disability rights organizations have also operated with a number of presumptions. The most problematic is the idea that "disabled people are just like nondisabled people." Numerous scholars, particularly in queer studies, have examined the ways in which this approach creates opportunities for some of its members, but severely limits access for others.[10] Most disabled people will never look like, think like, or act like nondisabled people. Some of us think that's a good thing. But whatever you think, the fact is that "we're just like you" means that the people who can't pass as nondisabled, are not "disability pretty,"[11] are left behind. This is most clearly seen in who is and is not the public face of disability rights organizations. Those people, those faces, nearly always have fluent speech, non-shaking bodies, appear middle class, and are usually white.

I was deeply involved in disability rights organizations in the 1970s and early 1980s.[12] For the better part of 15 years from the mid-1980s to

http://www.mfa.org/collections/art-americas

10. Smith, P. (2004). "Whiteness, normal theory, and Disability Studies." *Disability Studies Quarterly* 24(2). URL: http://dsq-sds.org/article/view/491/668

11. Naomi Ortiz. Twitter: @thinkfreestyle

12. This was the time period documented in the Disability Rights and Independent Living Movement oral history collection in the Bancroft Library at the University of California Berkeley.

2000, I was discouraged by the direction of disability rights organizations and the lack of sustained grassroots disabled-led alternatives. I kept observing that as the funding got tighter, disability organizations increasingly leaned towards what the funders wanted and not what the disability community needed.[13] When I went into disability rights organizations, the posters on the walls might have shown disabled people, but they were "disability pretty" people. There was nothing there to upset a nondisabled, white funder.

This is in stark contrast to the early days of disability rights organizations in Berkeley. In 1981 at the new Disability Rights Education and Defense Fund, founder Bob Funk (disabled)'s artificial leg sat on a short bookcase in the corner of his office next to the conference table. In the socket where Bob's leg stump would go there was a potted plant with ivy trailing down the leg. In the next office, Mary Lou Breslin (disabled)'s back brace had been bronzed and made into a lamp. These two objects, intimately connected to their disabled bodyminds, were proudly displayed in their offices and were never hidden when funders came around.

Today when I walk into disability rights organizations I cannot often tell the difference between them and other social service organizations. So I was thrilled in 2010 when I walked into the Silicon Valley Independent Living Center (SVILC), a disability justice organization[14] where Sarah Triano (disabled) was Director. Immediately inside the front door was a large sign stating how many disabled people have been freed from institutions in the past year by SVILC. Throughout the offices political posters positioned disability rights in the broader context of the struggle for human and civil rights, including gender, sexual orientation, and racial justice.[15] It's been a very long time

---

Although there are over 100 oral histories, this collection heavily favors white people, as 102 of the 109 individual interviews are white people. This collection also heavily favors people with physical disabilities (64), the vast majority of whom are people who use wheelchairs. Nondisabled people (29) are next largest group. And there are token numbers of people from other disability communities (21), queer people (7), and parents of disabled children (4). Even with these limitations, the oral histories are enormously valuable, particularly as they capture a number of people who have since died, but who provide critical historical information.

13. Typically grants matched programs, so anything that was hard to fund—for example violence against disabled people—just didn't happen.

14. "SVILC is a disability justice, rather than a disability rights, organization. The difference is subtle yet critical. Disability rights, as the name implies, focuses on one thing: disability. Disability rights activists fight for things like ramps, curb cuts, and personal attendant services. In disability justice, we recognize that all those things are important, but they don't go far enough. We see ourselves as part of the larger struggle for social justice in America. To this end, we work with other social justice groups outside the disability realm, from organized labor, the LGBTQ community, the immigrant community, and more." Source URL: http://svilc.org/index.php/about-us/disability-justice

15. "Silicon Valley Independent Living Center (SVILC) is a cross-disability, intergenerational, and

since I have been in a disability organization that was openly committed to fighting for justice for people of all disabilities, all races, all orientations and that showed their commitment by employing disabled people of color. SVILC also hosts an annual Thanksgiving day meal, in recognition of the reality that disabled people are poor, unemployed and far too often isolated. They also put on an annual Disability Pride Parade and Festival.

While I have been discouraged by the increasing tendency of disability rights organizations to act in ways that will make their funders more comfortable, I've been thrilled by the emergence of new models of disability empowerment. Disability culture has always been the place of radical self-expression. Comic Josh Blue (disabled) [16] incorporates his spasticity into his standup comedy act. Early in his performance he takes a thick-walled coffee cup and puts it in the little fingers of his most spastic hand. He knows that his fingers will hold tight to the cup for a while but that eventually they will lose their grip and the cup will drop. So while we are watching him perform, we are also watching his cerebral palsy perform. We wait with him for the inevitable but untimed release of the cup as it falls to the ground. Josh enacts his disability pride, showcasing his spastic bodymind, not for our pity but for our mutual enjoyment.

From 2006 to 2013, the BBC had a podcast called OUCH! cohosted by Mat Fraser (disabled) and Liz Carr (disabled). [17] The podcast was based in London, a hotbed of disability culture, and celebrated the disabled experience in interesting and challenging ways. They transformed the often boring station announcement, "This is BBC. Our call in number is…" by having a man with a significant speech disability make that recording. It was a lovely subversion of a boring sentence, and a celebration of the disabled voice. They also had a regular quiz segment titled "Vegetable, Vegetable, or Vegetable?" a blatant reframing of the history of disabled people being called "vegetables." In that segment, they invited disabled people to call and play a variation of 20 questions. Liz and Mat had 20 questions in which to figure out the disability of the person on the phone. Being performers, they were naturally competitive, and while trying to outdo each other, their banter

---

multicultural disability justice organization that creates fully inclusive communities that value the dignity, equality, freedom and worth of every human being. We do this by building disability identity, culture and pride; creating opportunities for personal and community transformation; and partnering with others to ensure that civil and human rights are protected." Source URL: http://svilc.org/index.php/about-us/our-mission

16. URL: http://www.joshblue.com

17. Some podcasts of OUCH! can still be found at: http://www.bbc.co.uk/ouch/podcast/

was more entertaining than actually discovering the person's disability. Those free podcasts leave valuable documentation of both the show and of the U.K. disability community's perspectives.

Sins Invalid is a "Performance project on disability and sexuality that incubates and celebrates artists with disabilities, centralizing artists of color and queer and gender variant artists as communities with and historically marginalized from social discourse." Based in Berkeley since its founding in 2006, Sins Invalid creates performance events that showcase artists rarely seen performing, either in traditional disability events or in public performance spaces. They frame their work in the context of disability justice and commit to training progressive groups on multiple intersections—race, gender, and disability. Their performances have included nonspeaking performers, nudity, poetry, video, and sexuality. Their artistic standards are high and their performances are always captivating.[18] Their 2013 film *Sins Invalid: An Unshamed Claim to Beauty* documents both their performances and their political work.[19]

There's always interesting and challenging disability work to be done. You don't have to look far for it. You can do it wherever you are. Nondisabled society is constructed to keep disabled people poor, unemployed, and always one step away from institutions. You can change that whether you are disabled or not. All you have to do is ask some disabled people "What do you need done?" or "Let's go make something happen." And don't forget to document your work!

To Infinity and Beyond

I love the phrase "To Infinity and Beyond," from the Disney movie *Toy Story*.[20] A toy spaceman believes that he can fly, even though gravity proves him wrong again and again. He is plastic, has short, fixed wings, has absolutely no ability to fly, and yet his preprogrammed speech tape has him saying, as he leaps off high surfaces with the total expectation of flight, "To Infinity and Beyond." I admire that kind of tenacity.

I see it in the most resourceful crips. The ability to acknowledge the limitations of the existing environment and yet throw themselves off the metaphorical ledge and leap into the unknown fully expecting to soar. They usually find a way to fly. Maybe not the nondisabled version of flying. Most often, it's a more interesting, more creative way of taking

---

18. Videos of some of their work can be seen at: http://www.sinsinvalid.org.

19. URL: http://www.sinsinvalid.org/film.html

20. Disney/Pixar. (1995).

flight. It might be the quad who adds velcro to her gloves to change her baby's diaper. Or the Autistic who wears headphones with the cord tucked into his pocket so it seems he is listening to music when in fact he is blocking out the cacophony of the subway train conversations with the silence of unplugged headphones.

We fly in so many different ways—sometimes in our hard-shelled wheeled chariots, sometimes signing until the space becomes a living environment, sometimes sitting quietly by the water communing. We dig deep through the attempts to silence us, incarcerate us, even kill us. Like human cockroaches, we keep surviving no matter how many times they try to get rid of us—the ones who are different, who are defiant, who are unwanted. We look around and find each other. Sometimes we can only look over and acknowledge each other when they are not looking. We let each other know that we know—you are seen, I appreciate you, the freak in me honors the freak in you. Other times we can openly embrace each other—we welcome each other publicly, naming our connection. Rarely do we get to openly celebrate our ribald joy in our gnarly bodies and minds that refuse to submit.

When we fly together our world dances. We slide and slither and bump and grind and flail and limp and rock and flap. We soar with and against the music showing each other our native moves which arrive unheralded by conventionality. We own our space. We celebrate our weird wiring. We unshackle from our shame. We are beautiful beings— varieties of human that frighten the rigid ones. We inhabit these bodies with grace and joy. We know ourselves to be worthy of life and we celebrate the worthiness of others who are often unwanted and undesired.

I look for these compatriots everywhere I go. Sometimes they want to be found, to be acknowledged. Sometimes they are still hoping to be given a pass into the nondisabled world, to be accepted there. But in that world they are always the "bipolar comic" or the "deaf professor"— never the clever entertainer or the brilliant researcher. They are tagged with their impairment, so the stereotypes stick to them like shadows, rather than the loving embrace of disability as valuable.

It is so very hard to be different, to say "I am proud." Pride is so much easier when we have people who validate our realities, who reflect our beauty, who support our struggles. Pride is easier when we have people who love our bodyminds, want our companionship and are grateful for our resourceful contributions.

Like a moth, I am drawn to people who allow their own voices to shine, who define their own beauty, who demand respect. They were not given these opportunities, they created them, often at great cost.

Maybe their check did not come, so they are eating the cheapest food they can find. Maybe their help did not come, so they lie in bed until someone arrives the next day. Maybe they do not have stable housing or food or money or family or work. Maybe they do.

I often say that mine is the first generation who has the possibility to live our entire lives outside institutions. Yet, most of us spend at least some time inside them. And for many of us, institutionalization nips at our heels, just waiting for us to fail. The system of nondisabled-run disability services ensures that the scale is weighted to institutionalizing us—that's what makes them the most money. We live in a country that has enough resources that no one need be hungry or homeless or broke. Yet disabled people are nearly all permanently unemployed and impoverished.

Do not be deceived by the cute young white man who sits tall in his manual wheelchair. Or the deaf child with the clear speech. Or the Autistic who does not flap his hands. Or the war veteran who plays sports. They are there to distract you, to fool you. They are not the majority. They are the one percent of us put there to make you, and us, believe that if we only try hard enough, work long enough we too can go into the nondisabled world without needing any accommodations.

In the late 1980s the city of Oakland, California had the following statement on their job application: "We do not discriminate on the basis of race, color, religion, sex, or unimpairing handicap."[21.] I love the honesty of that statement. "We do not discriminate on the basis of *unimpairing* handicap." The world will allow us in—but only if our differences do not impair. Impair whom? Us or them? We inhabit these bodyminds all the time. For us they are just the way we are, we move this way, we think this way, we feel this way, we communicate this way. We did not lose anything, we are not trying to gain anything. We are just trying to survive in a world that pretends we are not here, that "human" is a fixed thing—like the uber-buff daVinci drawing. We bring our drooling, stuttering, mad, gnarly, drooping, sometimes sick bodyminds into their world and say—How about a range of bodyminds? Can you grok that? Unfortunately the answer is nearly always no.

I am of the baby boomer generation. When we were young, we scared people because some of us were willing to use our race and class privilege to highlight inequities. Now as we age, we scare people because so many of us are becoming disabled so quickly. Now the discussions are about the costs of medical care and disability supports, about restrictions to care and services, even when loss of living skills,

---

21. I saw this on the job application for the Director of Special Education for the Oakland School District. (Note: they now just say disability.)

and even death, result. But that may be the point; dead people are not expensive.

We know this. We have been doing this a long time. We read our history, we know this is not the first time they've tried to exterminate us. They've always been trying. And we've always been surviving. They write us out of the history books, and then we write ourselves back in. Only this year (2014), archeologists realized that all those canes in King Tut's tomb were not ornamental, but needed by him for a physical disability.[22] Franklin Roosevelt hid his wheelchair and inability to walk independently for decades. Yet when his national monument was created without any image of his disability, activists joined with his family to create a statue of him sitting in his wheelchair.[23]

We have always been here. We will always be here. They will never exterminate all of us. They have tried to make us hate ourselves and hate each other, they have divided us into impairment categories, enforced disability hierarchies, restricted our movements and controlled our finances. Yet still we survive.

I don't want to just survive, I want to thrive. I refuse to be 'less than' and 'broken' and 'sick' and 'worthless.' I refuse to accept that for myself, or for anyone else deemed unacceptable. I am the fetus with Down Syndrome aborted. I am the Autistic who is shocked. I am the mad person locked up and drugged. I am the homeless veteran living under a bridge. I am the hemophiliac with AIDS. I am the unwanted and the unacceptable. These are my people.

I rock with Ibby (disabled), a human metronome. I sign stories with Lois (disabled)'s kids. I share child raising with Jessie (disabled), the blind mom. I celebrate the wondrous diversity of disabled bodyminds; the ways we inhabit space and defy rigid notions of 'body' and 'mind' and 'normal.' These people are part of my crip story, my crip life. I document them in the act of documenting myself. If you do not think your story is important to tell, you are wrong. We need all disabled people's stories. Some we will never know because they died before they got preserved, or they didn't think that their amazing act of surviving in this ableist world was important. How will the next generation know how to fight back if we don't tell them what we did? How do we stop the violence unless we offer our own life stories as stepping stones? We've spent a lifetime learning, why wouldn't we pass on this valuable knowledge to the people coming behind us? This book

22. Nuwer, R.. (October 2014). "Newest King Tut theory: He suffered severe disorders from inbreeding." *Smithsonian Magazine*.

23. Kilan, M. (January 10, 2001). "Revised FDR memorial shows disability: New statue depicts president who led from a wheelchair." *Chicago Tribune*.

exists because disabled people left their stories behind. Please document your life—the next ones need it all—your emails, letters, photos, stories. Give them the gift of yourself. They will need it. The world is a harsh place for disabled people. Make it a bit easier for them.

I will end with a poem[24] by Cheryl Marie Wade, a gnarly white woman who showed me the power of singing the freak's body.

I Am Not One Of The
By Cheryl Marie Wade

I am not one of the physically challenged—
I'm a sock in the eye with gnarled fist
I'm a French kiss with cleft tongue
I'm orthopedic shoes sewn on a last of your fears
I am not one of the differently abled—
I'm an epitaph for a million imperfect babies left untreated
I'm an ikon carved from bones in a mass grave at Tiergarten,
Germany
I'm withered legs hidden with a blanket
I am not one of the able disabled—
I'm a black panther with green eyes and scars like a picket fence
I'm pink lace panties teasing a stub of milk white thigh
I'm the Evil Eye
I'm the first cell divided
I'm mud that talks
I'm Eve I'm Kali
I'm The Mountain That Never Moves
I've been forever I'll be here forever
I'm the Gimp
I'm the Cripple
I'm the Crazy Lady
I'm The Woman With Juice

24. Wade, C.M. (1987). "I am not one of the." Published in *The disability studies reader, 4th edition.* (2013). Davis, L. (ed.). Taylor & Francis. Routledge. New York, NY.

JUST THE FACTS MA'AM

In addition to state history archives, there are currently five archives (libraries) that are actively seeking donations from disabled people. Contact the "Special Collections" Department to donate:

University of Toledo, 2801 W. Bancroft St., Toledo, OH 43606. Phone: 419-530-4480 URL: http://www.utoledo.edu/library/canaday/

Univ. of Massachusetts, Amherst, 154 Hicks Way, UMass Amherst, Amherst, MA 01003. Phone: 413-545-2780 URL: http://scua.library.umass.edu/umarmot/overview/collection-policy/

University of Texas Arlington Library, 702 Planetarium Place, Arlington, TX 76019. Phone: 817-272-3000 URL: http://www.uta.edu/library/spco/

The Bancroft Library, University of California Berkeley, Berkeley, CA 94720-6000. Phone: 510-643-3203 (voice) & 510-643-2548 (fax) URL: http://www.lib.berkeley.edu/BANC/

Disability History Museum, URL: http://www.disabilitymuseum.org/dhm/index.html

RESOURCES

Donating Your Personal or Family Records to a Repository. URL: http://www2.archivists.org/publications/brochures/donating-familyrecs

NeuroQueer. http://neuroqueer.blogspot.com

Sins Invalid. http://www.sinsinvalid.org

Wood, C. (ed.) *Criptiques: Exploring the Provocative Side of Disability.* Blog URL: http://criptiques.com/

A full bibliography is available at my website: www.corbettotoole.com

Index

How to use the index:

Entries are listed alphabetically. Names of people are last name first. Page numbers that have an "n" after the number are footnotes. Footnotes are the words in smaller print at the bottom of the page. "See" means to look for the term in another place. "See also" means to look for more information in another place or more than one place.

CPSIA information can be obtained at www.ICGtesting.com
Printed in the USA
BVOW06s1156110915

417255BV00009B/212/P